Passionate advocate for mental wellbeing and optimal health, Dawn Howarth is a sleep consultant and a teacher of mindfulness and yoga, with over 15 years' experience working with children, teenagers and adults. She is a member of the British Sleep Society and The Association for Child & Adolescent Mental Health. *The Family Guide to Better Sleep* brings together every aspect of her experience and knowledge. Dawn has written about teenage sleep for *The Times*, providing practical support for families. When not writing or teaching, she is an amateur potter, vegetable grower and knitter of socks. She lives with her husband, children and pets.

For Paddy

Dawn Howarth

THE FAMILY GUIDE TO BETTER SLEEP

Step-by-step Techniques for Healthier Sleep and Happier Children, Teenagers and Adults

AUSTIN MACAULEY PUBLISHERS®

LONDON * CAMBRIDGE * NEW YORK * SHARJAH

A CIP catalogue record for this title is available from the British Library.

ISBN 9781035890200 (Paperback)
ISBN 9781035890224 (ePub e-book)
ISBN 9781035890217 (Audiobook)

www.austinmacauley.com

First Published 2025
Austin Macauley Publishers Ltd®
1 Canada Square
Canary Wharf
London
E14 5AA

Table of Contents

Introduction

How did you sleep last night? How did your children sleep? How are you feeling today? The chances are, if you are reading this book, that the answers to those questions will be far from ideal. Under-sleeping—or not getting sufficient sleep—is so common that most of us take it for granted that we will feel tired for some or all of the day; that our children will be experiencing tiredness on a daily basis. Have you ever answered that third question with a resigned "tired" and had a sympathetic "me too"? The chances are you have because tiredness has been normalised and the assumption is that we all just have to live with it. We live with it day after day, in spite of how awful it makes us feel. We go through our days missing out on the amazing range of benefits that good sleep brings for the emotional, mental and physical health of every member of the family.

When we are tired, our mind is fuzzy, our memory is poor, our emotions are unregulated, our immune system is less effective, and we feel lousy. This applies to absolutely everyone, young, old and in the middle. Lack of sleep seriously impacts every aspect of our health. Tiredness literally kills—more road traffic accidents occur annually because of tiredness than of alcohol or drug consumption put together—but it also kills our joy for life and the ability to participate fully in our lives and reach our true potential.

It is my mission to help everyone to sleep better and to consequently feel better. I have worked with children, adolescents and adults for many years teaching skills that can radically improve sleep. Sleep takes place within the home and among the family, and this book will help you to diagnose common problems affecting each member of your family and will bring sleep solutions within this holistic context. You will find expert help and support along with practical, easy to apply, step-by-step techniques for healthier and happier bedtimes for everyone.

This may feel impossible right now. Behind many front doors parents are enduring nightly battles around bedtimes while adults undergo their own sleep challenges. Are any of the following scenarios happening in your home: children unwilling to go to bed or unable to settle when they get there; children waking frequently in the night; regular nightmares or night terrors; nocturnal teenagers who can't get out of bed in the morning; a chaotic bedtime routine; adult insomnia (acute and chronic); adults waking up either because of disturbances by young children or teens, or just through habit; adults unable to drop off even when completely exhausted? Parents and carers can feel at their wits' end even if only one of this list is a regular feature. Only extreme cases of sleep problems will receive referrals to specialist sleep units as our health systems are more stretched than ever before and the thresholds for intervention are getting higher and higher. In the meantime, parents, carers and children alike are getting up each morning after a night of broken or shortened sleep; families head off to school and work feeling exhausted and knowing that the whole cycle will begin again that night. It can feel overwhelming and that there is nowhere to turn for advice.

I am passionate about wellbeing and especially about the benefits that something as seemingly simple as a good night's sleep can bring us all. I want to support you on the journey to better sleep for your whole family with information and practical help. There are other books out there which focus on the science of sleep. They are fascinating and I have learnt a great deal from them. There are also lots of books that focus on sleep for children in the early years, but there is very little written about supporting teenagers with sleep and, crucially, about examining sleep and how it affects the whole family—and what to do to improve things.

This book will provide sleep solutions for that vast majority of people who don't choose or qualify for medical interventions. It tackles what happens in ordinary families night after night. If you want to understand more about what's taking place in the body and brain during sleep, how sleep cycles work, make bedtimes happier, support your teenager towards a realistic sleep pattern, get everyone using phones and technology in a healthier way, find ways to tackle anxiety, nightmares and stress, learn how to calm the mind and body so sleep comes more easily, have a better night's sleep with your partner—then this book is for you. We'll look at sleep issues that mostly affect adults such as snoring, sleep apnoea and restless leg syndrome. You will learn how to reset the whole family's attitude to and experience of sleep. I want to share with you the ways you can make small changes that can have a big impact and to provide you with a range of practical techniques so that you can choose the ones that most apply to the situation in your family. I want to empower you to improve the quality of life for the whole household so that everyone can get on with making the most of every day.

You will find plenty of ways to support yourself and your child/teen with the kinds of worries and anxieties that often surface at bedtime and prevent us sleeping. You will learn how to assess sleep hygiene, how to build a sleep diary and how to shift your mindset about how well (or poorly) you and everyone else sleeps at night. I share visualisations you can work through, body scans to enable relaxation and plenty of suggestions for practices you can put in place to build a bedtime routine that works for the whole family.

As a parent of three I thought I had dealt with sleep issues once they had all slept through the night, moved into their "big boy/girl bed" and come out of nappies. Support for parents and carers around the subject of sleep is everywhere at the baby and toddler stages; but there is little discussion around or advice available for problems that start or last beyond the preschool years. It becomes harder for parents to admit that their 8-year-old comes into their bed every single night or that they have given up trying to regulate their teenager's bedtime. Parents are exhausted, guilty and resigned to just putting up with it. We're all expected to have it sorted by then—but classrooms full of tired children tell the opposite story. A school leader recently told me: "the biggest barrier to learning in our school is tiredness." Parents often come to me with problems around their child's sleeping habits or around behaviour that, once you look more closely, is caused in part by insufficient quantity or quality of sleep. They share their own sleep issues and we work together to implement solutions.

My three children are now teenaged and beyond. Our carefully curated bedtime routines flew out of the window once they no longer believed their parents knew anything about anything, and we found there was a whole new set of issues to navigate. So, I have first-hand experience of dealing with the frustration and exhaustion when it comes to young people and their sleeping habits. The teenagers I work with are almost all experiencing tiredness, day after day. At such a crucial time in their lives, this is having a profound effect on their mental, physical and emotional development. There are a range of suggestions and strategies for parents of, and those who care for, teenagers in this book and you will find an examination of the changing world of technology and its impact on our young people and the adults who use it too. I've also experienced my own bouts of insomnia during times of anxiety and illness. I've tossed and turned too all night before a big day—exactly what you don't want to be doing. I will share tried and tested ways for the grown-ups to tackle their sleep issues. Adults are not immune either to the effects of technology and you'll be encouraged to re-examine your attitude to and use of tech in terms of your sleep.

As adults we can recognise the signs of tiredness and this book will help you create space around the issue and help to gently move towards changing that tiredness into the energy that we all desperately want. Ultimately, we want our children and young people to recognise this too, to be able to distinguish between feeling full of beans and feeling shattered—and understand why and how to remedy this. The advice in this book will enable them to fulfil their potential, flourish and feel good. They will need our support with this and our commitment to sleep better ourselves, modelling the behaviour we want to encourage. Getting adults in the home sleeping better and respecting the value of sleep has a positive impact on how children and teenagers embrace this. Change is hard and every household is different with its own challenges and own journey, but I hope you will gain a new respect for and understanding of sleep that will feel great for everyone. I hope that you will feel empowered to tackle the sleep issues in your family and to become an SAS family—one that is Serious About Sleep! I want parents, adolescents and children to use the interventions for both mind and body in this book that will enable sleep to be the powerful restorative foundation of health it is.

My fascination with sleep emerged from my work as a children's teacher of yoga, mindfulness and meditation where it quickly became clear to me how much benefit there is from learning to calm the mind and body. I knew this theoretically from my own practice, of course, but watching children and teenagers experiment with the practices and notice how much better this made them feel and perform is truly inspiring. Teaching young children and adolescents how to achieve calmness and stillness is incredibly rewarding and I feel honoured to be part of their learning experience. Being able to connect with yourself in a space of silence and peace can have profound positive effects. When did you last sit calmly and quietly with your own thoughts? For many of us it's incredibly difficult to turn our attention inwards from the demands of the hectic world we live in. This is especially important for young people to learn as they navigate an incessant rolling sea of social, physical and academic pressures.

I am a qualified sleep consultant and incorporate this knowledge when working with adults, young people, their teachers and families. I have talked with hundreds of people about their sleep over many years. The success I have had helping people of all ages is down to combining the protocols of sleep science, yoga, meditation and mindfulness; the modern with the ancient. These protocols find common ground in the fascinating relationship between the mind and the body. This is an area of science where exciting work is being done. The decades ahead will see the results and, I truly believe, life-changing implications for the treatment and prevention of disease as well as the possibilities for improving mental health and happiness for everyone. Sleep is the ultimate area where the mind/body connection occurs. As we all know, when the body is tired but the mind is racing, sleep is painfully elusive. Likewise, if the mind is relatively calm but the body is holding tension and stress, sleep can feel impossible. Learning how to make the mind/body connection work for your benefit can feel like a light switching on.

Research shows that everyone has the means to reduce their chances of cardiovascular disease, stroke, cancer, dementia, depression, weight gain and a host of other potentially fatal diseases in a way that is simple, pleasant and FREE—get 8+ hours sleep a night and, when possible, take a nap! It sounds so easy, yet we know that increasing numbers of adults and children fall short of the nightly sleep they require with serious consequences. By taking back control of sleep within our households, we will make major changes for the benefit of everyone. This book will show you why and how to make those changes. I hope the light switch goes on for you and yours as peaceful, restorative sleep becomes the norm.

The opening question in this Introduction was "How did you sleep last night?" Imagine if the answer was "deep and peaceful, thank you!" Imagine if the answer to how your kids slept was "nine solid hours actually." How different would your household be if everyone had slept brilliantly and woken up full of energy? We know that after a good night's sleep we've got energy for ourselves, our kids, our relationships, work, school, activities, fun. We're more able to be positive, creative, active, focused; we're more patient, more resilient, we laugh more. We are less likely to have meltdowns, lose our temper and say things we regret later, we're less likely to engage in risky or destructive behaviours. The adage says that "the family that plays together, stays together," I hope this book will equally prove that "the family that sleeps better, gets along better"—family harmony is what we all want and need. Sleep can be that gateway to a healthier, happier life.

Chapter 1
Why Sleep Matters

If sleep doesn't serve some vital function, it is the biggest mistake evolution has ever made.

Professor Allan Rechtschaffen, 1971

As parents and carers, the wellbeing of our children is at the heart of our lives, for many of us it is our number one priority. Our own needs can find themselves way down on the list of priorities in the hectic reality of family life but taking care of ourselves too is essential to the successful functioning of the whole family. Families are a living organism in their own right, and we all know how the sleeplessness of one member can impact on everyone else. Lack of sleep impacts us in so many ways, as the information I want to share with you here makes very clear. In real life, the sleep-deprived adult finds themselves short of energy, patience and good humour; the exhausted child has meltdowns; the teenager, already experiencing seismic changes to brain and body, flies off the handle and storms off.

As you read this chapter, you may have your children's needs at the forefront of your mind, but I hope you will also give yourself permission to think about yourself as well as other adults in the family—your sleep matters too as does the happiness and successful functioning of your whole family unit. Getting good quality and quantity of sleep is about a lot more than just not being tired, as you are about to learn.

The vast amount of parenting information available, combined with the messages we receive from marketing and advertising directs our focus onto several areas: nutrition, physical activity, mental development and social skills. A vast number of parenting books for babies and young children detail the foods they need for optimum health and growth. There are whole programmes designed to keep children of all ages fit and active, engaged in exercise and building the foundations for strong healthy adults. We can access advice about our children's happiness, the amount of fresh air and exercise they need, how to help with shyness and making friends.

Helping our children with their language and numeracy skills starts incredibly early with ways to stimulate a baby's cognitive abilities, followed by "brain training" advice for toddlers; it continues throughout their school years as parents are advised of ways to support academic progress. Increasing awareness of emotional intelligence and rising mental health issues puts parental focus onto supporting the development of children's resilience, confidence and happiness. Parents have never worked harder for the wellbeing of their children, and they are frequently doing this without the foundational support they need for their own self-care as well as for the care of those children.

All the above are doubtlessly important cornerstones of health and wellbeing—but why is so little attention and focus given to *sleep* when it affects the lives of every family? There is plentiful advice regarding sleep for babies in their early years, but it seems that by the age of five, it's a given that a child will be sleeping well and the long difficult months of night feeds, transfer from cot to bed and potty training are well behind. Yet we know that issues connected with sleep, for both adults and children, are at epidemic levels and that the health and wellbeing implications of this are extremely serious. The World Health Organisation has, in fact, declared a sleep loss epidemic throughout industrialised nations. The countries experiencing this epidemic are also those with rapidly rising rates of physical and mental health issues—this is far from a coincidence.

So, why is sleep so important? When our children are young their sleeping patterns affect us so radically that it can be easy to make it all about us. As a young mum I felt at times that I would give my right arm in exchange for a full night's sleep. Tiredness cripples us and, even though we expect it to happen when a baby arrives, nothing quite prepares you for the levels of weariness. So, getting to the magical time when baby sleeps through the night transforms everything and it's natural to turn our parental spotlight on to those other health cornerstones of nutrition, exercise and mental and emotional development.

Feeling we have conquered the issue of sleep with our very young children can come back all too often to haunt us. I have yet to meet a parent who hasn't experienced one or all of these common issues: children reluctant to go to bed; children going on walkabout in the night into another bed; fears and anxieties emerging just as the child gets ready for sleep; the child who reappears multiple times before you declaring "I can't sleep"; the teenager wandering the house in the early hours or seemingly permanently plugged into a device; rows about use of tech in bedrooms; the teen who can't get out of bed in the morning and becomes nocturnal during school or college holidays. And, goodness, how we all worry! We worry at the same time about our own difficulties in falling or staying asleep. Adult lack of sleep impacts on how well we can function at work, and it matters in whatever job you have or whether you work within the home and are trying to get through your day feeling you're on top of things.

All these common scenarios put pressure on families and often at times of the evening or night when parents are shattered and in need of sleep themselves. The worry about whether we will sleep well that night on top of getting the children to bed can become the normal way of feeling and it eats away at our wellbeing. Teenagers bring a whole new range of challenges from refusing to go to bed to refusing to get up in the morning. Add to this the amount of technology that all children use and love and frequently have in their bedrooms and it is not surprising that so many households experience nightly dramas around bedtimes and sleep behaviours. I am frequently asked by worried parents and carers for suggestions of ways to help their children.

Many parents are seeking help from the medical profession and the charities set up to provide assistance. In early 2020, data from NHS Digital revealed that thousands of children and teenagers in England are being admitted to hospital for sleep disorders, with admissions almost doubling in the past seven years. For most adults and children, the problems will not be acute enough to get themselves into the medical system but the issues still ruin the quality of our lives on a daily basis.

Sleep is a complex mechanism and a huge number of processes take place that affect our bodies, minds and emotions. Yet sleep remains a largely unexplored area of life for adults and children alike. Which is bizarre as we spend so much time doing it—36% of our lives, in fact. But what is absolutely unequivocal is that sleep is an unsung hero for the role it plays in our physical, mental and emotional wellbeing. The World Health Organisation stipulates that adults should get 8 hours of sleep every single night. For children, the recommendations are 12 hours a night for toddlers; 10–12 hours for children aged 3–6 years; 10–11 hours for 7–12-year-olds; and for teenagers 8–10 hours.

The statistics tell us that 25% of children in the UK get insufficient sleep—teachers will inform you that reality in their classrooms tells a much bleaker story. In a class of year 8, I recently taught, I found only one young person had had 8 hours sleep the night before; several reported fewer than 4. Almost all adults will experience disrupted sleep at some stage of their lives; unsurprisingly, adults who are parents will suffer the most. Most people know from their own experience that sleep is important for rest, recovery and repair but beyond that most of us are quite hazy about what exactly happens to our brain and body while we are tucked up in our beds and why the quantity and quality of our sleep matters so much.

In this chapter, the focus will be on exactly why and how sleep benefits us throughout our lives, with a focus on the areas that typically concern parents and carers. Understanding the wonderful ways in which sleep benefits our bodies and minds can help you prioritise sleep in a new way, perhaps changing your own approach to sleep as well as helping your child. I find the whole subject endlessly fascinating and I almost always get enthusiastic and positive responses from young people when discussing it with them. I find that giving them the facts about sleep can radically shift their perception and attitudes. They discover that sleep isn't wasted time after all—far from it. Arming you with this information will, I hope, enable you to talk with confidence to other adults in the house as well as your child/ren about sleep and make some positive changes in your household. It will give you the opportunity to re-examine your own attitude and approach to your sleep pattern.

Let's start off with a quiz to see how much you already know. I've already given you a few of the answers!

How Much Do You Know About Sleep?

1. What is the recommended amount of sleep required nightly for adults according to the World Health Organisation?
   a) 6
   b) 7
   c) 8
   d) 9

2. How many hours sleep a night should children aged 7–12 years be getting?
   a) 8–9
   b) 9–10
   c) 10–11
   d) 11–12

3. What percentage of UK schoolchildren are regularly getting insufficient amounts of sleep?
   a) 10%
   b) 15%
   c) 20%
   d) 25%

4. Which of these health conditions are you at an increased risk of when routinely getting insufficient sleep?
   a) Stroke
   b) Type 2 Diabetes
   c) Alzheimer's
   d) Cardiovascular disease

5. To which of these mental health conditions does lack of sleep contribute?
   a) Depression
   b) Bipolar disorder
   c) Anxiety
   d) Schizophrenia

6. The most accidents on the road are caused by…
   a) Drivers under the influence of alcohol
   b) Drivers under the influence of drugs
   c) Sleep-deprived, drowsy drivers
   d) Potholes

7. Which of these personal qualities are reduced by insufficient sleep?
   a) Creativity

b) Efficiency
c) Honesty
d) Ability to work in a team

8. Which of these aids a good night's sleep?
   a) Alcohol
   b) Caffeine
   c) Sleeping pill
   d) Hot bath before bed

9. What is the ideal temperature of a bedroom at night?
   a) Cold—16°C
   b) Cool—18°C
   c) Warm—20°C
   d) Hot—22°C

10. What is the annual cost to the UK economy caused by sleep deprivation in the workforce?
    a) £1 billion
    b) £10 billion
    c) £25 billion
    d) £40 billion

You will find the answers to these questions below. Some of them, hopefully, felt obvious to you but there will also have been questions that made you stop and think. I suspect some of the answers will surprise and shock you. More detail about all the issues raised in the quiz can be found in the rest of the chapter.

Answers: 1. c; 2. c; 3. d; 4. all; 5. all; 6. c; 7. all; 8. d; 9. b; 10. d

Sleep and Our Physical Health

The famously best line in the super-cheesy Patrick Swayze film *Roadhouse* (1989) is "I'll get enough sleep when I'm dead." How we laughed at this when we were young. The last laugh is on us, however, as it turns out that this has a solid base in reality. The shorter your sleep—we now know from two major epidemiological studies that have tracked millions of people over several decades—the shorter your lifespan. Any adult sleeping an average of 6.76 hours a night is predicted to live only until their early sixties.

Neuroscientists, psychologists and a whole gamut of scientists in universities and sleep laboratories around the world have revealed sleep to have a vital and powerful role resetting our minds and bodies each night. While you are sleeping, an extraordinary diverse range of bodily functions are being maintained and nourished. Those relevant to the physical body include:

- Immune system
- Cardiovascular system
- Hormone and blood sugar balance which affects weight management
- Repair and regeneration of cells
- Nervous system and processing of stress
- Hormone system

When you read that list carefully, it is clear that every single system in the body is dependent upon an adequate quantity and quality of nightly sleep to function properly. Furthermore, we now understand the complex relationship between sleep and the maintenance of our bodies enough to appreciate that, without this sufficient quota of sleep, we become vulnerable to a vast array of disease and disorders. Insufficient sleep:

- increases the likelihood of the coronary arteries becoming blocked which can lead on to cardiovascular disease, stroke, high blood pressure (hypertension) and heart failure. It alarms most people to learn that in adults aged over 45 who sleep fewer than 6 hours a night, the chances of having a heart attack or stroke are increased by 200% compared to those who sleep 7–8 hours.
- incontrovertibly contributes to diabetes and obesity. In the first place, tiredness, as we all know, causes you to reach for instant hit, sugar and carbohydrate-heavy snack food while making exercise much less attractive. Behind the scenes blood sugar levels are disrupted by lack of sleep causing us to gain weight. Our delicately balanced hormone system also tells us when we are hungry and when we are full and insufficient sleep causes it to misfire and we can find ourselves gaining weight even while eating healthily and exercising. There are far higher

rates of type 2 diabetes among people who report sleeping less than six hours a night than those gaining sufficient sleep.

- undermines the immune system which fights against sickness and infection. We know that tiredness makes people more vulnerable to contracting the common cold virus than when they are adequately rested. Additionally, and rather shockingly, tests have been performed that show that the standard flu vaccine is more likely to be successful for people who have slept enough compared to those who are tired.
- increases the risk of cancer. Research has been undertaken to measure the physical effects of working shifts when individuals' circadian rhythms (the body's natural wake/sleep cycle roughly equivalent to day and night-time) are disrupted. Their chances of developing cancer were considerably increased. This has caused the World Health Organisation to classify night-time shift work as a "probable carcinogen." We know that poor sleep quality in general increases cancer risk by 40% for people sleeping 6 or fewer hours a night. And for people who don't work shifts but for whom cancer cells have arrived in the body, a lack of sleep can cause them to spread faster and more dangerously.

Since learning more about the physical consequences of inadequate sleep, I have become a self-styled ambassador of sleep. Or sleep bore, according to my children. I have responded more and more fully to the tiredness of the children and young people I work with, and I have opened sometimes difficult conversations with parents and school leaders. My own sleep habits have changed as I reflect that, returning to the opening of this section, I saw *Roadhouse* at the cinema back in 1989 hence my sixties are not too far off and the statistics about a shortened lifespan are sobering. Everything I have learnt has told me that sleep is the single most effective thing I can do to keep my body and mind healthy and strong.

I use mindfulness and relaxation techniques to make sure my mind and body are in the best state for drifting off to sleep. I try to always get to bed before midnight and take a nap whenever life permits. Sleep is a priority for me and my family. Training as sleep consultant confirmed this and ensured sleep as a priority in our family and something I seek passionately to share with others.

Sleep and Our Mental Health

It will come as no surprise to learn that lack of quality sleep has a devastating effect on our mind as well as our body. There is no major psychiatric condition to which insufficient sleep or disrupted sleep does not contribute. These include depression, anxiety, addiction illnesses, bipolar disorder, schizophrenia and suicidality. Part of the reason for this is the extraordinary work our brains perform while we are asleep. This work manages much of what contributes to healthy minds and emotional wellbeing. Every night while we sleep the vast circuit of neural networks in our brains are recalibrated. Everything we have learnt or experienced that day is processed. Some things are stored in our long-term memory, others are deemed unnecessary and "pruned." This is a seriously amazing process and explains why you can remember certain facts and experiences from years ago but not cleaning your teeth two days ago. Our waking time activities are integrated properly, connecting with our previous experiences and prior knowledge and this builds and builds over a lifetime. The mental health benefits of adequate sleep include boosting the full potential of the vital parts of our inner lives:

- Emotional intelligence—Part of the nightly sleep cycle is spent in REM (Rapid Eye Movement) or dream-sleep, of which you may have heard. Matthew Walker in his fascinating book *Why We Sleep: The New Science of Sleep and Dreams* calls this "a form of overnight therapy" and, indeed, it is commonly acknowledged that you feel better about emotional events after a good night's sleep. This happens because the dream-sleep processes the previous day's events and aims to restore emotional balance for the following day. What an extraordinary gift it is, fundamental to our experience of happiness, if allowed to function properly. We all know how our emotions are affected by tiredness, especially chronic tiredness. Mood swings are common, overreacting to situations, inappropriate behaviours and extreme negativity or positivity can play havoc with our lives. Links have been made between lack of sleep and violence, bullying and behavioural issues. But just eight hours sleep for adults and the correct amounts for children (see p.18) help keep our emotions regulated and enable us to deal better with difficulties and stress—all of which leads to a greater likelihood that we will feel positive and happy. For families everywhere, children are tired and teasy, our teenagers are moody and angry—and we parents and carers are frequently too drained ourselves to deal with it.

- Creativity—This is a fascinating area of research with some wonderful anecdotes about famous discoveries or creative marvels that have occurred in dreams. Keith Richards claims he woke up one morning to find he had dreamt the introduction to "Satisfaction" and was able to write it down. The chemist who came up with the periodic table had struggled for years to order and arrange the elements but had a dream in which they were all laid out perfectly. While he was sleeping, his brain was able to take the pieces of the puzzle and put them together in a new way. Undoubtedly, deep REM sleep increases our capacity for creative thinking. This ability to solve problems has been experienced by most people. I once dreamt I was teaching puppies to meditate, which sounds bonkers, but on waking it gave me the idea to sit some of the younger children I teach on individual cushions used only for this activity. The cushions were like the dog beds in my dream and the results in the classroom were a huge success. My brain had solved the challenge I had been having with getting the little ones to sit still and shown me the solution while I was dreaming. I am sure you can think of a time that a dream has helped you process or problem-solve.
- Memory—A plethora of testing has taken place in sleep and science labs looking at the effects of lack of sleep upon people's ability to recall facts in the short and long term and the results are unequivocal. When we are tired, we retain much less information while we are learning and we forget a whole lot more than we do when we are well-rested. Most of us know this to be true in our everyday lives. Links between sleep disorders and Alzheimer's Disease have also been proven. Getting enough sleep makes a real difference in the ability to take in new information the following day because the filing away of yesterday's memories has successfully taken place. Apply this to the education process and the consequences for children are massive. When running sleep workshops for exam cohorts, they are shocked to learn their revision is undermined by 40% when they have had insufficient sleep.
- Concentration—Another experience we will all have had is difficulty following a television programme, reading a book, listening to a lecture, or paying full attention in a meeting when we are tired. Even the smallest

> amount of sleep deprivation affects our brain's ability to focus and the implications of this can be enormous. It's easy to make mistake, miss deadlines or forget important tasks because our concentration levels have waned. Tests performed on people who had been awake for 19 hours found they were as cognitively impaired as if they were legally drunk. The accidents caused by drowsy drivers outnumber those caused by drivers under the influence of alcohol or drugs and even more serious world events have been a result of human exhaustion, including the catastrophic nuclear explosion at Chernobyl in 1986. The engineers on the space shuttle *Challenger* famously worked around the clock and tiredness may have contributed to the terrible accident.

With rates of mental health issues for adults and children on an alarming rising curve, it would be negligent to ignore the clear links between these issues and sufficient sleep.

It can feel quite overwhelming to read all these facts and figures about the dangers of not sleeping enough and, of course, there are a whole host of other contributing factors to all health issues not least poverty and insufficient information and support for people trying their best. I certainly don't want hard-working parents and carers to feel guilty or frightened about this when we are all dealing with the challenges of modern life, but this is an opportunity for a reset or rethink and it's a good time to remind you that the benefits of a good night's sleep for you and your family are straightforward, pleasurable and free. The chapters below will deal with the practicalities and help you overcome the obstacles.

Sleep and the Development of Children

The baby developing in the womb spends almost all its time in a kind of sleep. Scans of the embryo brain measure similar frequencies to that of REM dream-sleep. I love to think of the tiny growing human floating in this dreamy state. From the moment of birth, however, there is much for the infant brain to be getting on with. Enormous amounts of neural pathways and connections build moment by moment as the brain and body rapidly grow and respond the world around it.

Sleep plays a vital role in enabling all this learning to take place. As a child sleeps, the huge array of physical, mental and emotional events of the day are processed, memories stored, new pathways in the brain built and that continuous recalibration of feelings takes place during REM. Unsurprisingly, intelligence and sleep are unequivocally connected. Tests have proven that children who sleep consistently longer go on to develop higher IQ than those who have had just 40–50 minutes less sleep a night.

The physical benefits of sleep are also profound for children whose motor skills are developing rapidly along with their immune systems and their overall growth. The growth hormone that performs a vast number of repairs to cells throughout the entire body is produced during sleep. I used to assure my young sons that they would definitely grow taller if they went to bed (this had its origins in truth although conveniently ignored the genetic factors). We also know that the links between sleep deprivation and obesity mentioned above apply powerfully in children. Three-year-olds sleeping just 10.5 hours a night or less have an increased risk of being obese by age 7 than children getting 12 hours a night.

I find in my work in schools and other youth settings that their focus on health tends to be around exercise and diet, which is essential, of course, but there is comparatively little in the curriculum or classroom discussion around sleep and the vital role it plays in our children's development. This is because sleep is something that happens in families, but it's clearly a neglected health consideration. As parents and carers we can try to instil an absolute cornerstone of wellbeing for our children by doing everything we can to ensure that they get enough sleep. To repeat the facts—for toddlers this is 12 hours; children aged 3–6 need 10–12 hours; those aged 7–12 need 10–11 hours. Your adolescent requires 8–10 hours.

In the chapters below, you will find a variety of support and idea for the issues that may be occurring in your house so don't despair if you are reading these recommendations and the scary consequences of not reaching them. As well as teaching mindfulness I have been practising it myself for more than 25 years. One of the core values is *non-judgement.*

Practising Non-Judgement

It sounds simple but we all know how hard it can be to apply in practise. This is because we will have taken on negative messages from childhood, and possibly for much of our lives, about ourselves and it's really hard not to carry them with us. We allow our inner critic to ride roughshod over our adult selves. Our brains are wired for survival, and this means that negative thoughts tend to "stick" in the mind more than positive ones—like Velcro; while the positive messages we receive from ourselves and others are more likely to slide off like Teflon. Take a moment to reflect on a time when you have batted away a compliment but taken on a real or implied criticism—it's normal, we all do it because our brains are wired this way. It can be harder to shift the negative messages and to properly register the compliments we may receive or really hear the appreciation of others—how often do we shrug off those warm words and choose instead to beat ourselves with the stick of perfection?

Mindfulness practice enables us to build resilience by *noticing* the impulse to pass judgement—those critical thoughts that pop up all by themselves in our minds and which we apply to others but, more often, to ourselves—and *choosing* not to go down that mental path. An awareness of this critical voice in your mind is the first step to quieting it down and creating some mental space. When it pipes up, you can then choose not to listen to it or to counter it with the opposite or with some kinder language. For example, a self-critical thought might be "I will never be able to sort this out"—take a breath, notice what the voice is saying and how it feels in your body, apply some kindness and rephrase "I find this difficult but am doing my best" or "I don't have to achieve perfection, but I can take small steps in the direction I want things to go," "Actually, I can make a positive difference." Breathe slowly and notice how you feel now.

Kindness is another core value of mindfulness and is sometimes easier applied to others than ourself, but winding down your criticism and judgement of others can be really liberating. We live in a pretty unkind world where social media interactions enable brutal verbal attacks on strangers and cause untold damage, especially to our young people. Modelling for your kids and practising a bit more tolerance and kindness feels better for everyone.

I hope you will apply some non-judgement to yourself now as it is easy for parents, carers and children, especially adolescents, on learning about the perils of inadequate sleep to give themselves a hard time or to feel hopeless about making changes. If you can communicate non-judgement to your children as well, all the better for making effective change. I work with real children in real schools and am well aware of the challenges in real families. These include dealing with illness, physical and mental. It is estimated that there are around 800,000 young carers in the UK—that is 6 in every secondary school classroom.

Young people often have responsibilities to contribute to the family business or to juggle part-time jobs with their school and social lives. An ageing family member or a new baby can cause disruption in family schedules. Parental conflict can cause severe difficulty for children—my parents would try to avoid arguing "in front of the children" but our bedtime would sometimes run against the low-level background noise of heated arguments that prevented us sleeping well. Bereavement, income insecurity and other adult pressures can act as a powerful source of unrest in all families that affects the ability to prioritise sleep. I live and work in Cornwall, top staycation destination for many UK families—yet it hides a significant amount of deprivation that can lead to issues such as housing insecurity, bedroom-sharing and sofa-surfing that all affect sleep, especially for teenagers. Keep reading and you will find plenty of support and strategies to help with a broad range of sleep issues.

Sleep and Teenagers

If you are the parent of a teenager, you will know just how many changes take place in diverse areas of their lives. Sleep is another noticeable area of change for adolescents as their sleep pattern takes a shift forwards—they naturally need to wake later and go to sleep later. For parents whose children have woken with the birds throughout their lives, the shift can be a welcome change, but it can make bedtime a more challenging matter. And when there are other challenges around aspects of teenage life, from schoolwork to social lives, another area of conflict is not what parents need.

Many hours have been spent in our house arguing about time spent—"wasted"—gaming. I've since been proved spectacularly wrong by our son heading to university to start an exciting career in video game design. However, it is important to understand just why and how the sleep needs of the adolescent matter so much. I know how challenging this can be, especially when they want to game, chat or consume vast amounts of cereal in the night.

As well as REM (Rapid Eye Movement) dream-sleep, mentioned above, our brains enjoy nightly cycles of NREM sleep—the imaginatively named Non-REM sleep. This NREM sleep works using different brainwaves and performs a different function from the REM sleep particularly in terms of neural connections. While REM sleep strengthens the connections in the brain, building emotional resilience, deep NREM sleep has the job of weeding out the unnecessary ones. Early childhood requires the creation of vast amounts of these pathways but with adolescence comes a consolidation and the process of pruning, carried out during NREM sleep. This enables the brain to free up space for the addition of new input the following day and thus this cycle of REM and NREM sleep continues throughout our lives. It signals the move of the adolescent away from the care of parents, who have made decisions for them, towards independence.

The change that comes during puberty requires the teenage brain to sleep for a minimum of 8 hours a night and preferably 10 hours. The combination of teenagers needing more sleep than adults, and the fact that they need it at different times, can play out in many difficult scenarios in households across the globe. You will find suggested ways to improve the situation in Chapter 5.

The important facts to take on at this stage are that insufficient sleep for the adolescent brain can lead to cognitive and emotional issues and set a pattern for poor growth and development. This is the time of life at which most psychiatric disorders first emerge, so long-term mental health is affected by under-sleeping. Abnormal sleep patterns are also associated with addictive substance use and this is of concern because the teenage brain is already programmed to take risks. Decision-making and critical thinking are impaired by lack of sleep. We know that children who did not sleep for long enough in their early years are more likely to use drugs and alcohol during adolescence.

Statistically, we know that fewer than 75% of children aged 11–18 get sufficient sleep which means the rest of them are going through the day without adequate rest. When I work in classrooms and ask teenagers about their sleep, I find this figure much lower. The role sleep plays in emotional regulation can have particularly serious consequences for young people and this is something I and many teachers see acted out regularly in classrooms and that parents across the world see at home. Tired teenagers have moods that can swing dramatically.

They struggle to manage their feelings and their relationships with each other and the adults in their life. They can become deeply unhappy and this is terrible to see.

The tired teenager is more likely to be aggressive towards others and, crucially, towards themselves. Incidents of self-harm are rising rapidly and help for these young people, a great number of them girls, is insufficiently funded so they are not getting support. When young people are tired, they cannot focus or concentrate as well and their performance in tests is directly affected by how rested they are prior to taking exams.

Add to all this the pressure from a school system that demands early starts and piles on homework and testing, and you can see why the levels of anxiety and depression among teenagers are at epidemic levels across industrialised nations. One motivation for my decision to train as a children's mindfulness teacher was my shock and sorrow at the rising levels of mental health problems our young people experience as well as the woeful lack of support for them.

It is estimated that 20% of adolescents may experience a mental health problem in any given year. One in six young people experience an anxiety condition at some point—these can manifest as social anxiety and shyness, exam stress, chronic worry, panic attacks and OCD (Obsessive Compulsive Disorder). Anxiety can escalate into dangerous behaviours such as self-harm. It is impossible to tell the exact figures as the teenagers self-harming are secretive and often afraid to ask for help. Other forms of self-harm are substance abuse, eating disorders (there has been a dramatic rise in hospital admissions for young people with anorexia and bulimia) and, tragically, suicide. Suicide is rising among young people and, while more males commit suicide, more young women are doing so than ever before. We know that every kind of self-harming is now happening among younger and younger children.

Getting enough sleep is not the cure for every physical, mental and emotional problem but research shows us that we should not underestimate what a powerful effect for good it is on our minds and bodies. This is particularly true for growing and developing children and adolescents. The most rewarding part of my work over the past decade has been the feedback from children and adolescents about the improvements they notice in their feelings of happiness and wellbeing when they have a set of practical tools to use to calm both their minds and bodies. Calmness, relaxation and connecting with ourselves feels good for adults and children alike. I have had whole rooms of children in deep relaxation, and I've looked around to see the teachers and teaching assistants with huge smiles on their faces at the palpable sense of peace in the room. Knowing that the children, their parents and teachers all perceive a definite improvement in wellbeing once these simple techniques have been learnt means everything to me. I have seen what can happen when we make rest, relaxation and sleep a priority.

Sleep as We Grow Older

We've learnt a lot about sleep so far and its vital role in development from the womb and through puberty as well as how it helps to protect people of all ages against disease, but what happens as we age? Learning about the changes that take place in our sleep as we grow older can help you set in place positive patterns for your cognitive and physical health during middle age. It will help you to support older family members, who may or may not live with you, and will empower you with the knowledge you need to create your own healthier future.

As we get older, our sleep patterns change. This is due in part to the body gradually producing less melatonin—you will learn more about the circadian rhythm and the role of melatonin in the next chapter. The reduction of this hormone brings about a change in sleep architecture. This refers to how people cycle through the various stages of sleep, such as NREM and REM sleep, mentioned above. As with teenagers, the sleep cycle moves forward meaning that we get tired earlier in the afternoon, it can be harder to fall asleep at night and we may wake earlier in the morning. The transition between being awake and asleep changes, and waking can often be more abrupt which means older people feel they are lighter sleepers than they used to be.

Less time is spent in deep restorative NREM sleep leading to feeling more tired generally. As we age, we may wake more frequently in the night due to needing the loo (this is known as nocturia) or because of anxiety, discomfort or pain from illness or disability. Nocturia may affect up to 80% of older adults. Medication for physical health issues can also have the side effect of fragmenting sleep.

Older people often experience daytime drowsiness and assume that feeling tired during the day is a normal part of ageing, but it can be a sign of underlying health problems that need medical advice. 40–70% of older adults have chronic sleep issues that may be undiagnosed because they think that it is just to be expected.

It is a myth that older people need less sleep. Good quality and quantity of sleep is required throughout our lives to restore energy levels and heal physical and cognitive damage in the body and brain. This means 7–8 hours of sleep every night and, ideally, a short nap during the early afternoon. Not only does sleep remain vital for cognitive function but a University of California team has found that partial sleep deprivation activates the molecular pathways that drive biological ageing due to the inflammation markers. Not getting enough sleep as we age can mean that we age faster—and feel less capable, confident and able to enjoy life.

Insufficient sleep causes reduced cognitive abilities which, for older people, can lead to feelings of confusion and to depression. People with heart troubles are at particularly high risk of depressive symptoms. These mental changes increase the likelihood of accidents and falls which can be catastrophic for older people. We know how crucial healthy sleep is to our memory as well as to cognition. Quality sleep consolidates the memory function. There are clear links between regularly sleeping less than 6 hours a night and dementia-related brain changes. These may begin in middle age. A Canadian research team has identified severely disturbed sleep as an early signal of impending dementia.

In my experience, I also find that accumulated stress is a major barrier to good sleep. Many people arrive in middle and old age carrying the baggage of life's difficulties which become hardwired into the brain and body. Our routines, beliefs and expectations tend to set firmly in place regardless of whether they are still serving us or not. Most of us don't sail through life without tough times. We may have experienced trauma, bereavement, hardship and long periods of anxiety or fear. The older we get, the harder it can be to release old patterns of thinking and to access the calm space of peace and relaxation that enables sleep to come easily. This is something I want to help everyone with.

Much of the focus of this book is on teaching these skills to our children and young people so that they can use the tools moving forward in their lives. Let me assure you, however, that it is never too late to make changes and to find that place of peace. I will be sharing practical suggestions and proven practices that will support your mind and body however stuck in your habits you may feel yourself to be. You'll be able to try out for yourself the ones that appeal and share them with the other adults in your life.

This chapter has, I hope, given you the inspiration to tackle the problems you may be facing in your family so you can all benefit from the many wonderful things sleep offers us all. The rest of this book is devoted to supporting you and providing you with those practical solutions and ideas.

Chapter 2
When Sleep Goes Wrong

Every major system, tissue and organ of your body suffers when sleep becomes short. No aspect of your health can retreat at the sign of sleep loss and escape unharmed.

Matthew Walker, author of *Why We Sleep*

There are over 100 diagnosed sleep disorders. These include many that you will have heard of, such as insomnia, sleepwalking, night terrors and narcolepsy. There are plenty you are unlikely to have heard of as well. If you think anyone in your family may be suffering from any of these, it is important to seek medical help. Some NHS trusts and universities have sleep clinics that can treat a wide range of disorders and you will need to go through your GP to find out whether you qualify for this specialist help. In addition, there are some excellent charities supporting families, details can be found in the Resources section on p.241.

The relaxation and mindfulness techniques I am qualified and experienced in teaching adults, children and young people are not a substitute for the review of health issues by a medical professional. However, I know that doctors often advise calming and meditative practices to help adults and children with anxiety that may be preventing sleep. Sleep consultants, myself included, teach clients relaxation techniques that improve their ability to fall asleep—you'll learn about these in the coming chapters. Increasing awareness of the efficacy of mindfulness means I am asked more and more to work with schools and youth groups and, as I said earlier, the proliferation of tiredness among the young people I see has led me to focus on it and to listen to parents, carers and children about what is going wrong with their sleep.

Schools invite me to teach sleep workshops to entire year groups where staff have identified tiredness as a barrier to learning and a key factor in behavioural, social and emotional concerns. All experienced teachers can spot a tired pupil a mile off whether it's the yawning, inability to recall information or from poor behaviour.

To better understand how some problems begin and are so challenging to solve, an awareness of how normal sleep cycles work can be very helpful.

How Sleep Normally Occurs

The wake/sleep cycle is also known as our circadian rhythm, sometimes referred to as our "body clock." Its daily pattern tells us when to wake up and when to sleep. Ideally, as discussed above, we all have 15–17 hours of being awake followed by 7–9 hours of sleep. We know that children and adolescents need longer and that older people, who may think they need less, actually need the same amount as they did during middle age. This cycle is controlled by several factors and, it should be noted here, has been radically changed by the development of technologies, from electric light to LED bulbs, and by aspects of modern lifestyle from air travel across time zones to shift-working. There is more detailed discussion of this in Chapter 6 (see p.156).

From the moment we wake up (ideally in the morning), our bodies begin to create a hormone called *adenosine*. This gradually builds throughout the day until it reaches peak when we need sleep. This is called sleep pressure and, ideally, we take notice of the tiredness and take ourselves off to bed. We all know how it feels when we don't do this in good time. Common experiences of excess sleep pressure include: a reduced ability to concentrate, feeling fuzzy headed, "gritty" eyes, grumpiness and short-temperedness, even weepiness.

My three children were frequently scratchy and grouchy in the first hour after school finished. I have taught many after-school sessions and have often had children arrive so tired they ask for a short lie-down before they start—I always have a bag of fluffy blankets with me and find a brief, quiet time-out means they perk up and join in before long. Some of the extremes of tiredness have already been mentioned and they include frightening facts about accidents and psychological and emotional consequences. When we sleep, the adenosine levels in the blood drop and the cycle starts over again once we wake. If you wake too early, there may still be adenosine in the body and it can last into the morning.

For me, as a night owl (see p.137 for more about the tendency of people to be "larks" or "owls"), this happens if I wake up before about 7.30am. I feel groggy, my eyes are gritty and I am aware of a real pressure to return to sleep. When I wake just an hour later, I feel much more lively and alert because the "sleep debt" has been paid. You may be more of a "lark" and feel as if you've hit a brick wall after about 10 pm unless you get to bed.

Also playing its part in the circadian rhythm is *melatonin*, a hormone you may have heard of in connection with jetlag and some sleep disorders. The brain starts to produce melatonin in the late afternoon, and it gradually rises throughout the evening enabling the body to sleep at night. The levels stay high while we are asleep then drop in the early mornings and signal the time to awake. Melatonin production is directly connected with levels of daylight and is a biological function that has kept the human body in tune with the rising and setting of the sun.

Melatonin Supplements

I am often asked about the efficacy and advisability of using melatonin liquid or capsule supplements to help adults and children with sleep issues. They are used by many people worldwide and sold in the United States as a dietary supplement where they are one of the most commonly used by adults and children. I am afraid they are marketed as a "quick fix" and, in my opinion, generally no solution to setting up long-term healthy sleep habits apart from in a few specific situations. Delayed sleep-wake phase disorder can occur when international travel has disrupted sleep patterns i.e. jetlag. Small research studies have shown that taking melatonin after you have travelled across time zones can be helpful to reset the body clock. Shift-working is another sleep disrupter but there is inconclusive evidence that taking melatonin will improve this.

The American Academy of Paediatrics (APP) states that melatonin may be a beneficial tool to help children and young adults while they are in the process of establishing better sleep patterns. Small study research shows it may particularly help children with certain conditions such as epilepsy and for those with neurodevelopmental disorders such as autism spectrum disorder. There is not enough evidence yet, however, about the long-term use of melatonin supplements or about the optimal dosage and duration for using it. This makes it a risky decision and is one you should only make in close conversation with your doctor or paediatrician. Side effects from melatonin use are relatively rare but some adults may experience daytime drowsiness, headaches or dizziness. Children may sometimes suffer agitation or increased risk of bedwetting so this makes that medical consultation even more essential

Having insufficient quantities of melatonin in the body is a very specific reason why sleep can go wrong—it can be remedied naturally by exposing yourself to enough daylight and sticking to a routine of rising and going to bed at roughly the same time. You'll learn how to track this for yourself and your children when we learn how to use a sleep diary (below). Melatonin's direct relation to time spent in daylight means that making an effort to increase this for ourselves and others will see an improvement in our sleep pattern. Teenagers who rise in the afternoon during school or college holidays will, especially during the winter months, struggle to get sufficient melatonin because its particularly linked to morning light. Similarly, older people and those who experience poor health or disability can find getting outside to be a struggle. I encourage a disabled relative of ours to get some sun on his face by helping him to a chair on the doorstep for half an hour. It means he can wave at his passing neighbours too and it is generally a success.

For good melatonin production, aim for a minimum of 1 hour outdoors every day for each member of the family. Half of this time outside is best taken in the morning, but a second half-hour exposure can be taken between 1–3pm when the body produces another brief spike of melatonin. Schools have this nicely worked into the timetable of playtime and lunchtimes and are always, in my experience as a parent and a teacher, determined to get the children outside! For adults and older people, however, it can be harder to motivate yourself to get outdoors. Getting outside when we have so much to do might feel like an indulgence. With many of us working from home more, that daily walk to the bus stop or train station might have vanished and plenty of people find they tumble from bed to the desk, via a slice of toast. We are seriously losing out on vital health and wellbeing benefits by staying indoors.

The Benefits of Getting Outside

Spending time outside, especially in the morning, affects our melatonin production which leads to better sleep. But there are multiple other ways we can all feel better when we expose ourselves to daylight:

- Vitamin D production is enhanced during sunlight exposure and plays a vital role in fighting fatigue, immune function, muscle and bone health and can improve our mood and reduce the symptoms of depression. Approximately 30 minutes of sun exposure daily will get both adults and children the recommended dose of vitamin D. Our body cannot get all the vitamin D we require from our food, the rest needs to come from sunlight.
- Skin health—we know to cover up and use sunscreen to protect skin damage from strong sunlight but there is evidence that certain skin conditions such as psoriasis and vitiligo will benefit from sunlight but check with your dermatologist for individual advice.
- Healthy weight and metabolism—a team of researchers studying obesity and diabetes disorders accidentally discovered that the blue-light spectrum in sunlight can have the effect of making certain cells in our body less likely to store fat. Our metabolism speeds up when sunlight causes our bodies to release nitric acid. However—don't go overboard as too much sun can still be damaging.
- Improved eye health—there are links between vitamin D3 and the slowing down of macular degeneration. Getting daily sunshine can help keep our eyesight sharp for longer. Avoid looking directly at the sun, of course, the benefits can be absorbed through the eyelids.
- Exercise—you can sit on your doorstep and absorb all the lovely benefits of the sun, but if possible, combine this with appropriate exercise. Calming the body at the end of the day so it is ready for sleep is considerably easier when we have moved and breathed deeply. Many people like to exercise indoors, I completely understand that, but whenever you can combine your sunlight exposure and a walk, gentle run or stretching routine it will improve the chances of a better night's sleep—which gives you energy for more exercise the following day!

It is easy to see how the circadian rhythm our ancestors experienced for thousands of years has altered post-industrial revolution. We no longer need to rise with the sun and go to bed when it gets dark. The invention of electric light at the end of the 19th century changed everything as people were able to go out, work and stay up as much as they wanted after dark. Shift work was also enabled and factories were able to maximise output by running work shifts throughout the night. In modern times, millions of people work through the night making up a global workforce. This includes the many call centres where companies employ thousands of night-workers to answer the phone calls of their daytime customers.

We live in this modern world, but our minds and bodies are happiest and healthiest when the circadian rhythm is permitted to send the hormonal signals for waking and sleeping—and when we listen to those signals. A culture of "sleep hacks" and burning the candle at both ends, taking work home and the FOMO culture of packing in as much as possible into a day means individuals are often fighting against their own body clock. When we can't fight the fluctuating levels of adenosine and melatonin beckoning us towards rest and sleep, many people, including children and teenagers, turn to the world's most popular, legal, psychoactive stimulant: caffeine. It impairs the production of adenosine enabling consumers to push their sleep times on and interfere with a healthy sleep cycle. That caffeine is also addictive makes it an essential part of any discussion about sleep and especially around young children and teenagers consuming it (more of this on p.142).

The Circadian Rhythm

In the womb, the developing baby is largely asleep and dreaming. Once born, it takes about 3 months for a baby to be able to settle into a rhythm of sleeping at night and being awake during the day, as all new parents can attest to only too well. This book is not addressing the often controversial issues around babies and routines. I will say for myself that I found it helped all three of my babies to sleep and feed better when they were in a routine and that I gently aimed for this from their early weeks. It is every parent's choice to navigate the early years of their baby's life in whatever way they think best.

By the age of 5, the majority of children will be in a routine because the rest of the family will be in a routine around mealtimes, nursery, school, work and bedtime. Children's hormone systems work in the same way as adults' do with adenosine released at their waking and melatonin in the late afternoon all signalling that sleep is necessary. Sleep needs to be at night and waking times during the day, as fits most of the world's natural rhythm. The biggest difference between adult and child sleeping patterns is around naps and this is an interesting area of study on its own with a major recent research project finding that taking a 20–45 minute nap a day can have a huge variety of health benefits from reducing the chances of heart attacks and stroke to actually prolonging life.

Bring back the siesta, says all the advice. My dad remembers when 1950s primary schools had nap time for all built into the day; my 1970s education saw us all often encouraged to lay our heads on our arms over our desks and rest. The mindfulness term for this would be "non-doing" or just "being," and I'm a massive fan.

Young children nap because they need much more sleep than adults to get done the vast amount of growing and developing the first few years of life require. This changes as they reach school age and they are able to stay awake for 12 hours plus. However, like adults resisting the call to snooze during those post-lunch meetings, children also have a natural dip in alertness during the day. Once a child starts school the opportunity for a nap is lost and this is a real shame as it would solve many sleep issues, prevent over-tiredness and enable better emotional regulation. Schools are not going to introduce sleeping facilities any time soon but, interestingly, now the benefits of the nap have been so well-documented, some businesses are taking notice.

Companies such as Google, Nike, Samsung, Zappos and space agency NASA have installed sleep pods in their offices. The impact of a tactical snooze on the ability of the workforce to concentrate, create and relate to each other are unequivocal and I suspect there will be a growth in this sort of office sleeping facility in the decades ahead. Needless to say, evidence finds increased productivity among the well-rested workforce. As much of the post-covid workforce continues to work from home some or all of the time, it could be easier to negotiate a "power nap" with employers—there is plenty of evidence to support you working better and for longer if you recharge your batteries in the early afternoon! Changing attitudes to sleep across society will benefit us all.

Children are often rising earlier than their bodies would like, roused by alarm clocks or parents rushing through the morning. Working parents often need to use school breakfast clubs to enable them to get to their jobs on time, so for some children the day starts extremely early. School days tend to be packed as teachers work to reach ever higher educational standards for their pupils. There is time allocated, thankfully, to play and exercise; to create, build and make. School can be exciting, stimulating, rewarding and fun. It is also where children navigate social situations by themselves for the first time. The classroom and playground can be daunting for all children and, as they become accustomed to it, other challenges may arise, including friendship issues and bullying. Enough sleep the night before can make a huge difference to how children process their emotions and regulate their behaviour especially when they feel under pressure.

Teenagers have a whole new set of challenges as their body clocks push an hour or two on and they tend to need to sleep longer in the mornings and go to bed later at night. This is due to the changes taking place in the teenage brain as well as hormonal differences post-puberty. The secondary school day often puts even more pressure on the circadian rhythm of teenage pupils as many need to travel further than they did when attending local primary schools. Some children need to rise very early to catch trains, buses or taxis. Breakfast clubs are found in over 85% of UK schools now and tend to start at 8 am; some schools have even earlier start times. These clubs are to help working parents but also to ensure that children get a good meal before they begin the school day.

After-school activities are part of life for many children in the UK with some clubs organised by schools meaning that children have a longer day on school premises. A survey in 2019 found that UK parents were paying up to £28,000 over their child's school years for extracurricular activities outside of school, including sports clubs and training, dance, drama, swimming, music, art, gymnastics and extra tuition. The benefits of activities for children are vast: mixing with children outside their school cohorts in local sports leagues and clubs; being part of community music and drama groups; learning lifelong skills like swimming, languages and musical instruments. It can be difficult to deny children opportunities that their friends may be enjoying or that parents feel will give them advantages they may not have had themselves. The average British child does three activities a week. The time spent taking children to and from activities is on average 156 hours over a childhood.

When you add the time spent in these activities to a school schedule that includes nightly homework of reading, learning spellings, completing projects for primary children and an onslaught of subject-based homework that arrives in year 7 and continues throughout their school life, it is no wonder that "over-scheduling" has been identified as harmful for children. Children who have too many scheduled activities lack time to relax with their families and embrace boredom and the creativity that can lead from it. We also know that some over-scheduled children suffer more from anxiety, eat badly, may have problems making friends and struggle to sleep well.

As a mindfulness teacher, I am a big fan of unscheduled time for everyone but especially for children. Downtime is vital for children's wellbeing: the opportunity to be bored, to play, invent their own games and past-times, pick up a neglected book or toy, to be spontaneous. Mindfulness is about being present, paying attention in the moment; boredom offers the perfect opportunity to notice where the inclination leads, and children need freedom to follow this.

Whatever the age of your child, a routine around bedtime is vital for the optimum function of the hormones governing sleep and the circadian rhythm. This applies to the adults in the house too although sometimes our working pattern can make this very difficult to manage. A routine will also make bedtimes more straightforward for you and your child and sets a pattern for a lifetime of healthy attitudes around sleep. Chapter 1 explained why sleep matters so much. Readers will know the impact of lack of sleep or poor sleep habits on their lives. You will know your own child's behaviour around bedtime and sleep and the impact it has on everyone in the household. Bed-hopping, waking frequently, refusing to go to bed are not diagnosable sleep disorders but they can make life a misery for the whole family and create a tension around bedtimes that is hard to eradicate.

I juggled multiple children with different bedtimes for many years and often found as soon as I'd got one sleeping happily in their own bed, an older child would appear needing a drink, or the eldest hoping for special dispensation and a chat. So, I understand how challenging it can be. I found sticking to simple rules about not coming back downstairs once we said goodnight helped but that meant consistently enforcing the rule night after night until it sunk in. You have to stick to your guns once you've decided what's best and the following chapter will help you do so.

For adults experiencing any difficulties around falling or staying asleep, a routine is also essential. When we work with our body clock and not against it, the whole process becomes more natural and effective. It can be hard to establish a regular bedtime if you are shift-working or caring for a disabled or unwell person and I wholeheartedly sympathise. Moving towards a schedule that best supports your sleep is done via experimentation and mindful awareness of how each change makes you feel. You may be surprised how much better you will feel after making one simple change such as avoiding screens for an hour before sleep or cutting out late-night snacking.

One person's winding-down ritual may be vastly different from another's but building in time devoted to relaxing the mind and the body means the process of sleep will become easier. We will look more closely at sleep hygiene and sleep routines in the following chapter.

Diagnosing Sleep Problems in Your Family

Hopefully, by this point in the book, you will have been thinking about your own family sleep issues and identifying areas where you might be able to make changes or at least prioritise. Perhaps your issues are around children staying in bed once the lights are out or it might be that getting them into bed and in the right frame of mind for sleep is where the issue lies. Do worries surface at bedtime that require lots of calming? Or your child may be one who wakes in the night after a bad dream or who is difficult to resettle once they have woken up. Children who are very tired at the end of the day may fall asleep straight after dinner but then wake again a few hours, just as you've headed off to bed, and the challenges may be here. Adults with different sleep patterns can disturb each other and this puts pressure on relationships. A routine consistently stuck to can help with all these areas.

The quiz below is designed to help you focus on the habits in your household and how they may be impacting on the bedtime issues you may be experiencing. There is no judgement happening here at all so please be honest and remember there is no such thing as the perfect parent, perfect child or perfect family. It may look like certain answers are "better" than others but this is not the point at all. I want to help you focus on aspects of sleep and to assure you that there are solutions for all the difficulties that may be identified in this quiz. The answers to some questions for yourself and your child/ren may be different so make a note of where those differences are for each member of the family. Here goes!

1. Is there a regular bedtime routine in your house for adults and children?
    a) Yes, we follow one every night and it is pretty much the same
    b) We have a vague routine but it is affected by activities and busy lives
    c) We used to have one but it didn't work/children are older now
    d) Routines are not for us

2. Are you and your child/ren getting enough nightly sleep—reminder: 3–6-year-olds, 10–12 hours; 7–12-year-olds, 10–11 hours; teenagers, 8–10 hours; adults, 8+ hours? Be honest!
   a) Pretty positive that we all are
   b) Unlikely to be enough every night but it's not far off
   c) No idea
   d) Definitely not

3. Is bedtime a time of tension in your house?
   a) No, my child enjoys the attention and winding down
   b) Sometimes it is, when we are rushing or running late
   c) We have nightly dramas about something
   d) It's always a battle and we dread it

4. Do the adults have a bedtime routine?
   a) Yes, there's an enjoyable wind-down period
   b) It depends on social/work demands
   c) Life is too hectic to manage this
   d) We collapse into bed after cramming in as much we can

5. Does your child have a very busy schedule?
   a) Not at all, there is a lot of empty time to just be
   b) A few after-school clubs and the odd regular lesson or activity after school or at weekends
   c) Most days have activities after school and playdates, and we keep busy at weekends
   d) My child's diary is fuller than my own and I spend my life ferrying them from club to club

6. Does your child worry or experience anxiety at bedtime?
   a) No, bedtimes are about feeling secure
   b) My child will sometimes share worries at bedtime and this affects how well they settle
   c) My child can be worried about bad dreams, friendships, school work and it all seems to surface just before bed
   d) Most nights they express anxiety and we have tears or tantrums

7. How often do you or your partner struggle to fall or remain asleep?
    a) This is seldom an issue
    b) Disturbances from the children interrupt my/our sleep
    c) Stress and worry can keep me/us awake but this is usually down to specific issues
    d) I/we experience disrupted sleep at least 3 nights each week

8. How dark are the bedrooms in your house?
    a) Very dark, blackout blinds or curtains with blackout lining; or I/my child uses a sleep mask
    b) Normal curtains or blinds which let in some light especially during the summer months
    c) The door is left open with a light on outside the room; or a low nightlight stays on throughout the night
    d) A light remains on all night including light from television, phone or computer screen

9. How warm are adults and children at night?
    a) Cool—room is about 18°C, nightclothes are light
    b) Warm—room is about 20°C, warm pyjamas worn, sometimes socks
    c) Cold—room is about 16°C
    d) Hot—room is about 22°, onesie worn, socks often

10. What technology is in each bedroom?
    a) Digital alarm clock
    b) Kindle or other e-reader
    c) Television, laptop or iPad
    d) Phone, computer

11. Do adults or children regularly drink caffeine?
    a) Never
    b) Occasional soft drink containing caffeine (many popular soft drinks contain caffeine with the diet option often having most)
    c) 2–3 cups of tea and coffee a day
    d) More than 4 cups of tea or coffee every day

12. Do adults and children get regular exercise outside?
    a) Yes, everyone walks/plays daily outside at home and school
    b) Yes, several times a week
    c) Walks to work/school or exercises once a week
    d) Seldom takes any outside exercise or spends time outdoors

13. How would you describe your/your partner's overall sleep?
    a) I sleep like a log
    b) It always takes me ages to drop off
    c) I usually wake in the night or earlier than I need to
    d) I am a terrible sleeper

During the process of answering these questions, you may have been able to identify the areas where things are going well. There aren't right or wrong answers: it's a consciousness-raising test that flags up aspects of lifestyle and attitude that impact on sleep. If your child isn't over-scheduled, has plenty of fresh air and exercise and doesn't drink caffeine, these can all be eliminated as considerations. All these habit-based issues are the focus of Chapter 3 when the bedtime routine is covered in much more detail. Questions 3, 6 and 7 flagged up emotional issues and these may be the areas you need help with. These will be covered in Chapter 4. Make a note of the issues you most need help with. Some problems can be solved quite easily while others will take a little time.

Adult Insomnia

Question 7 focused on the thorny subject of insomnia. Question 13 examined any set beliefs you may have about your or your partner's sleep in general. We'll be looking in Chapter 9 at how those expectations you hold about the quality of your sleep might be preventing you from making changes and you will learn ways to shift these beliefs and reset your sleep habits. Insomnia, however, is the most common of sleep disorders and, as you may know from experience, can play havoc with how you feel and behave the following day.

Short bouts of adult sleeplessness are common and may be due to short-term stressors. Insomnia is typically characterised by looking at the duration of this pattern. If it happens now and again, it is likely to be acute insomnia. It can happen before a job interview, for example, or when an important deadline is looming. It can happen when we are worried about a family member or a friend.

Life is full of stresses and when the mind cannot switch off, this passing sleep disruption can be incredibly frustrating. It is also very challenging when one adult is going through a period of insomnia that is disturbing their partner. It can be very hard to drop off when your partner is clearly struggling to do the same—and two tired people are undoubtedly worse than one. We'll look at this and other sleep challenges that take place between adults sharing a bed shortly. Acute insomnia usually resolves itself once the stressor has passed but you will learn ways to improve this using relaxation and mindfulness in the following chapters.

Chronic insomnia is diagnosed when sleep patterns are disrupted for more than 3 nights each week and when this has been happening for 3 months or more. While we expect this to happen during those new baby months, when it lasts for much longer it can be truly debilitating and action needs to take place whether resolving your own sleep pattern or helping your children to sleep better so you can get that much-needed sleep too. A National Sleep Foundation survey in 2005 highlighted that approximately 57% of women and 51% of men had experienced insomnia for a several nights a week or more. Women may be experiencing more insomnia than men due to biological changes around menstruation and the menopause.

Chronic insomnia is frequently co-morbid—in other words, it is linked to other factors such as these hormonal ones. Other co-morbidities include the wakefulness of children but also clinical disorders, medication, PTSD (post-traumatic stress disorder) or health problems that cause pain or discomfort. If you think your sleeplessness may be linked to one of these, it is important to have a conversation with your doctor about ways to improve things—don't just put up with them, help may be available.

Solutions to insomnia may lie in making changes to where, when and how you approach sleep. However ingrained those beliefs about your sleep may be, use this as an opportunity to look holistically at all the factors that contribute to quality sleep. A key way to do this is to build a sleep diary for yourself and any poorly sleeping adults or children.

Building a Sleep Diary – Adult, Child, Teenager

If you answered question 2 in the quiz above about the amount of sleep you or your child gets with any uncertainty, please don't feel bad. You are not alone. A recent survey found over 70% of parents believing their children were getting enough sleep, while fewer than 25% of teenagers were really achieving this. You can usually assess the quantity of sleep you yourself have managed, but how do you know how much sleep your child actually gets? It is easy to account for a baby's hours of sleep as they tend to notify their parents in no uncertain terms when they are awake. Checking young children are asleep after it all goes quiet is something most parents do just before they turn in themselves or via a listening monitor. Older children may be reading or playing quietly in bed for quite some time before they fall asleep; and teenagers can be getting up to all sorts behind closed doors!

Once my teens had computers in their bedrooms, we had to reach an agreement about usage that didn't involve me or their dad bursting into the room to catch them out. Promising we'd switch off the Wi-Fi at a prescribed time did the trick and we tried to put the focus on that mindful awareness of how much better it feels to have had a decent amount of sleep. Our children shared with us how hard it can be to voluntarily switch devices off—it helped when they understood how social media and gaming companies deliberately create an addictive experience.

The answer to question 2 is extremely important for all the reasons set out in Chapter 1: the physical, mental and emotional health of adults and children is impaired by a lack of sleep. In addition, the benefits are vast: from improved concentration to mood regulation. Getting this right or at least moving it in the right direction can have a profound effect on the wellbeing of the whole family.

Adult Sleep Diary

If you are keen to improve your own sleep or that of your partner, start to build a picture of what this actually looks like. This is an essential tool for solving your sleep issues and would be an early part of the consultation with a sleep expert. You can get yourself a notebook for this or use the chart provided below for adult sleep tracking. Commit to doing this every day for 1 week. Record times and details for the following:

- What time you head off to bed
- Estimate when you fell asleep
- How easy or difficult it was to fall asleep
- Any night wakings (cause and duration)

- What time you wake up—then calculate for each night the total amount of sleep that night, deducting time spent awake
- Exercise taken (when and what kind, including sex)
- Caffeine use (what time)
- Alcohol consumed (how much)
- Meals and snacks (when taken and what kind)
- Exposure to daylight (quantity and time of)
- Any mindfulness practice or mindful movement (e.g., yoga or qigong)
- Any specific worries/stresses
- Any naps taken (time of and duration)
- What time you last use an electronic device (e.g., TV, phone, laptop—backlit e-readers are OK). If you use blue-light blockers, you can ignore this (see Chapter 6 for greater detail)
- Your general mood during the day
- Any physical pain or discomfort experienced during the day or night

Complete in the morning			
Start Date: Date of week:	Day1	Day2	Day3
What time did you get into bed?	PM AM	PM AM	PM AM
What time did you try and go to sleep?	PM AM	PM AM	PM AM
How long did it take you fall into sleep?	PM AM	PM AM	PM AM
What time did you wake up this morning?	PM AM	PM AM	PM AM
How many times did you wake up during the night?			
No. of times:			
No. of minutes:			
Last night I slept a total of:	HRS, MINS	HRS, MINS	HRS, MINS
How would you rate your sleep quality?			
Very poor Poor Fair Good Very Good	o o o o o	o o o o o	o o o o o
Was your sleep disturbed by any factors? {eg, allergies, noise, pets, discomfort/pain, etc.}			
Any other comments about your sleep worth noting			

Complete in the morning				
Start Date: Date of week:	Day4	Day5	Day6	Day7
What time did you get into bed?	PM AM	PM AM	PM AM	PM AM
What time did you try and go to sleep?	PM AM	PM AM	PM AM	PM AM
How long did it take you fall into sleep?	PM AM	PM AM	PM AM	PM AM
What time did you wake up this morning?	PM AM	PM AM	PM AM	PM AM
How many times did you wake up during the night?				
No. of times:				
No. of minutes:				
Last night I slept a total of:	HRS, MINS	HRS, MINS	HRS, MINS	HRS, MINS
How would you rate your sleep quality?				
Very poor Poor Fair Good Very Good	o o o o o	o o o o o	o o o o o	o o o o o
Was your sleep disturbed by any factors? {eg, allergies, noise, pets, discomfort/pain, etc.}				
Any other comments about your sleep worth noting				

Complete in the Evening			
Day of Week:	Day1	Day2	Day3
I consumed caffeinated drinks in the: (M)orning, (A)fternoon, (E)vening, (N/A)			
M/A/E/NA	PM AM	PM AM	PM AM
How many?	PM AM	PM AM	PM AM
How much exercise did you get today?			
No. of times:			
No. of minutes:			
Time of day (morning, afternoon, evening, night)			
Did you take a nap? (Circle one)	Yes No	Yes No	Yes No
If yes, for how long?			
List all medications you took today			
Approximately 2-3 hours before going to bed, I consumed			
Alcohol A heavy meal Caffeine Not applicable			
In the hour before going to sleep, my bedtime routine included: (List activities including reading a book, using electronics taking a bath doing relaxation exercises, etc.)			

Complete in the Evening				
Day of Week:	Day4	Day5	Day6	Day7
I consumed caffeinated drinks in the: (M)orning, (A)fternoon, (E)vening, (N/A)				
M/A/E/NA	PM AM	PM AM	PM AM	PM AM
How many?	PM AM	PM AM	PM AM	PM AM
How much exercise did you get today?				
No. of times:				
No. of minutes:				
Time of day (morning, afternoon, evening, night)				
Did you take a nap? (Circle one)	Yes No	Yes No	Yes No	Yes No
If yes, for how long?				
List all medications you took today				
Approximately 2-3 hours before going to bed, I consumed				
Alcohol A heavy meal Caffeine Not applicable				
In the hour before going to sleep, my bedtime routine included: (List activities including reading a book, using electronics taking a bath doing relaxation exercises, etc.)				

Child Sleep Diary

While you can complete a sleep diary for yourself easily, it is harder to do that for a young child and is all about observation as well as their feedback and input. Spend a week or so monitoring your child's actual sleep-time or "sleep efficiency" as well as you can and try to build a picture of normal sleep patterns. Try to do this discreetly without them knowing, as creating anxiety around sleep can turn it into a bigger issue than it might be. On day 1 start from the time when they wake up. For many children on a normal school day, this will be with an alarm clock and enables accuracy as you build up the picture.

Without trying to make any changes at this stage, make a note of any naps they may have had in the car or on the sofa post-school and what times these occur. Then see if you can identify what time they fall asleep later that night. This may mean a few more trips up and down the stairs than usual but it will be worth it. I know how tempting it is at the end of a long day to shut the door, hit the sofa and hope for the best—I've done it myself many times. The effort involved in building an accurate picture of sleep efficiency will be worth it in the end I assure you. You can use the chart below to help you or make your own—whatever works best and will enable you to gain an overview of sleep patterns.

Sleep Diary				
Sleep Tracker	**Schedule Start Date**			
ACTIVITY	**Monday**	**Tuesday**	**Wednesday**	**Thursday**
My child got into bed last night at:				
Last night my child fell asleep: [easily, after some time, with difficulty]				
My child woke up during the night: [#of times, #of minutes]				
My child got out of bed today at:				
Last night my child slept a total of [hours]:				
My child's sleep was disturbed by: [noise, lights, temperature, pets, allergies, nightmares, stress, discomfort, pain, etc]				
When my child woke up for the day, he/she felt: [rested somewhat rested, tired]				
Notes: record any others factors that may affect your child's sleep				

Sleep Diary			
Sleep Tracker	**Schedule Start Date**		
ACTIVITY	**Friday**	**Saturday**	**Sunday**
My child got into bed last night at:			
Last night my child fell asleep: [easily, after some time, with difficulty]			
My child woke up during the night: [#of times, #of minutes]			
My child got out of bed today at:			
Last night my child slept a total of [hours]:			
My child's sleep was disturbed by: [noise, lights, temperature, pets, allergies, nightmares, stress, discomfort, pain, etc]			
When my child woke up for the day, he/she felt: [rested somewhat tested, tired]			
Notes: record any others factors that may affect your child's sleep			

Make a note of any times your child reappears, clearly not yet asleep, perhaps jotting down their reasons. We all know this can be anything from an itchy label in their pyjamas to suddenly remembering some uncompleted homework; fears about bad dreams; lost toys, sore tummies; worries about an upcoming event or, several times in my house anyway, the climate emergency and the end of the world. It's very normal and there are lots of ways of reducing anxiety and worries, as will be covered later. If you allow unlimited reading after saying goodnight, then note what time the light goes off and check shortly afterwards that your child is asleep. As per advice for the adult diary, try to include brief details of:

- Exercise and daylight exposure
- Temperature of the bedroom
- Any particular stresses and worries
- Meals and snacks (especially sugar intake)
- What time electronic devices go off
- Any mindfulness or mindful movement (e.g., yoga)

As the sleep diary takes shape, you may be able to quickly get a picture of your child's sleep pattern as you add up the nightly hours. If it is quite erratic, keep going for a further week until you have an accurate overview. It may come as a shock. The 8-year-old whose light is turned off at 8 pm, but who reappears several times in the evening and doesn't finally nod off until 11 pm, is only getting 8 hours if they wake at 7 am: this is 2–3 hours less than the recommended quantity.

I appreciate that compiling a sleep diary can be a time-consuming task and I wouldn't want anyone to become stressed by it. If you're attempting an overview of the entire family that might include children, teenagers and adults, I would advise doing them one at a time over a period of several weeks. Prioritise the person who seems to have the most difficulty with sleep and start there. It is also wise not to include young children in the process as it might cause them to become anxious and might also skew your results.

Teenagers often enjoy being part of the solution so if you can involve them, it will benefit in multiple ways. Try to record accurately. While you might not enjoy seeing your child's sugary snacks laid out in black and white, nor the time you stuck them in front of the iPad because you had a mountain of housework or a looming deadline, don't give yourself a hard time. Remember our non-judgement? It will be much more effective to have the whole truth set out and you'll be better able to make those positive changes when you've got the full picture. We'll shortly be learning what we do with all this valuable data.

Adolescent Sleep Diary

Teenagers are a whole different challenge and the only way to do anything with them, as we all know, is to get them onside and involve them. I am being a little flippant here about teenagers and the challenges of parenting them. In fact, I have huge respect, admiration and affection for teens and Chapter 5 is focused on them. For the purposes of putting this diary together, you can let your teenager know what you're trying to do—and why—and ask them to help. Explain you are concerned about their tiredness and how it's affecting them and everyone else. Share with them what you've learnt about how better sleep can improve their mood, schoolwork, relationships and health. They may enjoy being the focus of your attention and let you know when they plan to put out the light.

On the other hand, they may resist your interference in their habits and especially resent you invading their rooms to "check up" on them. You may have to use some guesswork about when they actually fall asleep at night. Just noticing how tired they are in the mornings is not necessarily a sign of them staying awake too late; it is more likely they have had to wake up too early, as discussed above. I noticed that my children, as they got older, became much more aware of their own tiredness and it eventually resulted in the eldest taking himself off for an early night without prompting—miraculous! This happened at the same time the youngest was finding bedtime was when her worries surfaced and I would often be in with her, talking things through or helping with a relaxation technique while we could hear big brother's snores through the wall.

Technology is the big area of potential conflict when assessing teenage sleep, as all parents and carers will know. Their phones can be running all night long, pinging social media alerts, newsfeeds and messages. A 2019 survey reported that 68% of teenagers keep their mobile devices within reach at night and nearly a third of them sleep with their phones or tablets in bed with them. The same survey found children were checking their phones in the middle of the night. The links between mental health problems, lack of sleep and unhealthy phone habits are unequivocal and of great concern to medical professionals, charities and parents alike. I have devoted Chapter 6 to tackling this serious topic and you'll find support, information and suggestions there.

The weekday sleep diary may look very different to the weekend one as children, especially teenagers, take the opportunity to sleep late and catch up on sleep. Sadly, this isn't the cure-all it may seem and, while it feels better to wake naturally than with an alarm clock, those extra hours in bed are no substitute for the sleep lost during the week. Adequate sleep is needed nightly for optimal wellbeing and lost sleep cannot be replaced by a binge-sleep on a Sunday, however nice that is. I encourage lie-ins as much as possible, but they are not a replacement for healthy nightly rest.

You can add into the sleep diary any exercise or fresh air your adolescent has had that day, any caffeine or excess amounts of sugar, plus if there were any particular stresses or events that day such as a big test, friendship issues or sports fixture. You can also ask them to choose a couple of words about how they felt that day and record those. You are building up a picture that is going to enable you to consider how best to make tweaks to the routine or where to begin a major overhaul. Just as it might be alarming to see the reality of a young child's sleep pattern, you may find you have a 14-year-old who finds it hard to sleep before midnight but wakes at 6 am for an early school run—which means they are getting 2–4 hours less sleep a night than they actually need for optimum growth and development. Don't panic, I'm here to help.

You will find below a template I use with teenagers when supporting them with sleep and wellbeing. It is designed for them to fill in themselves and it enables them to recognise the factors that may be making a difference to how they feel and how well they sleep. So, they may realise, when they see it written down in black and white, that the days on which they exercise are better sleep days; likewise, those days when there is a lot of caffeine consumption or late-night tech use coincide with a poor night's sleep.

Mindful awareness is at the core of this activity as is taking the time at the end of the day to reflect on how their day has been. I told my youngest I didn't mind if she swore on it if that summed up the kind of day they had—you may not agree with this but you can use this template as it is or come up with a version that better suits your adolescent. Involving them in the design and making the intention clear before they start will make it more likely to be useful.

Complete in the Morning				
Start date: ----/----/----	Monday	Tuesday	Wednesday	Thursday
I got into bed last night at:	PM AM	PM AM	PM AM	PM AM
I fell asleep Easily: After some time: With difficulty:				
I woke in the night: # times # minutes				
I got up this morning at:	PM AM	PM AM	PM AM	PM AM
Last night I slept a total of:	hours	hours	hours	hours
My sleep was disturbed by: (e.g., noise, lights, temperature, nightmares, pain, etc.)				
When I woke, I felt rested: somewhat rested: tired:				
Notes: Any other factors affecting sleep last night (e.g., worries)				

Complete in the Morning			
Start date: ----/----/----	Friday	Saturday	Sunday
I got into bed last night at:	PM AM	PM AM	PM AM
I fell asleep Easily: After some time: With difficulty:			
I woke in the night: # times # minutes			
I got up this morning at:	PM AM	PM AM	PM AM
Last night I slept a total of:	hours	hours	hours
My sleep was disturbed by: (e.g., noise, lights, temperature, nightmares, pain, etc.)			
When I woke, I felt rested: somewhat rested: tired:			
Notes: Any other factors affecting sleep last night (e.g., worries)			

Complete at the End of the Day				
Start date: ----/----/----	Monday	Tuesday	Wednesday	Thursday
Today has been a…day—find one word to describe your overall day. E.g., great, good, OK, boring, tiring, stressful, terrible				
I consumed caffeinated products (tea, coffee, energy drinks, chocolate) in the M(orning), A(fternoon), E(vening), N/A				
M/A/E/NA How much?				
I exercised for at least 20 minutes in the M(orning), A(fternoon), E(vening), N/A				
M/A/ E/ NA				
I got at least 20 minutes of daylight outdoors today	Y/N	Y/N	Y/N	Y/N
I took a nap today: For how long?	Y/N	Y/N	Y/N	Y/N
During most of today I felt Tired: Moderately alert: Awake and alert:				
My mood today has mostly been Very Pleasant (VP), Pleasant (P), Unpleasant (UP), Very Unpleasant (VUP)				
VP/P/UP/VUP				
In the hour before bed, I used an electronic device	Y/N	Y/N	Y/N	Y/N
In the hour before bed my routine included (e.g., bath, reading, relaxation)				
I have practised mindfulness today	Y/N	Y/N	Y/N	Y/N

Complete at the End of the Day			
Start date: ----/----/----	Friday	Saturday	Sunday
Today has been a…day—find one word to describe your overall day. E.g., great, good, OK, boring, tiring, stressful, terrible			
I consumed caffeinated products (tea, coffee, energy drinks, chocolate) in the M(orning), A(fternoon), E(vening), N/A			
M/A/E/NA How much?			
I exercised for at least 20 minutes in the M(orning), A(fternoon), E(vening), N/A			
M/A/ E/ NA			
I got at least 20 minutes of daylight outdoors today	Y/N	Y/N	Y/N
I took a nap today: For how long?	Y/N	Y/N	Y/N
During most of today I felt Tired: Moderately alert: Awake and alert:			
My mood today has mostly been Very Pleasant (VP), Pleasant (P), Unpleasant (UP), Very Unpleasant (VUP)			
VP/P/UP/VUP			
In the hour before bed, I used an electronic device	Y/N	Y/N	Y/N
In the hour before bed my routine included (e.g., bath, reading, relaxation)			
I have practised mindfulness today	Y/N	Y/N	Y/N

How to Use a Sleep Diary

Now that you've got your sleep diary complete, you are ready to become a forensic data analyst! Don't be daunted. With a true picture of who is sleeping how much—or little—and when and what daily habits are built into that picture, you are empowered to work with the data and bring about real and positive change. As you examine the diary, you are looking for patterns. Look at the days you or your child sleep the least well. What factors are there in common? This might be late-night access to screens or a lack of exercise or daylight. Look at the days people sleep best—what links those occasions, and can you build on those? In my experience, teenagers are brilliant at this. They can often see straight away that they sleep better on PE days and worst when they've had a midnight feast.

Over the course of the rest of this book, you will learn about routines, reducing anxiety and stress, healthy tech use and the ways mindfulness and relaxation can help everyone. As you learn more, you can start to make changes and see how they impact on you and your children. The diary shows you how much sleep everyone is getting across a period of time. The chances are that it is not as much as they require and your aim is now to move closer to that ideal amount, as an average over time. You can begin to tweak the areas that jump out at you.

You have a lot of lifestyle factors to work with as well as anxiety tools and tech rules. If adults or teens are consuming caffeine, you can try reducing that (follow the advice on p.142). If late-night snacking is a habit of yours, see what happens when you cut it out. Your teenager may be getting woeful amounts of exercise—how could you increase that? What happens when you do? Your partner may be sleeping poorly due to a specific stress. Are there ways to resolve this or to support them with the issue? If you try one thing and it makes no difference, look again at what the diary is telling you and try another. Keep noticing what happens.

The sleep diary is a foundation for experimentation, and it requires you all to hold an open mind about what might or might not happen as a result of making changes. There is no one-size-fits-all solution because every family is unique and every individual within it is their own person. Alongside non-judgement, a core aspect of mindfulness practice is curiosity. Holding a position of not knowing can be hard for people, it's especially hard for parents who can be expected to know everything. We don't, of course. We're just doing our best. But not knowing can be a gift when we are implementing change and it requires that we step up that other core mindfulness quality of observation: paying attention and taking notice of what is actually happening, not what we expect to happen. This can be really liberating. When we change an aspect of our own sleep such as doing a short gentle yoga routine before bed, or we stick to the tech-free rule for our child or spend time with our teenager or partner talking through a worry they have, it's vital that we pay attention and notice what effect the change is having.

The Power of Curiosity

As well as non-judgement, another quality of mindfulness practice is curiosity. Mindfulness begins with awareness of what is going on for us in this present moment. Holding expectations of what that might be is a barrier to encountering, and staying with, whatever comes up for us. When we cultivate an attitude of curiosity, we are inviting whatever is there to simply be—and this can be the way forward to feelings of peace and clarity. Curiosity is a way of enquiring into our unique moment-by-moment, breath-by-breath experience of life. Along with kindness it can be a great antidote to judgement—our judgements often turn out to be untruths when examined in the light of mindful awareness. Liberating ourselves from judgement and expectation opens the possibility that things may not be as we initially assume, that there might be more space around the issues in our lives than we might have thought. With this knowledge, we can respond more skilfully to the challenges we face.

I teach this approach to children and teenagers by gradually introducing them to the practice of stopping, allowing the body to become still, giving the mind the task of enquiry—how am I right now? What can I feel/smell/taste/hear/see in this unique moment? Without curiosity they would be unable to participate fully and it's gratifying when they embrace the invitation. Enthusiastic children often surprise themselves with what they observe. An early exercise I do in the classroom is to take a spotlight torch and focus the beam on a random place on the ceiling. I ask the children what they notice. It's amazing what they see when choosing to focus this way with an open and curious attitude—I've had everything from a small spider, flaking bit of paint, tiny crack, to a change in the brushstrokes of the paint used. With mindful awareness, we can choose to try and look at life with more curiosity and notice what is actually there, not what we think or expect to be there. It can open life up for us in unexpected ways. For young people studying in a formal setting, it can enhance their studies and their experience of learning.

The sleep diary is the place to record the lifestyle and habit changes you decide to try. Write down when you notice that anything improves for your family as a result. Sometimes it really can be a simple change that makes a big difference. Likewise, if you are lying awake worrying about your energy bills, a warm milky drink isn't going to fix that. But learning stress release and mindfulness techniques will certainly help. We need to match the right solution to the right problem. Using the sleep diary methodically will reveal what works best.

People ask me how long they need to keep this up and I can appreciate what an undertaking it is, but I urge you to stick with it as it's invaluable. Once the core data is there you should be able to see the area most in need of attention and start experimenting with tweaks. Noting down overall sleep times and consequent feelings of wellbeing is the most important thing, alongside whichever specific lifestyle changes seem to be a priority. This means you might be running the experiment for several weeks, even months. If you run out of energy to keep the diary going, try and stick to the whatever change you're trying out and complete another diary a few months later. Or you can do a snapshot diary of exactly what's happening on a single day, which may give you a great perspective of what you've achieved or inspire you to try a different tack. It won't give you much of an overview but it's a good way to see how things are progressing. The sleep diary is a diagnosis tool and then a tracker that you can use in whatever way best serves your family's needs.

How Adult Sleep Habits Influence the Family

The survey about technology referred to above found 68% of teenagers with phones in their bedrooms at night—but 74% of parents surveyed had theirs in reach all night as well. When you are assessing your child's sleep habits, it is important to look at your own and those of the other household members even if you don't have any specific sleep issues yourself. Despatching a 10–year-old to bed is more likely to be unsuccessful in a house where there are teenagers and adults clearly up late and enjoying themselves. Adults working shifts can affect the routine of children in the house. Households where people need caring for will also find children's sleep affected. Likewise homes with babies face challenges if older children's sleep is disturbed.

Your reason for picking this book up might have been solely to help your child or teenager with their sleep problems. Adults confidently tell me that they would have no difficulty getting enough sleep themselves if their 7-year-old didn't come into their bed every night. This is undoubtedly true, but I hope by now that you've learnt enough about the importance of quality sleep to know that it matters for you too in the short- and long-term and addressing sleep is essential for adults. As I have said, parents tend to put themselves at the bottom of the list of priorities, but I hope it's clear that for the best possible outcome for the whole family, everyone needs to get on board and make sleep a priority. This is what it means to become an SAS family and have everyone Serious About Sleep.

It can be easy to undermine all your good work around improving the sleep of your children and teens if you are not joining in too and setting that good example, modelling the behaviour yourself of someone who values sleep. This applies to all the adults, I'm afraid, so if you need to win over a partner or other adult in the house, share this book with them or join me in being a sleep bore and tell them everything you've learnt. If you're not sure of how well the grown-ups are doing, try this audit of family behaviours. Answer honestly about the ways your family values sleep in these areas:

- Do the behaviour and routines of the children affect each other's sleep patterns?
- Are the needs of elderly, disabled or ill members of the house impacting the sleep of children?
- Are bedtimes for adults reasonably regular?
- Is bedtime and sleep held in sufficient respect by those still awake?
- Is falling asleep on the sofa in the evenings a regular adult habit?
- Do adults have a phone, tablet, television or computer in the bedroom?
- What is your own routine like and how much sleep are you getting?
- Do you often lie awake worrying?
- Do you complain about tiredness in front of your children?
- How able are you to relax and do nothing?
- Do you use bedtime as a punishment for children?
- Are there times of quietness and peace during a normal day?

- Are all bedrooms a place of calm?

These questions are a starting point for you to examine what might be causing the sleep difficulties you experience as a family. Can you make changes to the environment or to your attitude? The next chapters are designed to help adults and children get into healthy bedtime routines, look at sleep hygiene, tackle anxiety and worry, re-examine tech use and learn mindfulness techniques that will lead everyone in the direction of sleeping better, feeling better and enjoying happier, healthier lives.

You and Your Partner

If you generally sleep alone, this section will not apply to you, but the majority of adults share a bed with a partner for some or all of the time. In most cultures, it is ingrained that part of intimacy and a good relationship is being in the same bed at night, but it can be really problematic for lots of couples. A clash in sleeping behaviour is incredibly common and can disrupt proper rest for one or both of you, as well as cause stress in your relationship. We're all scratchy after broken or inadequate sleep so it's easy to see how this can build into resentment and conflict in the cold light of day. In long-term relationships, the poor sleep experiences of one or both of you can go on for many years and feel impossible to shift. As with our modern acceptance of tiredness as the norm, poor sleep is just another burden we feel we must bear. Let's see if we can open this up a little. Some issues you may experience include:

- Insomnia experienced acutely or chronically by one or both of you. We looked at this above, but from the perspective of the sufferer rather than the person sharing the bed. Lying next to someone who is tossing and turning or getting up frequently in the night makes sleep incredibly difficult. Once we reach the deeper NREM phase of sleep we are less likely to be woken but the hypnogogic (falling asleep) phase of sleep generally lasts 5–30 minutes and we can be jolted out of it very easily by the person beside us; likewise the phase of REM sleep from which we can easily wake. A short-term way to combat this might be for the person not experiencing insomnia to go to bed at least 60 minutes before the other so as to reach a deeper phase of sleep. This doesn't always work as there's nothing like the pressure of "I must get to sleep right now" to keep you awake. Try to resolve the insomnia by talking through stresses well before bedtime, using the body/mind calming tools and techniques here, by improving sleep hygiene, having a relaxing wind-down period prior to sleep (this can include sex) and making adjustments to lifestyle by using the sleep diary. Remember that if insomnia becomes chronic in spite of all your efforts to resolve it, it may be co-morbid with another underlying condition that requires medical advice.

- Snoring and sleep apnoea. I have been with my other half for over 25 years and can honestly say that his snoring has ruined my sleep more times that I could possibly count. So, I sympathise wholeheartedly with anyone lying beside their loved one listening to the noise. Snoring is the hoarse and harsh sound that occurs when air flows past the relaxed tissues in the throat causing the tissues to vibrate. Nearly everyone (apparently even me, according to my husband) snores now and then and it, not only disturbs the other person, but can indicate a serious health condition when chronic. Snoring is often associated with another sleep disorder called Obstructive Sleep Apnoea (OSA). Not all snorers have OSA but an evaluation by a doctor is vital if there are periods when the sufferer snores loudly followed by a period of silence when breathing stops or nearly stops. People with OSA usually experience periods like this at least 5 times during every hour of sleep. Snoring happens when the airways relax and this is more likely following alcohol consumption, a blocked nose due to a cold or allergies, being overweight, sleeping position and the anatomy of the mouth (e.g., an elongated soft palate). Once you have good medical advice, some solutions for the snorer are to try to lose some weight, cut back on the alcohol, use a nasal spray or menthol inhalation just before bed to unblock the nose if you have allergies or a cold, find pillows that support side sleeping which is better for snorers than sleeping on the back or front. Earplugs can help the snorer's partner and, after many years of searching for solutions, I have invested in some active noise-cancelling earbuds which don't completely cut the sound out but reduce it to a manageable level. If there is a spare bed or sofa-bed in the home that can be used during a bad bout of your partner's snoring, try to start the night in it rather than stomp off there clutching your pillow at 2 am. You can probably anticipate a bad night if there has been a lot of alcohol consumed or your partner has a bad cold or allergy flare-up.

- Nightmares or night terrors. These are discussed fully in Chapter 4 in relation to children, but they can be a feature of adult sleep too. If you or your partner experience regular nightmares, it is not good to ignore this and it might be wise to consult a doctor or a therapist to help resolve underlying mental health issues. PTSD is a common feature of modern life, sadly, with men and women suffering long-term anxiety following trauma or bereavement. Cognitive Behavioural Therapy can be a great support and is often available free via your GP.
- Incompatible sleepers. You might get on with your partner famously during the daytime, agreeing on family issues large and small, but your sleep cycles and sleep hygiene needs might be out of kilter during the night. I've mentioned the tendency of people to be "owls" or "larks" and if this is the case for you, it might require some honest conversations about going to bed and getting up at different times so you can each be more in tune with your natural body rhythm. It might take some negotiating about one person reading while the other sleeps or one person getting up quietly so as not to disturb the other. It's OK to have different body clocks, don't forget to talk about scheduling in time for intimacy too. Shift work also requires a level of sensitivity and respect for sleep within the entire household, so have those conversations with the family and agree the ground rules. Sleep hygiene can also be a point of controversy when one person wants the window open and the other claims to be freezing. A previously agreed room temperature can fly out of the window during menopause when many women experience night sweats and need the room to be cooler. If you're the chilly partner, add a blanket to your side of the bed or take a hot water bottle with you. Tech use can also cause conflict if one person wants to use their laptop or phone in bed while the other would prefer the bedroom to be a no-tech zone. You'll have to talk openly about this together and try to resolve on a compromise. Sharing the facts about the impact of blue light on the brain before sleep might give your tech-loving partner the impetus to re-examine this habit. If you have compiled sleep diaries for you both, it might be clear when alcohol, late-night snacking and lack of exercise have contributed to poor sleep and you could set yourselves some new

goals around these habits in the interests of improved health and wellbeing for you both.

- Restless leg syndrome (RLS). This condition causes an uncontrollable urge to move the legs that typically happens when the sufferer is sitting or lying down, usually in the evening or while in bed. If you or your partner experience this, you will know it can disrupt sleep for you both. It may also be associated with another more common condition called periodic limb movement of sleep which causes the legs to twitch and kick and this can happen during the night. People who suffer from this often feel reluctant to talk to a doctor because of worry they won't be taken seriously but the sleep loss consequences are serious, as we know, and I would urge anyone suffering to have that conversation. There is no known cause for RLS but we know it gets worse as people age and that it can run in families. During pregnancy, women may experience it for the first time, especially during the last trimester, and this suggests there is a hormonal link as it usually disappears after the baby is born. An iron supplement can sometimes improve RLS and there is anecdotal evidence that magnesium supplements also relieve symptoms, but these must be taken under the advice of a medical doctor who will also check for underlying health conditions that may be related. Lifestyle changes can also help and these include regular exercise, gentle yoga stretches, a warm bath before bed, massaging the legs and avoiding caffeine and alcohol. Good sleep hygiene and a bedtime routine can also see improvements.
- Children joining you in bed. Everyone has their own feelings about co-sleeping and I would never tell anyone what to do on such an issue but my own experience is that the interruption to sleep that occurs as the child hops under the covers with you, the increased temperature of more bodies in the bed and the likelihood of wriggling and kicking doesn't help anyone to get better sleep. Using the sleep solutions in this book should help decrease the likelihood of this happening. If it's become a habit, then breaking it will be a challenge but start slowly by explaining to your child that they will sleep better in their own bed, deal with worries and anxieties and, of course, offer lots of praise and enthusiasm when they stay in their own bed all night. We'll talk later about beloved pets in bedrooms and beds!

All the above challenges to sleeping well with another person can cause tension and see resentment build which will place an unwelcome strain on your relationship. It's important to make time to talk about the issues during the day and when you are both in a positive frame of mind. Communicating calmly can be difficult, I've certainly done my share of door-slamming and sulking after snoring incidents, but do your best to summon up those mindfulness qualities and try to listen with kindness, patience and tolerance. Seek creative solutions together or with the help of a neutral third party such as a doctor or therapist. Ultimately, the reward for you both getting a good night's sleep is all-round better health in the short- and long-term, which will benefit the wellbeing of your entire family.

Chapter 3
The Bedtime Routine

The previous chapters will have armed you with a fuller understanding of why sleep is so important, for adults and children alike. You have had the opportunity to look closer at the sleep habits and behaviour of everyone in your household and, using the sleep diary, you will have a more accurate picture of who is sleeping for how long, and where any regular interruptions occur. The diary will contain the information you need moving forward as we take a close look at the benefits of a routine and how to make one work for you.

The Benefits of a Routine

A routine is important because our bodies are driven by their circadian rhythm or body clock, which, as you will recall, is a hormonal and chemical process. This exists in all living creatures and we flourish when we stay in tune with ours and when we listen to our bodies. If you have ever tried to exercise when you're exhausted, you will know how hard it can be, even if you do feel pleased afterwards—but compare the experience of exercising when you're feeling bouncy and looking forward to it. It is difficult for most of us to be totally tuned into our physical, emotional and mental needs at all times. Tending to those of our children takes up much of a parent's time.

We have jobs and responsibilities; our children have their education, relationships and experiences to manage. Modern life has taken us all a long way from nature and particularly from the patterns of rest and wakefulness dictated by daylight and darkness. Yet our body clocks are ancient and the hormonal imperatives remain the same as ever. So, we need enough sleep to function properly and feel good, but we must make it work within the boundaries of our lives. This makes a routine the only realistic option. A bedtime routine means that bedtimes are agreed, set and stuck to and that the period of time allotted to the routine involves the same actions (e.g., a bath, story, relaxation or mindfulness practice) and atmosphere (e.g., low lights, calming music) each day. You will find lots of suggestions below to experiment with and help you design your own. Routines for adults support better sleep too and you'll be using your sleep diary to track what works best for you and the other adults in the house.

Setting a pattern of consistent behaviour around bedtime can provide children with security; it can also be very soothing and comforting for them to know that there will be a little bit of time in the day that is about cuddles, stories, listening, relaxing music, a warm bath or whichever aspects of the routine you decide will work best. It also signals to your child that this is what happens at bedtime, it's enjoyable and it leads to feeling good. Family life can be chaotic enough at times, as we all know, but establishing a routine around bedtime takes the drama out of the situation and clearly communicates that "this is what we do in our house". Establish that getting into bed, allowing tired eyes to gently close, letting go of the outside world and all the busyness of the day and trying to go to sleep are "the sleep rules"—if you meet with resistance you can offer a reward the next day for keeping to the rules. The reward should be something small but enjoyable. I used to give my kids one of those tiny 20p toys the local swimming pool used to tempt them with but you can try something simple you know will inspire them as you get the routine up and running. Don't forget to give lots of praise and encouragement when it does all go well. Never negotiate on the timings: they are not for discussion! The benefits to everyone of sufficient sleep cannot be underestimated. Happily, they are easily seen in yourself and others so they can be celebrated and enjoyed.

The barriers to establishing a routine around bedtimes are many and can include work patterns, social commitments, caring for ill or disabled family members. It also includes a totally understandable reluctance to run life around the time displayed on the clock because this can preclude spontaneity, late-night treats and the total change of routine during holidays. There can be considerable resistance from the children themselves, particularly if bedtimes have been random and unstructured for a while. But regardless of all these barriers, the body's autonomic processes require sleep and require it to be regular. As with most things in life there is a balance to be sought and this must be reached by you and your family in the way that benefits most of you, most of the time.

If anyone in your family is experiencing what could be classed as a sleep disorder, and remember that there are over 100 of them, you may well seek professional help. As a qualified sleep consultant, one of the cornerstone practices I studied was the importance of going to bed and rising at more or less the same time each day when trying to tackle insomnia or other irregularities. This makes a routine essential when trying to improve the sleep quantity and quality of your family.

Sleep Hygiene

This term which refers to environmental factors that contribute to a good night's sleep. This differs from the behavioural factors which are those that the mindfulness and relaxation techniques you will learn in the next chapters can help with. Sleep hygiene focuses on creating the best sensory environment for sleep and good habits that support better sleep. In the meantime, a simple checklist of what you can do to give adults and children the best chance of sleeping well may be useful. If you can't tick them all off, don't worry; just get as many as you can sorted and work with the other suggestions. If sleep is an area of concern for yourself or any other adults in the household, you might find some of these make a positive difference. Teenagers can join in with any changes made and feel empowered by doing something to help themselves.

Sleep Hygiene Checklist

- Keep the bedroom cool at night, ideally about 18°C
- Shower or bath prior to bedtime
- Nightclothes should be light, cotton if possible, no socks, no onesies
- Keep the room as dark as possible
- Avoid devices with blue LED lights for an hour prior to sleep
- Remove electronic devices from the bedroom
- Daily exercise is important but avoid exercise right before bed
- Avoid going to bed too full or too hungry
- Avoid caffeine for several hours before bed
- Avoid sugar and carbohydrates before bed
- Wake up and go to sleep at the same time each day whenever possible
- Establish a bedtime routine and prioritise sleep

I have put together a sleep hygiene checklist for teenagers to fill in on their own. You will find it in Chapter 5 on page 146. It will help them to feel they have more agency around their sleep and how they can make good choices for themselves.

Family Pets

This is an area I find needs increasing consideration as the number of pets we collectively live with has grown over recent years. Animals can be a huge part of family life and provide us all with a fun focus that gives many children a source of comfort and love and often gets us outside for exercise as we walk our dogs. Our house has always featured pets over several decades including dogs, cats, hamsters, guinea pigs, chickens and fish—every one of them loved by all. Sleeping with pets, however, can be problematic and you'll need to think about whether it's doing your child more good to have the cat curled up by their feet for comfort or whether the animal is disturbing the sleep of their best friend.

Pets sensibly spend a large amount of time asleep—lucky them—but they have zero respect for the sleep needs of their human family members. So, a cat or dog that is contentedly snoozing when your child gets into bed can be disturbed by noise or by early morning light or by just wanting to move about in a way that wakes a child from their much-needed rest. If your child is used to having a pet in the room at night, you'll have to make a judgement as to whether this is doing more harm or good. The animal will be fine wherever it sleeps. A child who insists they can't sleep without the animal could start off the night with it but you would be wise to sneak in and relocate it once they are asleep. Explain that the beloved pet needs to be in its own bed as well and will be waiting for them in the morning for lots of cuddles.

Likewise, nocturnal animals or birds kept in cages in bedrooms can create a lot of noise that may disturb sleep or interrupt the process of falling asleep which requires peace and quiet. We once moved a hamster cage to several different places in the house after the excited all-night wheel spinning kept everyone awake. Find a balance that works for you—but prioritise your child's vital sleep.

Getting Everyone Onside

There is little point working out the details of a bedtime routine to improve your child's sleep quantity and quality if they are dead set against it and fight you every step of the way. When planning how the routine is going to look and work, it really helps to take children's focus away from bedtime signalling the end of the day's fun, banishment to their bedroom while the grown-ups carry on having a good time—and towards bedtime being a happy, positive, nurturing time. Likewise, your evenings will doubtlessly be precious time to unwind from the day and you may want to prolong and enjoy them, even when you are feeling tired. Finding the routine that feels best for you might involve turning off the telly before you really want to and shortening your leisure time, but the extra sleep pay-off enables us to enjoy our lives more fully and with more energy.

Hopefully, you took the quiz on page 44 and recall the question about routine. Some people will have answered question 1 about regular bedtime routines with answers c) We used to have one but it didn't work/children are older now or d) Routines are not for us. The wide-ranging consequences of lack of sleep for adults and children, plus the issues around sleep in your own house will, I hope, encourage you to at least experiment with a routine if you've never had one or, if you have let go of it over the years as your children have grown older, to reinstate one.

A routine is not a punishment; it is not controlling or rigid—try to think of it as a gift that honours the natural rhythm of the body as it moves between wakefulness and sleep. Giving everyone time to rest properly, recharge their batteries and be ready for a new day is an act of loving care. I used to put my "parenting effort" into trying to feed the family the best I could and into their activities but when my children became teenagers, I realised how much that simple bedtime routine had mattered to them—they have all shared with me that the bedtime stories and chats and goodnight kisses made them feel loved and nurtured during those years. They certainly don't say that about my cooking! I felt quite bereft when my story reading was no longer required and I was politely asked to leave them in peace to read by themselves.

If you want to try to instil a routine or reorganise a lapsed one, you may need to make some changes—not least of which will be getting the whole household onside. Start by talking to everyone. I find that children of any age can understand more than we often give them credit for. Take the first chapter of this book and, making it relevant to the age of your child, see if you can present them with three "sleep facts" that will get them onside. Some easily-digested facts about the areas of life that getting enough sleep helps with are:

- Friendships and relationships
- Focus and concentration that makes schoolwork feel easier
- Better memory
- Test and exam performance
- Sports, drama, music performance
- Keeping well and not catching colds, etc.
- Anxiety and stress
- Weight management
- Decision-making
- Feelings of happiness and positivity
- Creativity and great ideas

Hopefully, several of these benefits of enough sleep will help your child understand why you are making sleep a priority in the whole house. If you set a good example, it will be even easier to improve things! For us this meant turning the telly down in the evenings and trying to limit noise. I'd also talk about the "big bubbly bath" as something I enjoyed before bed and make sure they saw that our phones are always left downstairs at night and never kept in the bedroom.

If you have used bedtime as a punishment, it will be challenging to change but it can be done. If bedtimes have been rushed, tense or hotspots for drama, then it is going to take some time to establish the new culture of calmness we want to pervade the whole of the bedtime hour. It can help if you explain to your child honestly that you are worried about their lack of sleep and that you know they will feel a lot better and happier if they get a bit more sleep. See if you can engage them in an experiment—try the new routine and see what everyone notices. Bringing some mindfulness to the experiment will fit in with the other practices you will be introduced to below. It's hard to argue with waking up and feeling good after a decent night's sleep. It's hard to argue with the improvements that they will notice in different areas of their life.

Take a look together at your child's bedroom. Ask them how they feel about the position of their bed in the room, about the light, the temperature, the bedding. Can you make any changes to turn their bedroom into a calmer environment, where the emphasis is on sleeping? Some suggestions:

- Declutter toys, projects, clothes, etc. to create a calm atmosphere
- Cushions go a long way to make bed appealing and are cheap to buy or make
- Cosy blankets make the bed look enticing but make sure they aren't keeping your child too hot
- Buy, or borrow from the library, books to read just at bedtime, choose together with your child and keep a selection near the bed
- Soft toys are OK in bed but watch out for any sharp or bulky "friends" smuggled into bed for late-night games
- Nightclothes should be light, cotton if possible. Keep onesies for Sunday mornings and TV watching
- No socks unless your child has very chilly feet or the room is very cold—socks can keep the body temperature higher than the ideal for sleep
- Remove as much tech as you can
- Alarm clocks can help teenagers wake gradually (see p.175)
- Low lighting is a must for the end of the day, especially remove LED lighting (see why on p.144). Buying a lamp that can be dimmed by touch goes down well.
- Calm music helps everyone unwind and you can find mindful mix or yoga playlists on all the music apps
- Keeping the room cool is essential, check that radiators aren't too high and that a window is open when possible. The temperature should be about 18°C. This may not be possible depending on where you live and a hot summer may mean it is very difficult to keep cool at nights. Keeping the curtains shut during a hot day will prevent the room from holding on to as much of the sun's heat. My menopause hot nights have been hugely helped by a cooling pad or "chillow" kept in the freezer during the day then placed under the pillow—when it gets too hot, flipping the pillow over to a deliciously cool side has really helped me.
- Try to make the room as dark as you can, using blackout blinds or lined curtains. Sending a child to bed on a summer evening to a well-lit room is unlikely to end in sound sleep. Making changes to your child's sleeping environment will hopefully have achieved some buy-in about trying a new routine together. Make sure you also ask them for their thoughts about bedtimes and sleep—what do they like and not like? What does their ideal bedtime look like? Are they disturbed by noises

elsewhere in the house? Try to do as much listening as you do explaining: it will go a long way to getting them onside. My youngest was kept awake for weeks by a "beeping noise" that no one else could hear—after sitting in her room with her, I realised the boiler right next to the room was the source of the sound and once the plumber had been and fixed it, sleep was a lot easier. As well as explaining the theoretical benefits of good sleep, it will help enormously if you can focus with them on how it actually feels to be rested and full of energy for the day ahead and all its challenges.

Use the same eagle eye in your own bedroom or those of other adults—check the temperature and the comfort of the mattress and pillows. Are there streetlights preventing the room from being dark enough? Blackout blinds are not just for children's bedrooms. As we discussed above, negotiating with your partner over any incompatibility is important.

Sleep and Self-Care

Self-care is a term used more and more these days, I am delighted to see. Back when I started teaching one of the things that excited me most was introducing children and young people to the concept of self-care. This is a novel idea for the majority of children as, quite rightly, the adults in their lives have the job of caring for them. Few children consider the concept of taking care of themselves, but it is a skill they will need to gradually build as they make their way through childhood. Understanding what nurtures them and makes them feel happy and healthy is at the heart of self-care. The way this is achieved by adults and children alike is, over time, to practise tuning in regularly to what's going on in the mind and body and then make an appropriate response to what we find.

For all of us, our attention is largely focused outwards into the fast-paced modern world where so much competes for our attention—but mindfulness is all about reversing that and *looking inwards*, with curiosity, to see what's going on. Luckily, children pick this concept up much faster than most adults and it's a joy to engage with them about the things they notice in their minds and bodies. It's never too late for adults to try this out for themselves.

As a parent, you can do this too and you can support healthy sleep and the bedtime routine by helping your child understand not only the theory of tiredness and sleep, but the physical feelings too. At school, children learn about the importance of good food and exercise for their health and wellbeing. Only limited focus is given in the curriculum to sleep as the vital contributor to wellbeing that it actually is.

Psychologist Suzy Reading is the author of the brilliant *Stand Tall Like a Mountain: Mindfulness and Self-Care for Anxious Children and Worried Parents*, which is full of strategies for families to improve resilience and wellbeing. She writes: "Self-care is any life-giving act that tops up your energy bank and the healthier your reserves, the better placed you are to cope with the daily challenges you face." An unequivocal life-giving act is the simple but essential good night's sleep. Enabling children to recognise the value of this is best achieved by helping them tune into the feelings in their minds and bodies when they are tired and, by contrast, when they are well-rested and full of beans.

Checking In—a Mindfulness Exercise to Do with Your Child or the Whole Family

- Explain that you are going to do a short, fun mindfulness exercise called Checking In. Tell them it will only take a few minutes and that it is like a science experiment.
- Tell them that you are going to give them a few things to do and that they can tell you all about it at the end when you ask, but to stay quiet for the next few minutes.
- In a quiet, comfortable place where you will not be interrupted, make sure everyone is comfortable, been to the loo, etc. Use cushions or blankets if you like. Children can lie or sit. You can use relaxing music if you choose.
- Encourage everyone to close their eyes and take 3 deep breaths in and out. If possible, ask participants to rest their hands either on their chest or tummy. Ask them to notice their hands gently moving up and down as their lungs fill up with air and empty again.
- Ask everyone to turn their attention to how they are feeling right now, to what they can notice going on for them. Everyone can ask themselves "How is my body right now?" and be really really interested in whatever they notice. Older children will also be able to ask "How is my mind right now?" and see what's happening. Again, this is done with gentle curiosity.

- Keep the calm breathing going for as long as you think appropriate to the age and mood of the children then you can signal the end of the Check In and encourage eyes to open and a nice big stretch for everyone.
- Now is the time to enquire what everyone noticed about their body and/or mind. It is vital not to interrupt nor to pass any comment or judgement ("I felt tired"—"I'm not surprised, you wouldn't go to sleep last night" or "I feel hungry"—"well, you should have eaten your dinner"), tempting though this may be! Listen carefully and encourage any and all responses. One-word answers are fine. Especially praise children who are able to notice what their mind is up to—they may use words like "fuzzy" or "jumpy" or "clear."
- Make sure you share your own experience too and finish by thanking everyone for sharing.

To introduce the concept, start with self-care as related to food and exercise. Ask your child, in an age-appropriate way, if they notice how they feel after riding their bike, swimming, running, playing outside, etc.? Hopefully they will tell you that they feel good or great, even if they feel tired afterwards. Ask them what "good" feels like? How do they know they feel great? What are they noticing in their body? Endorphins are the chemicals released by the body when we exercise and they trigger positive feelings that can last for a couple of hours. Even very young children can recognise this and will usually tell you all about it if you ask! Answer these questions for yourself too and share them with your partner or, if suitable, your children.

Turning the focus to food is trickier because, as we all know, so much food that is actually bad for us, sadly, tastes really good. If you are concerned about your child having issues around food and eating, then don't attempt this conversation without seeking advice from your GP or health visitor. But if you are happy to talk about eating with your child, keep the focus of your question to delicious healthy foods: it will be easier to get the response you are looking for. Asking how your child feels after eating a juicy orange or a handful of grapes should get a positive response. Ask similar questions about what feels good? Do they feel the food is giving them energy or vitamins or goodness?

I always include mindful eating with my pupils and it is extraordinary to hear them respond to eating a slice of apple or pear or carrot in a mindful way. They love the chocolate too when eaten super slowly and savoured in great detail!

Mindful Eating—a Mindfulness Practice to Do with Your Child or the Whole Family

- Prepare ahead some food items and ensure they are laid out and ready before you start. You only need one small item per person. Try a satsuma segment, a grape, an apple slice, a raisin.
- Explain that you are going to do a short, fun mindfulness eating practice. Tell them it will only take a few minutes and that it is like a science experiment.
- Put the plate where everyone can see it and invite them to sit comfortably, and take 3 deep breaths in and out. Ask them to focus on the plate of food now and to let go of everything that has been happening today or what will be happening later on.
- Invite everyone to take an item of food from the plate and to hold it in their hand. Look at it very carefully; imagine you have never seen this food before in your life! Look at the shape and colour. Feel the weight of it in your hand. Bring it to your cheek and feel the texture. What does it smell like? Can they notice the mouth watering in anticipation? What does that feel like? Children can share their observations as they go along or you can ask them at the end.
- Next, place the food gently on the tongue and avoid talking for the next few minutes. Suggest that eyes are closed to focus better on what's happening in the mouth. What is happening on the tongue as the food moves around? What does it feel like to bite into it? How are the flavours released into the mouth? What does it taste like? Can they feel the food becoming smaller as it is chewed? What is it like to swallow? How does the throat feel as the food moves down? Once the mouth is empty, what does that feel like? Does any trace of the flavour remain?
- Suggest that eyes are open now and be prepared for some fun feedback as this very different way of eating can inspire some wonderful responses.

- Repeat this as often as you like. You may notice that mealtimes are more enjoyable when the food is appreciated. Remind the family that it is much better for us all to eat slowly, chew our food properly and really enjoy the flavours and tastes.

Whether you have had detailed responses from your child or children about how exercise and healthy food make them feel, or just a few words, doesn't matter. The process of stopping to *check in* with how they are feeling in the moment is usually fun and interesting. The next step is to bring it round to tiredness and energy levels. It can be as simple as asking them to stop and shut their eyes at a time when you can see they are tired—but without pointing that out or using the "T word". My children have all been furious with me at times when I've smugly commented that their behaviour is due to tiredness. I've been right, of course, as you will be since all parents can spot the signs of tiredness a mile off. Your child, however, will seldom thank you for pointing it out to them. If you can help them to identify it in themselves, you will get a long way to helping them understand the remedy.

Asking your child to stop, close their eyes, take a few deep breaths and tell you what they notice going on will frequently result in them discovering that they are tired. You can ask how do they know this? What does it feel like? They might notice stinging eyes or a heaviness in the limbs or a drifting sense in the mind, they might feel weepy or grumpy. It can come as a revelation to them that what they are feeling is tiredness. We don't always realise how tired we are until we stop. I am sure many adults notice exactly the same thing. We can be incredibly busy at work or around the house, engaged in the normal human process of rushing to fit in tasks, often working to some sort of deadline, then we sit down for a well-deserved coffee or flop onto the sofa in the evening and, hey presto, we notice the weariness in our muscles, heaviness behind our eyes.

We can keep underlying tiredness at bay in so many ways: constant stimulation and activity, the distraction of busyness, pushing ourselves on to the next thing on the to-do list, fuelling ourselves with caffeine and, of course, a massive dose of the stress hormones that so many people have lurking behind their everyday lives. Building the habit of stopping to check in with yourself a few times a day is a great foundation for building mindful awareness and taking care of yourself.

Focusing exclusively outwards and rushing about is the same for children, maybe substituting sugar for caffeine, but the same imperative to be busy, to achieve, to dash from activity to activity—to do do do. For many of us, there is virtually no time in the day to just BE. I can't begin to count the number of people who have told me they would love to have a mindfulness practice but they simply can't fit it into their busy lives. It's true that there are only a finite number of minutes in a day, and we tend to only fit in what we prioritise, so if mindfulness isn't a priority, you'll be unlikely to find the time for it. So, as you consider the role of sleep and rest in your family I urge you to look at the amount of time in your child's life, and in your own, that is dedicated to quietness and the freedom to just be.

As well as tuning in when they are tired, it is vital that you ask your child to check in with how they are feeling when you are confident the answer is going to be that they feel the opposite: full of zest and energy. Ask how this feels? Where can they feel it in their body? Encourage them to be as detailed as they can—you might hear about tingly fingers, bouncy feet, wide open eyes. What does it make them want to do? Don't ask this at bedtime!

Enquiries into a child's response to exercise, healthy food and energy levels become the learning of self-care because the parent or carer who has asked and listened is better equipped to guide that child towards choosing what makes them feel good. Using mindfulness in this way creates space to pause, notice what's going on and to make healthy choices. The ultimate aim of a self-care strategy for children is that they recognise the various signals in their minds and bodies related to their own physical and emotional wellbeing and then make the best decisions to meet these needs.

Many children, with some guidance, are able to realise they are hungry and that they feel better after eating a healthy meal than they do after consuming empty calories. They can recognise that running around in the fresh air, swimming or riding their bikes makes them feel good. They know when they need a hug or reassurance. Equally, I know that children as young as 6 or 7 are able to recognise feelings of tiredness in their own minds and bodies and to compare them with contrasting feelings of energy and alertness. When there is concerted focus on developing the ability to recognise how the mind and body are feeling, you will hopefully find your child learns to welcome the time to rest and relax. You may even find they take themselves off to bed when they are tired. My older children can now manage this but there have been many discussions and experiments around bedtimes to get to this stage and I will be sharing them with you now.

What Does a Good Bedtime Routine Look Like?

A good bedtime routine has at its heart a time at which sleep should start. This needs to be calculated by working backwards from the time we wake in the morning. Many early bird adults and children wake naturally while others are woken by alarm clocks. Whichever way the day starts you will need to count backwards until you reach the number of hours of sleep you or your child needs in order to function optimally in physical, mental and emotional terms. If you need reminding of why this matters so much, please go back to read Chapter 1. To refresh your memory, the amount of sleep we all need is:

Toddlers: 12 hours
Children aged 3–6: 10–12 hours
Children aged 7–12: 10–11 hours
Teenagers: 8–10 hours
Adults: 8 hours

If, when you calculate this, the hour at which your child should be going to sleep seems impossibly early, look at the morning wake-up time. Are there things you can do to enable them to sleep a little longer in the morning? If you allow a long time to get up and ready for school because they are useless in the morning, it may be that the extra sleep will make a big difference. It is certainly worth experimenting to see whether your mornings are better after a later start time. Some strategies you could employ:

- Check homework has all been done before they go to bed
- Pack schoolbags the night before
- Prepare packed lunches
- Lay out uniform and check any kit needed is ready for the morning
- If there are morning chores to do, can they be done after school instead?
- Can any breakfast preparations be made the night before?
- Can travel arrangements for school be made any later/easier?
- Can your own routine change to allow more time in bed?

This may seem like a massive faff but just one small change that enables an extra half hour of sleep could make a huge difference. This is especially true for teenagers whose circadian rhythm has changed, requiring them to wake later in the day than they did as younger children. My teenagers perfected getting up at the last moment humanly possible in order not to be late for school and I have encouraged them to do so. They are certainly less grumpy as a result. The evenings are the time teenagers are often full of beans, just as the adults are thinking of heading off to bed. You can encourage them to use their spike in energy to make their preparations for the morning with the promise of extra morning sleep. Just beware of the teenager clattering around the house at 11pm gathering items for the morning and disturbing the sleep of younger children. I know all too well that these are the challenges families face.

Instilling in your children the packing of their own bags and laying out of uniform the night before as early as you can in their lives encourages independence and taking responsibility; and it will save everyone a great deal of angst over the coming years and is worth persevering with. Yes, it's quicker to just do it yourself, but they will soon get the hang of it and, hopefully, take pride in organising themselves. Like all aspects of the bedtime routine, the gentle repetition will ensure it becomes a habit and there will gradually be fewer arguments or procrastination around it. A calmer morning is possible for the whole family if there is less rushing around trying to locate a vital football boot or, memorably once in my house, create a World Book Day costume in 10 minutes flat.

Once you have decided on the time at which your child needs to sleep, you can share this with them. Remind them why it matters and be prepared for arguments that their best friend goes to bed at midnight, etc.

One Hour Prior to Sleep

Your routine will work well if it looks approximately like this. One hour before your child needs to be asleep remove access to screens. This is easier for younger children and may not be possible with your teenager. Knowing the reasons why this is important can help you convince children of any age that it is sensible. Chapter 6 discusses aspects of technology and sleep and I suggest you read this before you talk to your older child or teenager. Run through the reasons why sleep is so important to them.

Make preparations for the next morning in order to maximise the amount of time spent sleeping before the alarm goes off. If your child wakes early, then this won't be necessary and you will probably find they become tired earlier in the evening. Go with the flow of their natural rhythm if you can but don't allow them to nap at all after 5 pm if you want them to settle down for a full night of sleep later.

Next comes a shower or bath. This can be lovely time of fun and games away from screens and phones but it has another important function that aids a good night's sleep. Our bodies are generally at a temperature of 37°C but in order to sleep, we need to reduce our core temperature by one degree or so. This change is in tune with the melatonin levels in our bodies which, you will recall, are linked to daylight. For millions of years, as the sun set in the evening, human body temperature would also drop in tune with rising melatonin levels signalling the need for sleep. This is why the quiz on page 44 included questions about how warm your and your child's bedroom is and how warm you are in bed. This is covered further below.

The bath or shower has the important benefit of helping the body cool down as the water evaporates from the skin. Adults and children will sleep better and more deeply following a shower or bath. Allow enough time for this to happen and try not to rush through it. The sensations of warm water, maybe some bubbles and nice scents, are simple ones but they can dramatically reduce stress levels and get the mind ready for a calm and peaceful drift off into sleep. If you bathe children together try to keep the peace as much as you can. There is a great array of bath toys available nowadays, even waterproof books. Avoid the temptation to involve technology and make sure bath time stays simple but as calm as you can.

My kids used to love taking their favourite cars, trains, zoo animals, dolls, etc. into the bath with them. For adults, showering is more often a part of the morning routine but if your sleep is not as good as you'd like it to be, experiment with an evening bath or shower as well, add in some relaxing scents and take it as an opportunity to relax.

When your child gets out of the bath or shower, try not to smother them in anything too hot and allow them to cool down; equally, don't encourage them to sleep in overly warm onesies and, especially avoid socks. The head, hands and feet are the ways in which the body seeks to cool down prior to sleep so keep those parts free of clothing if possible. After teeth cleaning, there will hopefully be about 20–30 minutes left before the time your child needs to be asleep. You can get them into bed at this point or spend the final half hour in another part of the bedroom, a beanbag or cushion pile.

Half an Hour Before Bed

This half hour is crucial and spending it well, giving it your focus and attention, will pay off later. During this time, you will be aiming to calm both your child's body and their mind using *relaxation* and *reflection* techniques. The quiz on page 43 revealed that many of the reasons children find it hard to go to sleep are emotional. Feeling frightened or worried about issues small and large is completely normal for children and adults alike. Worries and anxiety that we experience throughout the day can be avoided by keeping busy but when, we head to bed, the day's issues surface. This happens to children in exactly the same way as it does for adults, and especially if they have had little downtime in their day and few opportunities to share the day's events with parents or carers.

Incorporating some *reflection* time into the final half hour of the day can be a powerful wellbeing tool which will benefit much more than sleep. Chapter 7 goes into this process more deeply and offers a series of options to suit you and your child. These include practising gratitude, which we know that has the power to rewire the brain; active listening as the parent allows the child to talk about any worries from the day; prayer and blessing, which may be part of your family culture. These practices can help dispel emotional worries and clear the mind ready for sleep.

It's also crucial to *set the intention* of having a good night's sleep, with happy dreams and waking full of beans for tomorrow. Praise your child for everything they do related to calmness and relaxation and how it will lead to great sleep. You're trying to build their recognition of the link between good preparation for bed and a consequential restful sleep—it's a virtuous circle as the day that follows this good night's sleep will be easier for them in many ways.

The body is often as active as the mind before sleep, as you will know from the times your child seems unable to be still. The warm bath or shower will have gone some way towards *relaxation* as will the restriction on use of screens and phones, etc. Once your child is settled following their bath you can decide whether to first have a "mind calm" by using a reflection tool or start with a "body calm" relaxation. For the body, you can choose a short mindfulness visualisation, body scan and relaxation the scripts of which are in Chapter 8.

I haven't yet mentioned the more traditional bedtime story. Reading stories with your child can be a moment of closeness and calm in a busy day. Many of my happiest memories of my children when they were young are when we cuddled up together with a pile of picture books or the latest chapter of a longer book. Children well into their primary years can beg for stories to be read to them, even when well able to read by themselves. You can fit in a story around the other relaxation practices. If your child is physically restless, try the body scan (page 183) first, then a reflection chat, then the story. Some nights the reflection chat can take longer if your child has had a bad day at school, so you will have to adapt time spent on the relaxation. There are many wonderful books available that can tackle emotional issues such as shyness and being different, please see the Resources section. None of this has to take more than 20–30 minutes, which may seem impossible to fit in but the investment now will pay off later with fewer reappearances or wakings.

Experiment with the Routine

I am aware that bedtime in many households can often be fraught because of the myriad other tasks that need completing in what can be a very small window. For many parents getting in from work, feeding everyone, checking homework and rushing through housework can be a daily challenge. Instead of seeing the bedtime routine as yet another job on the long list before you can collapse on the sofa, perhaps try an experiment. A shift in perspective, even if it starts as an experiment, can make it about you as well as your child. Putting aside your other "jobs" and accepting that the next hour or so is going to be unproductive in terms of answering emails and sorting laundry, means you'll end up with a longer and more peaceful evening if this is done well and done once. So, take the opportunity to play with your child during bathtime; have a big towel cuddle; make a cosy nest to read stories together in; put on relaxing music and lower the lights for the last half hour. You might find yourself nodding off too! Enjoy the relaxation yourself after your own busy day.

The hardest times for me were trying to give an older child this kind of one-to-one attention while needing to feed and settle a baby. As with all things parenting, do not beat yourself up about what you don't achieve; just give yourself the credit for managing whatever aspect of this that you can. And remember that a child who settles well into bed, shares worries and relaxes their body will sleep a whole lot better and your evenings will be less disturbed by upping and downing.

Below are a few sample routines for children of different ages plus some sibling examples. You can plan your own. Use the body calm tools in Chapter 7 and the mind calm tools in Chapter 8. Once the routine is planned, you can make a start and just come back to it every day, trying to make as much work as possible, not getting anxious when it doesn't. There will be points of resistance for you and your child; there will be late nights that are out of your control and there will always be dramas. Just keep trying to establish the rhythm of the routine, tweak it as you need to and see what works best, and you will see it embed itself and make changes for everyone. Repetition, repetition, repetition!

Sample Routines for Families

These are sample routines for children of various ages and with various wake-up times. If you are finding it hard to work out a routine for your family, using a template may help. Tweak it back and forth to fit your family best. Keeping some notes might help as you notice when things work well and when they don't. For example, the week may go very well until Thursdays when Brownies or football practice goes on until 8 pm and the knock-on effect of the later night affects everyone. Can you make any adjustments on Thursdays to keep things running more smoothly?

Being somewhat forensic will pay off as sometimes the smallest adjustments can make a big difference. I recommend turning off tech but am also suggesting that using relaxation apps can be helpful—seems contradictory? If you're going to try out some of these apps, make sure that all notifications are switched off so that there are no interruptions to what your child is listening to. Remove the device straight afterwards. With teenagers, encourage them to use the apps without checking anything else on the device. Easier said than done, I know, but this is where their mindful awareness comes in—"I notice I drift off to sleep well after listening to a calming app, but if I start scrolling afterwards, it wakes me up again and I can feel worried." I've heard comments like this over and over and see my role as congratulating the young person for such great noticing and encouraging them to stick with the plan, let the app help their mind and body to get ready for a good sleep—and don't sabotage that by opening up other parts of the device. If this proves tricky, using entries on the sleep diary to record when those temptations arise and what effect it has can help them to raise that awareness and, ultimately, make better choices.

Age of child:6
Wake-up time: 7.30am
Sleep time: 8pm
Routine: at 7pm turn off all tech and run the bath. Lay out clothes and schoolbag for the morning. Bath fun! 7.30pm ready for bed, play calming music, body scan to relax, 3 Things gratitude practice; story. Lights off.

Age of child:10
Wake-up time: 7am
Sleep time: 8.30pm
Routine: at 7.30pm turn off all tech and run the bath or shower. Lay out clothes and schoolbag for the morning. 8pm ready for bed, play calming music; reflect on the day together; pebbles visualisation; next chapter of story. Lights off.

Age of child:14
Wake-up time: 7.45am
Sleep time: 10.30pm
Routine: at 9pm turn off all tech and remove phone if possible. Teenager to lay out clothes and prepare kit, etc. for the morning. Shower or bath. 10pm ready for bed, suggest playing calming music. Use app with body scan to relax; journal. Lights off.

Ages of children: 3 and 7
Wake-up time: 6.30am
Sleep times: 6.30pm and 7.30pm
Routine: Turn off all tech at 5.45pm and run bath. Bath children together. 6.15pm read stories together then settle younger child into bed while older child lays out school bag and clothes. With older child play calming music, use reflection tool such as best things; relax with Beditation; read a chapter of a book together.

Ages of children: 8 and 12
Wake-up time: 7am
Sleep times: 8.30pm and 9pm
Routine: Turn off tech at 7.30pm for the younger child, followed by and bath/shower. While the younger child lays out tomorrow's things, turn off the tech for the older child and send them for a shower. With younger child, reflect on the day planning activities for the weekend/holidays; relax using a visualisation, read together. At 8.30pm, encourage older child to reflect about their day; suggest they use an app for relaxation or mindfulness; allow them to read by themselves until 9pm.

Ages of children: 13 and 15
Wake-up time: 7.30am
Sleep times: 10.30pm and 10.45pm
Routine: Turn off tech at 9.30pm and send the teens for staggered baths/showers. Pop in to see them and check they have got everything ready for tomorrow. Use tips from Chapter 5 to engage them in discussion about their day. Reflective listening can be helpful. Respect their privacy and give them space while letting them know you are available for listening. Encourage use of meditation apps, relaxing music and journalling. Wish them goodnight, every night; don't expect a kiss!

Applying the Routine

If you have introduced a new bedtime routine to your family with great enthusiasm and determination, you will likely get off to a great start. Hopefully, there will quickly be benefits and it is important to focus on those and allow everyone to give their feedback. Like many projects begun in a wave of vigour, there will be times when it is difficult to stick to and, like those new year resolutions we all make, things start to slip backwards and you can end up feeling worse and more helpless than you did to start with.

To avoid this experience, make a realistic assessment of your family's areas for improvement and their temperament around change and rules. Some children respond happily to instructions and rules and some children are less keen. Knowing what you know about your own situation, choose the elements of the routine you feel will most benefit the family, think through how you are going to practically apply them, then try your best to stick to it. Common pitfalls are the weekend late night, parents or carers going out to work or leisure in the evenings, child procrastination and your own sheer tiredness.

As I have said before, never beat yourself up about things going wrong, it's tough work being a parent day in and day out; let it go and try again tomorrow. The late night, whether at the weekend or weekday, can be disrupting but if the routine is the default "normal" then it will quickly slot into place again. It's very hard for a babysitter to fill the exact same role as the parent at bedtime but you can ask your childminder/sitter to help you (and themselves) by sticking to your lights-out time and to reading a story, checking the ventilation and that there are no smuggled devices under pillows!

With procrastinating children, you can gently speed things up with a shorter bath or shorter stories but it can add to your stress levels and this can be communicated to your child so try and stay calm if you can. When you're tired yourself, it is really hard, I know, so see if you can take the time for yourself too, to curl up for a bit, have a cuddle and not think about all those jobs that still need doing. I've frequently gone to bed myself shortly after settling my kids—they just looked so snug and cosy in bed, I couldn't resist heading off myself.

As with all things parenting, it is important to acknowledge that it's hard. It is especially hard for single parents or those dealing with children with diverse or multiple needs. It's hard when you're tired, it's hard when you're working and it's hard to keep going with what you know is right when you meet opposition from the children or lack of support from other adults in the house. And because it is hard, it is vital that you cut yourself some slack, don't try and be super Mum/Dad and, above all, don't beat yourself up if it doesn't seem to be working. Changing habits takes time. Keep aiming at the routine, some days will be easier than others, and eventually it will fall into place and life will improve.

Monitoring progress over the weeks and months is important and will encourage you. By looking at the original sleep diary you put together, you can see how much more time your child is sleeping now. If your starting point is way off from where you think it needs to be, aim to shift it by 10–15 minutes every 4 days. So, if you want your 8-year-old to be asleep by 8.30pm but they have got used to 9.30pm, start with 9.20pm for 4 days before shifting it back to 9.10pm, etc. It will take a while (approximately 2 weeks) but if you keep the focus on feeling good rather than reducing their fun time it can help keep them onside. It can be tough doing this on your own so try and involve other supportive adults to give your child positive feedback about their new improved sleeping habits.

Direct or indirect compliments from family members, friends or teachers can be very helpful—these could include praising the child for handling a tricky situation well or getting a better mark in a test or playing well in a sporting activity. We're building that neural pathway: sufficient sleep equals feeling good.

Track everyone's sleep patterns for a week and see how much more rest everyone is getting since you began the routine. Don't forget to include yourself—parents are happier, healthier and more likely to enjoy life when they have had enough sleep. Best of all you can monitor progress through everyday improvements. Bringing mindfulness practices into your lives and promoting self-care will enable everyone to reflect on how they are feeling around tiredness and rest. Even young children will be able to notice changes in how they feel when they are well-rested by comparison. More sleep will, over time, result in:

- Better concentration
- Fewer tantrums
- Better emotional regulation
- Improvements in friendships
- Better academic work
- Memory improvement
- More energy
- More resilience
- Better decision-making
- Improved performance in sport, drama, music, etc.
- Increased sense of wellbeing and happiness
- Brighter complexion
- Fewer coughs and colds

Keeping the sleep conversation going with your child is important. Give them as much positive feedback as you can, sticking to non-judgemental observations and avoiding smugness! So don't open with "you're so much less grumpy since we moved your bedtime" or "I told you you'd feel better after a proper night's sleep." Instead, focus on what you or others have noticed that will make them feel good. Above all, ask them questions and listen carefully to what they say in response. You are very unlikely to find your child offering you thanks for their earlier bedtime, but they might let you know in their own way that it's good to have more energy for football practice or that they haven't had a falling-out with a friend for a while or that their maths test was easier than they'd thought it would be. Complimenting teenagers on their appearance can go a long way. Dark circles under the eyes aren't a great look for any of us.

Sharing your efforts to improve your own sleep will also be helpful, especially if they have involved a certain amount of effort, such as switching your phone off before you get ready for bed. If you feel better as a result of getting more sleep, your children will have noticed and you can ask them for their thoughts and observations. Try and avoid becoming a sleep bore like me! Holding the balance between being confident about what you're doing and being neurotic is important. Just keep going with it. The challenges will come, as always, when someone is experiencing stress and anxiety and these times can come hard and fast in families. The next chapter looks at this and how mindfulness and relaxation practices can help.

Some Tips and Tricks

Before moving on to adult bedtime routines and the next chapter, I'd like to cover a few issues that often come up in conversation with parents.

Weekends and holidays: When your routine is based on the average school/work day, it can be challenging when those rising times change at the weekend and during school holidays. As we know, sleep once lost cannot be recovered—the sleep debt builds. Weekends offer the chance for everyone to get a bit longer in bed if working patterns allow this. Personally, life would lose a great deal of joy if I didn't get to wake naturally twice a week rather than to the hated alarm clock. Children tend to feel the same, so my advice is to let them sleep in. Teenagers will need much more of this lie-in time than younger children due to the forward movement of their body clocks and the fact that they tend to fall asleep much later than their younger siblings.

A horrible myth perpetuated by many parents and carers is that not getting up early means you are "missing the best part of the day". I say horrible because it's an adult-imposed attitude that actually works against what adolescents require—and also because of my own teenage memories of having the curtains yanked open and a rude awakening when I was deeply and happily catching up on my sleep. The problem with this, however, is obvious once you understand how the hormonal cycle works: without sufficient building of adenosine (sleep pressure) and the melatonin levels that are influenced by exposure to light, falling asleep on Saturday and Sunday nights can be very difficult. Allowing lie-ins at the weekend and during holidays will not be a disaster but it's important to ensure children get some fresh air, exercise and, whenever possible, sunlight.

It's strongly advisable not to allow older children to become nocturnal during the school holidays, sleeping all day and gaming/socialising all night—this leads to poor mood management and isolation within the family. If bedtimes move a little later, that's going to help with sleep but try to keep as much of the sleep hygiene in place such as removing screens in good time, a shower or bath and some end-of-the-day reflection time. It's also a good idea to keep an eye on the amounts of sleep that are happening on weekend nights too—if they swing wildly from the functional weekday routine, look for ways to tweak the routine at either end. A 15-minute shorter lie-in and a 15-minute earlier bedtime can gain a whole half hour and make returning to the Monday-Friday routine less of a jolt.

As the long summer holidays come to an end, start to gradually move towards the term-time sleep routine at least a week before they return to school. If you've had little or no routine for the whole of August, it is unwise to wait until the night before school to start insisting on an earlier bedtime. The night before starting a new school year can be stressful for many children, especially those starting at new schools and they are likely to find it harder to sleep when they are worried. The strategies in the following chapter can help at this time and at other times when we know our children are experiencing anxiety.

Different households: It's very common for children to spend nights in different households when their parents are separated and this, along with a host of issues, can be extremely challenging. If you're a primary carer who has put lots of effort into establishing a bedtime routine, it will be painful to find your ex has undone all your good work. This is just another aspect of parenting that will need to be negotiated. Share this book with your child's parent and explain how much everyone will benefit from enough sleep, not least the lack of night-time disturbances and a happier child the next day. A child who may be struggling with this change of circumstances will find comfort in the continuity of a nurturing routine regardless of where they are sleeping.

Sleepovers: Ah, the dreaded sleepover...This was one of my least favourite words when my children were young. Much as they absolutely adored having friends stay over, the knock-on effect was often disastrous. It was a badge of honour to get as little sleep as possible and one memorable occasion involved my cleaning up vomit after a poor visiting child was exposed to normally forbidden sweets. The shame of explaining this to the mum the next day still makes me flush all over. If you don't want to be a total killjoy, you will likely find yourself agreeing to host one of these or to despatch your child to one at someone else's house. There is very little you can do to contain the situation but my main advice would be to tire them out as much as possible during the day with outside activities. If they sit indoors in front of screens all day, the chances of them getting any sleep reduce dramatically. Often the whole household is also disrupted so try to find the balance between letting the fun happen and ensuring the next day zombie effect isn't too bad. Keep sleepovers as a rare treat!

Early Night Wednesday: My husband came up with this genius strategy and it forms a core foundation of good sleep for everyone in our household. It's something we regularly use and I hope our older children will find it helpful in adulthood. Napping certainly seems to be part of their university life. The early starts of the average weekday when combined with the pressures of schoolwork, sporting activities and social demands can easily build into tiredness as the week progresses. We all know how good it feels to get to Friday.

A mid-week intervention can really help physically and psychologically. If this appeals to you, try introducing the concept when you get complaints of tiredness in the mornings or after school. Explain that everyone will feel much better and aim for just a half hour earlier bedtime for everyone. It has a surprisingly positive effect and seems to give a little reset to the week.

Bedtime Routine for Adults

If you've been reading this chapter with your kids in mind, you've likely come across strategies and tips that could just as well apply to you. Maybe you sleep soundly every night and wake refreshed and are the envy of your family and friends—certainly you're the exception rather than the rule. Looking at our own routine around bedtime can be a great opportunity to identify areas that could be changed to improve how long and how well we sleep ourselves. All of which enables us to better tackle the next day.

Sleep hygiene is the first place to start. Run through the same checklist you did for your child, checking the bedroom temperature and light are optimal. You might not have had the time or inclination to complete your own sleep diary, especially if your main concern is around a child's sleep pattern, but the aspects you can consider are caffeine, alcohol, exercise, screentime and stress. Are you getting enough daylight to ensure healthy melatonin production?

Making some tweaks here and setting some new self-care practices can have a major impact. For example, swapping to the decaf option, trying some gentle stretching before bed and stopping screentime one hour before bed or experimenting with blue-light filters. I spoke recently with someone who walks an average 10 miles a day on his postal round shifts so gets plenty of exercise and doesn't drink alcohol. The improvement to his sleep came unexpectedly when he stopped following the news for a month. Late-night TV news can send us off to bed feeling anxious and angry which is far from conducive to an enjoyable drift into sleep. If that rings a bell for you, maybe try cutting it out in the evenings.

A good bedtime routine is ideally enjoyable and part of a self-care habit that sustains us beyond getting those magic 8 hours. It can feel impossible with life's other pressures and not everyone has the option of a pre-bed hour for themselves. Take whatever you can from the suggestions below but try to stick to the core practice of having a set time for sleeping and rising as we know that this better regulates our metabolism and enables sleep to work its wonders. It can be hard to make changes but stick with whatever you decide will suit you for a month and take note of what differences result.

- Decide on the time you need to be asleep by for a 7–8 hour sleep then 30–60 minutes later begin your routine.
- Working into the evenings is a common practice for many people but try not to work right up to the wire and pack away the laptop or put the files away before the bedtime hour.
- Avoid falling asleep on the sofa. If you're nodding off, take the signals from your body and go to bed for some quality sleep. The last time to take a nap should be 5pm for a good night's sleep. Sleeping on the sofa is never as comfortable as bed and can lead to neck pain or becoming overheated if you're still in your daytime clothes. A late-evening snooze disrupts the sleep pattern and can make it harder to fall asleep properly later when you really need it.
- This is the hard bit—turn your attention away from the day you've had and the one coming up and commit to focusing on yourself and your own needs. Being in the present moment during our bedtime routine will make it more enjoyable and easier to commit to.

- Turn off the telly, especially if the news triggers you. And put away your phone and any other devices. Ideally don't sleep in the same room as them. Doom-scrolling or looking at images of other people's perfect homes, holidays, car, lives, etc. will only keep your mind busy and anxious. You might have a spot of nomophobia (see p.168 to find out) but experiment with this and see what differences you notice. Giving our brains a break from external stimulation and blue-light frequencies will better enable sleep.
- Take a bath or shower to relax and get your body temperature to the right place.
- If you're one of the 30 million women in the UK experiencing peri-menopause or menopause, make sure the room is cool enough and you have what you need for any night sweats. This might be a damp flannel nearby, a cooling pad under the pillow or a fan by the bed.
- Any pampering around skincare or beauty, relaxing music and smells will help get you ready for sleep.
- Experiment with the mind calm and body calm exercises you will find in Chapter 9 to release tension and relieve worry and anxiety. There are plenty to choose from to support your mental, emotional and physical wellbeing.
- Once in bed, read a book or do something you find relaxing such as writing, drawing, or knitting. If you have the energy, sex is a good release for mind and body. If reflective practices appeal to you, take time to run through the best moments of your day even if there are only a few simple ones—that cup of tea when you got home, a hug from your child. There is more below about gratitude practice, but we know that appreciating the good things in our lives rewires the brain to positivity and makes us feel better, all of which supports good sleep.

Navigating this with a partner can be tricky but persevere to find a routine that suits you both. None of this is easy to do when you have had an evening of interruptions from children or you fear being woken from your much-needed sleep by children having bad dreams or by teenagers foraging around the kitchen for food. This is where the family routine comes into its own. By tackling your children's sleep issues, you are then far more likely to remember how a good routine supports and nurtures you. We're now going to look at fears and anxiety and the role they play in the sleep patterns of adults and children and what can help the whole family.

Chapter 4
Fears and Anxiety

Put your thoughts to sleep. Do not let them cast a shadow over the moon of your heart. Let go of thinking.

Rumi

My youngest child aged about 7 was, by day, a confident and bubbly girl enjoying school, her friendships and activities. Bedtime often saw a different child emerge as she would claim to be frightened of having bad dreams or would have a new nightly worry to share. To us, they would sometimes seem valid worries: "I haven't learnt my spellings for the test tomorrow"; sometimes small worries about toys or clothes; and sometimes such enormous worries our hearts would sink at the prospect of trying to answer "what will happen to the polar bears?" or "will you die?" This is entirely normal, and we went through similar bedtime conversations with both older children but when these fears and anxieties appear just before bedtime, it can be difficult. It can be especially challenging when teenagers want to have a late-night heart-to-heart with you and share the worries that come up for them; they are perky and alert for this, while you are on your knees and desperate for bed.

As adults, we often have a very similar experience as our busy days finish and we settle into bed only to find our minds racing over what we haven't done or need to do, things we should or shouldn't have said that day. We also all know what it's like to find major issues such as mortality, money and relationships dominating our minds as we struggle to get much-needed sleep. Knowing how much we need to get some sleep in before it all starts again, doesn't help either. Insomnia is a global problem, especially in the industrialised nations with about a third of the general population having symptoms. Unsurprisingly, parents are more likely to experience insomnia than those adults without children. Many people have discussed their sleep problems with me over the years and the most common reason for being unable to sleep is the mind running while the body feels tense: classic symptoms of anxiety.

If you are concerned about your own levels of stress or anxiety, it is important to seek medical help via your GP. There are many charities and organisations that can help with mental health, you will find details in the Resources section of this book. Thankfully, mental health issues are no longer something people have to feel shame or embarrassment at experiencing from time to time in their lives. The global pandemic has been, of course, a source of intense stress across the world and affected people of all ages, gender, ethnicity and socioeconomic status. The long-term implications of it upon us all are yet to be assessed but we already know how much children and young people have suffered.

Anxiety in Young People

There is no doubt in the minds of professionals working in any capacity with young people that the experience of anxiety is at an alarming level. It used to be that a report about youth wellbeing conducted by one of the mental health or children's charities would hit the media and cause a reaction of horror when it revealed the numbers of children experiencing severe worry, depression, self-harm or even suicide. These reports largely tend to track children and adolescents self-reporting the symptoms they experience rather than clinically diagnosed mental health disorders, but that's alarming enough for me. It is always shocking to hear about the pain our children are suffering.

Over time, this has somehow become normalised and we seem to just accept that this is the nature of the modern world, the reality of the complex lives children lead on and offline; that mental health issues are normal and to be expected. A young person recently told me, as an aside to something else we were discussing, "I've got my anxiety, of course"—as if it were completely par for the course. My heart ached for her.

The pressures on our young people are stacked high. At school, they must perform and succeed to compete in an uncertain employment market. They are tested and examined from a very early age by teachers under pressure themselves to keep their schools performing well in league tables. Once they leave school, they will likely struggle under the burden of student debt however much the repayments are arranged or in a precarious labour market; they face the decreasing likelihood that they will be able to afford to buy their own homes for decades. Adolescence brings a whole new bunch of things to worry about as bodies develop and changes in the brain bring about new ways of thinking about themselves, other people and the world—more of this in Chapter 5.

Meanwhile, poverty, inequality, discrimination and exploitation remain issues for society as a whole and their impact on the lives of young people can be devastating. Throw in a climate catastrophe and a pandemic and you have a perfect storm for mental distress in people of all ages and background. However, if we can take one thing away from the global pandemic it is that the human spirit is resilient and often thrives under pressure. Young people featured in the news, as well as many known personally to me, including my own kids, showed throughout a wealth of compassion, creativity and positivity in the face of that threat. Young people were among those whose resourcefulness and generosity helped their families, friends and neighbours through those dark times whether it was fundraising for the NHS, shopping for neighbours, walking dogs, volunteering at foodbanks, sewing surgical scrubs on the kitchen table or just keeping spirits up with zoom quizzes and kitchen discos. My eldest son's A-levels and gap-year plans were scuppered but he signed up and worked the year as a carer and we've never been prouder.

The issues above can keep anyone awake at night. Our young people are also having to live an online life and to navigate a world of social media and that is totally alien to many of the generation above them. One of the UK's leading charities for young people is the Prince's Trust and it has undertaken vast amounts of research into many aspects of children's lives. In 2019, it identified that more than half of 16–25-year-olds think social media creates an overwhelming pressure on young people.

A further report by the Prince's Trust in May 2020 found that 43% of young people across the UK feel their anxiety levels have increased as a result of the coronavirus crisis, with 32% saying they are "overwhelmed" by feelings of panic and anxiety on a daily basis. Studies have also emerged, however, that show us there were some young people who did better during lockdown and I know many children were reluctant to return to "normal" once it became possible again. We're all different and some of us thrive in the world of normality while for some, less social pressure and more freedom released tension and anxiety.

In October 2020, the Department for Education published "State of the Nation 2020: children and young people's wellbeing" which found that more than a quarter of all young people reported having had sleep problems in the past seven days, with more girls than boys experiencing this (32.4% to 24.7%) Sleep problems were more common among children and young people with a probable (i.e., symptomatic but undiagnosed) mental disorder with more than 50% of those participants reporting difficulties sleeping.

When we know how powerful sleep is as a protector of mental health and emotional regulation, we can see how this sets up a vicious cycle of sleep deprivation leading to difficulties around resilience, low mood, challenging behaviours, difficulties with relationships—all of which keep people awake, and so on. Interventions are necessary and while schools and colleges are increasingly equipped to provide support and advice for children and young people experiencing mental health issues, sleep remains an area of limited focus and priority. This is understandably so when sleep happens at home not at school (hopefully) but the knock-on effect in classrooms everywhere means educators are well aware of the quantity of tired children they see every day.

Adult anxiety is also a common feature of normal life as pressures stack up to be good parents to our children; sons and daughters to ageing parents; keep friendships going; work and provide for our families and take care of our homes, bodies and minds. Anxiety is experienced by everyone at times and has a profound effect on our wellbeing and ability to function.

Anxiety and the Stress Response

It is important to say that anxiety is extremely common. This is because it is an absolutely normal human response to feelings of fear or panic. Stressful situations set off a whole process in the brain which many people are now aware of as the "flight or fight or freeze" response. It is a complex biochemical process that the brain triggers in order to enable us to survive. It begins in the area of the brain known as the amygdala. When we experience stress, the amygdala is activated in a split second. Stress hormones such as cortisol and adrenaline flood the body, the "reasoning" part of the brain (the prefrontal cortex) is overtaken as we prepare to tackle the challenging situation before us. It's a little like a smoke-filled room: your brain is so full of smoke that it's impossible to see anything clearly—we react rather than respond. The smoke eventually clears but it leaves behind a "smell" that can last for many hours if nothing is done to "neutralise" it. This bad smell stops us enjoying life and from being at our best.

The physical responses to stress are well-known to everyone, they include: increased heartrate and blood pressure, rapid breathing, blood being diverted to the muscles which tense for action, the bladder or bowels needing to empty. This amazing self-protective set of responses to danger is rooted back in evolutionary history when the dangers faced by humans were very real. Rapid, effective reactions were needed to ensure the survival of the race. The energy generated would have been expended during the fight or flight and the body would then be able to rest and recuperate.

Modern life in most parts of the world, thankfully no longer requires us to regularly fight or flee for our lives but our brains, evolved over thousands of years haven't caught up yet. We don't face wild animals on the whole, but the identical stress response kicks in when our mother-in-law is due to visit or when we are running late for an important meeting. For children, it can happen when they haven't learnt their spellings for a test or when a friend doesn't return their friendly greeting or text. We can recognise the same physical signs—sweating palms, rapid heartbeat, dry mouth. We recognise that under stress we often "can't think straight". This is exactly right and occurs because the brain is busy at lightning speed running scenarios, creating the conditions for our escape from danger and the areas of the brain best equipped for reasoned thought are temporarily overwhelmed.

When under stress, we don't think as we normally do and people often experience their thoughts leaping around wildly. If you have tried to help a partner, friend or child who is experiencing a stressful moment, you will know that they tend not to make much sense, and they can find it hard to follow your calm or logical thoughts. Their emotions can swing dramatically and they may be panicking. It can sometimes be painful to be with someone suffering in this way.

After the stressful situation has passed and the visit or the spelling test is over and the friend explains their phone was out of charge, we may experience relief and a release of the tension built up by the stress hormones. Follow this up with a restful night of sleep and mostly we will feel better. Sleep enables this emotional reset as well as the recuperation that happens in our cardiovascular and nervous system.

The problems occur when this stress response is repeated over and over, when the "downtime" between incidents of stress is reduced, giving the body less time to let go of the overload of hormones and recover. An animal in the wild might escape from a predator following a huge rush of chemicals that enable it to run incredibly fast and, in a matter of moments, the zebra or antelope will be calming munching grass again. Humans, unlike animals, are gifted with imagination. This is one of our greatest strengths, but it can also be our greatest weakness as we find ourselves going over and over something stressful that has happened to us. We turn it over in our minds, imagining much better things we could have said or done; we imagine different outcomes or we see it playing out again in our mind's eye. This keeps us in a state of low-level stress, like the smell of the smoke in the room, and it prevents us from returning to homeostasis (our point of stability).

When sleep is affected by stress, the reset function happens less well. This is when stress becomes chronic and anxiety becomes an issue. Anxiety occurs when people feel worried or panicky even when there is no obvious stressful situation. The symptoms can affect people's enjoyment of everyday life and include:

- Difficulty concentrating
- Feeling nervous, edgy or panicky all the time
- Feeling overwhelmed or full of dread
- Feeling out of control
- Not feeling hungry or over-eating for comfort
- Feeling moody or grouchy
- Sweating
- Feeling shaky or faint
- Stomach cramps and needing to go to the loo more often
- Difficulty sleeping

You will not be surprised to see that last one on the list. Anxiety affects us all for many of the reasons covered at the start of this chapter. The children I work with find themselves experiencing anxiety for a wide range of reasons that include friendship problems; bullying on- and offline; worries about money; schoolwork and exams; problems at home; they are anxious about their appearance, sexuality, identity; even the purpose and meaning of their lives. Their worries are large and small, life-changing and every day, but every child experiences the same feelings of anxiety in response to those worries, regardless of what triggers them. It is my job to help them understand what is going on in their brains and the bodies when they are feeling anxious and to give them practical tools they can use to restore feelings of calm and wellbeing.

One of my fellow mindfulness teachers told me about a boy who had taken part in a mindfulness course along with his classmates. Several weeks later he was on a school activity trip descending an abseiling board. He was overcome with fear and froze halfway down. Neither the instructor nor the teacher was able to get him moving again but one of his friends called up: "it's just your amygdala" and a lightbulb moment occurred enabling him to easily make it back down to the ground.

Understanding what's going on in our brains and our bodies can be incredibly liberating as it was for a young pupil I taught, about to go on stage in a big drama performance who was convinced she couldn't remember a single line or when she was meant to move. She was very frightened but was able to use the petal breathing technique (see p.186) she'd learnt, find her breath and connect her feet to the ground. She did this while recognising that it was just a stress response and her thoughts were not real things. I was so impressed and proud of her!

How to Help Someone Having a Panic Attack

It can be alarming if you are with someone who is experiencing a severe moment of intense fear, generally called a panic attack. They might be having trouble breathing, they may shake or sweat and be in distress. Try to remain calm when you are with someone in this situation; stay with them but give them space. The most intense feelings tend to last between five and ten minutes but the person experiencing it will not have much sense of time. Speak calmly and gently to them, reassure them that you won't leave and that this won't last long, tell them they are safe. You can put your hands on their shoulders or hold their hands if they are comfortable with this. Their breathing will be rapid and will be frightening for them.

Encourage the person to slow their out-breath down by making an "oh" shape with their lips and blow the breath out, as through a straw. Do it with them until their breath steadies. If they are able to speak or engage with you, ask them to try to name three things that they can see right now. Anything will do—their shoes, the floor, try and see if they can open their eyes. Then ask them to tell you three things they can hear. Then three things they can feel. Anything they can smell. Anything they can taste. If the person having the panic attack can engage with any of their senses in the present moment, it can help anchor them and enable them to interrupt the cycle of fearful thoughts that have overtaken their brain.

For someone who is prone to having panic attacks, the mere thought of having one can in itself be frightening. Encourage them to practice these grounding techniques when they are in a calm state. That way it becomes a habit that can be fallen back on when a challenging situation arises. Jon Kabat-Zinn describes this as weaving your parachute before you jump out of the plane. Wise words, as ever.

Mindfulness and Mental Health

Nowadays, there is a widespread recognition of the role that mindfulness can play in supporting mental health for adults and children alike. My military, no-nonsense dad recently asked me to recommend a mindfulness book for him! For those of us who have been practising for a long time and have seen the positive effects it has on young people, this is a much welcome shift in approach. Mindfulness is now prescribed by some GPs in the UK who recommend the flagship book, *Mindfulness: A Practical Guide to Finding Peace in a Frantic World* by Mark Williams and Danny Penman. The book follows the well-established 8-week *Mindfulness-Based Cognitive Therapy* course that has seen powerful results for many people around the world and is as effective as drugs for treating depression.

What Is Mindfulness?

At every introductory session, I always ask the children or young people if they have heard of mindfulness. It's wonderful that every hand goes up among the older age groups and the majority of hands even in the younger ones. Most of us have heard of it, many of us will try it, for some it will be life-changing and for others it is fine to take the bits that work for you and use them to help in everyday life.

The best way to capture moments is to pay attention. This is how we cultivate mindfulness. Mindfulness means being awake. It means knowing what you are doing.

Jon Kabat-Zinn

This was written back in the 1970s by the man credited with bringing Eastern practices of meditation to the West, making them secular and accessible for everyone for the benefit of physical and mental health. For details of his wonderful books and to see where you can watch him talk movingly about his life's work, please see the Resources section.

Put simply—mindfulness is a very simple form of meditation that can be practised by absolutely anyone, including very young children. I might even argue that they are the ones we can learn from as their attention is so often in the present moment and their absorption in what they are doing is an inspiration to all we weary adults juggling our attention between so many things. Typically, it involves focusing your full attention on your breath. As you focus on the breath coming in and out of the body, you find you can take a mental step back from your thoughts. With practice, you will be able to observe your thoughts as they arise in the mind.

As you get better at this—as your practice grows—you are able to remain detached from your thoughts for longer, and you learn how to let them go. Your thoughts no longer grab hold of you, dragging you along the pathway of anxiety. When we are lying awake with our thoughts racing, this ability to create a bit of space around those thoughts can bring the mind and body to a calmer place, making sleep come more easily. I have been doing this for most of my adult life. I am just human though and I have nights when my mind is racing about and sleep is elusive. But I am grateful for the reliable practice of tuning into the breath, again and again, until that clear quiet space grows in my mind.

The wonderful thing about mindfulness practice is that it enables us to treat all thoughts, big, small, trivial or serious, with the same calm compassionate detachment. As you breathe, you notice your thoughts with *friendly curiosity*. You are able to catch negative thought patterns before they send you off along the same old spiralling pathway. You are able to observe what triggers certain thought patterns; and what thoughts make you feel good. You take control of your thoughts and save yourself a great deal of anxiety, depression and that horrible feeling of being trapped inside your own repetitive thought cycle as feelings of tension and anxiety ripple through your body. This is what happens to us when we can't sleep. We simply can't find a way to let go or manage these wild and whirling thoughts that race through our minds.

Mindfulness can be a powerful tool in breaking negative thought patterns which directly improves how you feel. Mindfulness builds resilience and empowers the practitioner. It is not a cure for everything but for many people of all ages it is a significant step towards better mental health, wellbeing and—of course—sleep.

Myths About Mindfulness

Mindfulness is not Buddhism and meditation is not religious. It is a method of mental training.

- You do not have to sit in a yoga position or under a tree or chant "Om". It helps to sit in a chair with a straight back and place your feet on the floor, but you can bring mindful awareness to everything you do, including movement, eating and most aspects of life.
- Mindfulness practice doesn't take a lot of time. It can take as little a few minutes daily but it needs some patience and persistence. One benefit of practising is that you feel less pressured by time. It won't happen by itself, however, so a commitment to those daily minutes is needed.
- Mindfulness is not complicated. Nor is it about "success" or "failure". You are not trying to get somewhere. This is radically different from most things we undertake which have goals and targets. For this reason, it takes some getting used to. It is incredibly liberating to "just be" without have to achieve anything. This is what many young people love about it.
- Mindfulness will not give you rose-tinted specs or make you passive about life, letting it drift by at a distance. It is not about accepting the unacceptable but about seeing the world with greater clarity. With self-compassion, people find they can take wiser, more considered action towards identifying goals and priorities. It helps us make better, clearer decisions. In fact, mindfulness is a practice of some of the world's most successful individuals and is promoted by some of the largest global corporations.

Mindfulness has become well-established now in some schools and workplaces. There is even an all-party parliamentary group at the House of Commons. A wealth of research has been undertaken proving the positive impact it can have on mental wellbeing. For a long time, the available courses and literature were only aimed at adults. The Mindfulness in Schools Project (MiSP) is a charity that set out to fill this gap, identifying that children could benefit just as much as adults from learning these skills. In its own words, the charity's aim is to inform, create, train and support the secular teaching of mindfulness to young people and those who care for them.

Since 2009, MiSP has been working to train teachers like me to deliver courses in mindfulness to primary and secondary aged children. They have added courses over the years to support teachers in their stressful working lives and to bring the foundations of these practices to preschool children. It is an honour and privilege to teach these courses because they have been developed with great care, impeccable research, and have the wellbeing of every child at their heart. We all want children to have the skills to manage difficulty and to flourish. We want everyone to feel more peace, to embrace and fully enjoy the good parts of their lives while accepting that difficulties arise for us all and we can learn from them and learn how to let go of them too. Best of all is the feedback I have had over the years from the teachers, teenagers and young children who have learnt how to calm their minds and boost their wellbeing.

Feedback from Children and Young People Who Have Learnt Mindfulness with Me

- *"I think that mindfulness helps me share my ideas and feelings and also I can have time to relax and not worry."*
- *"I love mindfulness as I used to get really anxious, but when this came along, I started feeling better."*
- *"Mindfulness is very helpful because I have trouble going to sleep at nights and it has helped me."*
- *"It helped me not look into the future or back in the past, but think about now."*
- *"It has helped me with stress, sleeping and making the most of the good things."*
- *"The course helped me realise that stress is normal and that there are ways of dealing with it."*
- *"I have enjoyed being able to connect with myself and my thoughts."*

Explaining Mindfulness to Your Child

Adults will be able to learn more about mindfulness for themselves but there are ways to introduce it to your child that will help to engage them and hopefully inspire them to try it with you or, in the case of older children, by themselves.

Recent development of neuroscience has enabled much insight into the way the brain reacts during times of stress but also into what's going on during times of relaxation and when we practise mindfulness, yoga and other stress-reducing activities. You can teach your child the basics of this by explaining the relationship between different parts of their brain. You can assure them that scientists have been working hard for decades to understand this so that people of all ages can learn more about how their bodies respond when they are frightened or worried. You can explain it as below; I have inserted some suggested talking points that you can adapt to the age and suitability of your child:

1. **Prefrontal Cortex**—put your hand on your forehead. The incredibly hard bone you can feel under your hand is there to protect your amazing brain. And right under your hand is the bit we call the prefrontal cortex. It helps us in really important ways, especially it helps us to concentrate [*When do you use this power of concentration? What does it feel like?*], to make choices [*What choices have you made today? What choices have you made in the last few weeks?*] and to be our best [*What does it feel like to be your best?*]. When we feel frightened or worried, this part of our brain stops working normally because it has to take second place to another part of our brain…
2. **The amygdala**—you can't put your hand on this bit of your brain because it is tiny and it is right in the very middle of your head. For such a small area of the brain, it is surprisingly powerful! It is the oldest part of our brain and evolved when we lived in prehistoric times and needed to be able to stay safe in a lot of dangerous situations. [*Can you think of any?*] Its job is to help us to survive and it helps us to react really quickly when we are in danger. If we have to move fast out of the way of danger, we haven't got time to think about the best way of doing it (which is the job of the prefrontal cortex) we just have to move! So the amygdala helps us by enabling our bodies to respond to danger in one of three ways: fight, flight or freeze.

3. **The Stress Response**—is what we call our fight, flight or freeze reaction to fear or worry. When we are frightened or worried, the amygdala doesn't know that we aren't being chased by a scary bear and it just gets on with its job of keeping us alive. We might need to move fast or defend ourselves or keep very still. We will need all our energy and focus for the danger in front of us, so the amygdala orders the body to get ready [*What might our bodies need when we are in danger?*]. Our hearts beat faster, energy rushes to our muscles, our breath comes quickly, we might sweat as heat is generated. This is called the Stress Response. [*Can you think of a time you have felt frightened/stressed? How does it feel?*]
4. **Taking control**—sometimes we might need all the energy and focus that the amygdala organises to keep us safe [*Can you think of times when this might be helpful?*] but a lot of the time the things that cause us to feel afraid or worried don't need us to be ready to fight or run away. Think about seeing a spider and how it might make your heart beat hard for a moment until you remember that you are 100s of times bigger and it is probably scared of you. Our minds and our bodies confuse real danger (such as a car speeding along on the road you want to cross) with feelings of anxiety and worry (such as a friend not replying to a message or being late with homework). A metaphor I use is of the smoke alarm in your house. We all have one (hopefully) and its job is to wake us up in the night if our house is on fire and to save our lives. But it sometimes goes off when someone burns the toast. The amygdala is like the smoke alarm—it doesn't realise when the danger is very serious or just a "false alarm". Using mindfulness enables us to recognise this and to take control of the way our brain works and *to create a bit of space*. In this space, we can enable the prefrontal cortex to take back control, look at the big picture and make good choices. [*What would that be like?*]

Simple Mindfulness for Your Child

We have already discussed bringing mindful attention to everyday activities like eating. If you have had fun and success with this practice, it will be straightforward to explain to your child that mindfulness is just about *paying attention*. Our attention is our superpower. Wherever we choose to put it, the whole force of our energy and mind follows and amazing things can happen. Children are often so much better at this than adults. My kids would become totally absorbed when their attention went into building a Lego creation, drawing their masterpiece or doing keepy-uppies. As parents we have all called to children who can hardly hear us because they are so deeply engaged in their activities. Adults may experience that feeling of being "in the flow" when exercising, being creative, gardening or having sex. Practising *using this attention deliberately* is the cornerstone of mindfulness.

Chapters 7, 8 and 9 contain comprehensive lists of mindfulness and relaxation tools to use in whichever way is most suitable for the children, teenagers and adults in the family. You can start, however, as soon as you are ready with some simple breathing exercises. These form the foundation for many relaxation or mindfulness techniques so it can be very helpful to get used to switching the attention to the breath and noticing what it is like to do so. See if you can try the following exercises. They will need to be adapted to the age and suitability of your child. Don't worry if it's a total washout the first time and they get a fit of the giggles or become very excitable! Allow the outcome to be open and see if you can do the exercises without expectation or judgement.

This can be hard for many people as so much of life is about performing better than others or being "good" or "bad" at something. There is no right or wrong here, no good or bad. Have a go and enjoy yourselves—the more positive the experience, the more likely your child will want to repeat it. If you can bring a sense of curiosity and fun, it will help. Older children might enjoy seeing it as an experiment where certain conditions are applied and the result is observed. As with all experiments, it is important to let go of any expectation or judgement and just see what happens.

- **Balloon Belly**—sitting or lying somewhere comfortable, close your eyes and place the hands on the tummy. Take a big deep breath in, imagining your tummy is a balloon that is filling up with air. Notice what happens to your hands as you do this. Breathe out again steadily, letting the balloon empty. See where your hands are now. Continue like this for as long as appropriate. Once normal breathing returns and the hands are removed, discuss what it felt like.
- **5/7 Breathing**—sitting or lying comfortably close the eyes and see if you can find your breath. It's always there but we don't take much notice of it generally! As you breathe in next count in your head up to 5. As you breathe out, count up to 7. Notice how this feels. Rather than count

faster on the out-breath, try to slow the out-breath down, just enough so you can get to 7. See if you can continue counting 5 in, 7 out for a few breaths. After a while, drop the counting, breathe normally and open the eyes. What was it like?

- **Petal Breathing**—this can be done with the eyes open or closed; try it each way. Sitting up with the hands resting loosely on your lap, knees or on a table turn the palms upwards. Imagine the fingers of the hands are like the petals of a flower. As you breathe in, open the petals up to the light and spread the fingers wide. Keep them soft! As the breath goes out again, slowly bring the fingertips together softly, like the petals of the flower closing for the night. Keep breathing gently in and out and match the movement of the fingers to the breath, open and closed. Talk afterwards about what that felt like.
- **Buzzy Bee Breath**—this is particularly good for young children as it's noisy and fun. Sitting tall with eyes closed, take a deep breath in. As you breathe out make a long zzzzzzz sound, like a buzzy bee. Notice the sensations in the body, especially in the lips and maybe the teeth. Where else can it be felt? What does it feel like afterwards? You can incorporate this into a version of the hot/cold hide-and-seek game—one person hides a flower (maybe a hair bobble flower or a toy representing a flower) somewhere in the room and the other searches for it. The hider makes the buzzy bee breath which gets louder or quieter as the seeker gets closer to finding the flower. After the excitement dies down, ask what it was like? This exercise is a good introduction to breath practice and can lead more easily into the other, quieter ones.

When doing any of these exercises for the first time, start really small. If you can do the breathing together for a whole minute, give yourself a big pat on the back. It can be difficult to persuade some children to give these exercises a try and perhaps this isn't surprising. So much of what captures their attention is "out there" and many children are accustomed to non-stop demands on their attention from parents, siblings, teachers, friends, devices, social media and busy schedules. How often is your child asked to "pay attention" over the course of a day? Ask them! Stopping to turn that attention *inwards*, to do nothing, achieve nothing, might seem very strange and alien to them. Persevere with whichever exercises they enjoy and see if you can creep the time up slowly.

Many children find they grow to love moments of silence and stillness. They often enjoy the chance to hear their own thoughts, recognise that they belong to them and to value them. A child having problems with a particular friend she kept trying to please told me that mindfulness had enabled her to hear her own thoughts properly and to realise that she actually didn't like this friend very much after all; she felt lighter and more empowered as a result. Sometimes our thoughts are tiny little voices hiding under all the external noise—when we choose to be quiet we can hear them properly and really listen to them. This enables us to develop our sense of self and strengthens a sense of identity. Without this, how else will we know what or who we like, what makes us happy or sad, what we want to do and what we don't want to do? These moments can make a great contrast to a child's hectic days and enable them to get in touch with themselves and whatever is happening for them.

I often challenge new yoga pupils by asking "Who thinks they can sit completely still and watch their breath for a whole minute?" Hands shoot up at first then some waver as they think about it and how it might actually be quite tricky and a few put their hands down again! We often think together about what might make it easier to sit still and breathe for a whole minute. We might conclude that being warm and comfortable will help. Not having distracting noise or bright lights on might also be good. Going to the loo first; removing glasses or hair bobbles; putting on some socks. Whatever it takes is fine by me.

More time is frequently spent getting ready than actually practising the breathing, but it's worth it. Keep this in mind when introducing your child to mindfulness: that it is a practice and like anything that we practise, it isn't always easy but it will become easier the more often we do it.

If you can keep doing any or all of the above exercises for a few minutes each day, you will be doing your child an enormous service. Helping them learn tools to calm themselves, ground themselves and listen to themselves builds resilience and increases feelings of happiness. The tools they learn and practise now could last them a lifetime. You can keep this fresh by mixing up the practices or doing them in different locations, indoors and outside. I always take a class outside for a yoga session whenever I can and I love that the children who find it hardest to lie still and relax are often the ones most content to lie on the grass and look up at the sky. Joining in yourself can also help it stay a joy and not a chore.

You may be familiar with some of this yourself, in which case I hope this specialised child-focused approach fits well with your own experience. If you can make time for calmness and quiet in your family life, it may well have a positive impact on everyone. Practising mindfulness or relaxation alongside a child can bring you benefits, it may even inspire you to commit to a practice of your own or to reassess your pace of life. Many of the parents I know are constantly busy, juggling work and family, often at a cost to their own wellbeing.

Our busy world doesn't easily accommodate permission to do nothing, which can be seen as wasting precious time. Among all the terrible consequences of the global pandemic, one positive that I can identify is that people have, by necessity, had to spend more time in their homes and with themselves. For the most sociable among us, this was terrifying at first. The amount of time we spent locked down removed some social pressures, creating more time and space for many people. It has also inspired more people to learn about mental health practices and take up classes online that they may have previously resisted in person.

Many people were able to reconnect with the simple pleasures of walking outside, appreciating the green spaces in their neighbourhoods. People took up simple pleasures that life didn't allow before—baking, gardening, making. I taught myself to knit socks and fished out enormous jigsaws from the loft. We have yet to see the effects of the pandemic in full and we know there have been many disastrous ones, sadly affecting children and young people adversely. Finding positives matters to me and I remain hopeful that time to reflect and experiment may have helped more people discover how mindfulness, relaxation and yoga support their wellbeing. When adults understand these benefits, they are more likely to apply similar ones to their children. And children and young people have never needed these skills more than they do now.

The Breath and the Nervous System

The reason that learning these breathing skills is so vital is because of the relationship between the way we breathe and our central nervous system. In yoga, breathing practices are known as *pranayama* because *prana* (rhymes with "banana") is the subtle life force carried to us by the air we breathe; *ayama* (rhymes with "prana") is directing and allowing the prana to flow though our bodies. Many people go through their whole lives taking their breath for granted, not giving it a moment's thought—yet it has a profound influence on our physical, emotional and mental wellbeing.

The nervous system is one of the body's key systems and it helps us function in the world and assimilate the information around us. It is the seat of our emotions and our bodily functions which include digestion, respiration and, of course, sleep. The nervous system is made up of two main parts: the Central Nervous System (CNS) which is the brain and the spinal cord. The CNS is the control centre of our nervous system. The second part is called the Peripheral Nervous System (PNS) and consists of millions of sensory and motor nerves that run throughout the body. Part of the PNS is the Parasympathetic Nervous System (PSNS) and its work is around the relaxation, rest and repair activities that take place when the body is calm and safe. It is an *unconscious* or autonomic system. The other part of the autonomic nervous system is the opposite of the PSNS and is, unsurprisingly, known as the Sympathetic Nervous System (SNS). This system stimulates the stress response as discussed above.

The reason for sharing this with you is that in all aspects of the PNS the brain sends signals and instructions to the rest of the body. Much of it is unconscious as we respond and react to what is happening around us. Think about a normal day in your or your child's life and the number of events that take place for you, her or him or them. Each conversation, each activity, each thought you have sends a multitude of signals along the neural pathways and those signals trigger events in the body.

When we become stressed and anxious, our SNS is dominant and, while this might be useful in the short term, we know that spending too much time in a state of stress is extremely bad for us. It raises our heart rate and our blood pressure, upsets our digestive system and generally makes us feel discomfort. Children might describe this feeling as butterflies in their tummies, a tightness around their chest or throat, short shallow breathing leading to dizziness; they may have the urge to release this uncomfortable tension by crying, shouting or kicking or punching something. The urge to express this is perfectly understandable because it feels bad.

As adults, we accumulate stress and our bodies become accustomed to carrying it. Life isn't easy and people face very real challenges which their minds and bodies have to cope with. For children, the contrast between feelings of wellbeing and those of anxiety can be much more pronounced than for adults. I applaud their ability to identify their feelings of tension and encourage them to work with those feelings until they release.

We know that the body is at its optimal state when the parasympathetic nervous system is in control. This is when we are able to think most clearly, digest our food most effectively, sleep more deeply, heal more fully and feel happiest and most peaceful. Strengthening and supporting the PSNS will enable us to be more resilient during inevitable times of stress. The best way to do this is to learn to use the breath to bring the body into a place of calmness, thus suppressing the stress response and allowing the PSNS to kick in with all the benefits. Breathing is the only function of the autonomic nervous system that is both voluntary and involuntary. In other words, we breathe without thinking about it much of the time but when we learn how to use the breath, we can help ourselves to function better and, more importantly, to feel better. This makes it our central tool for dealing with fear and anxiety.

Bedtime Fears

Which brings us to what may be a major reason for you choosing to read this book and I apologise for taking such a long time to get to it! My aim was to provide enough information about the importance of sleep, about good sleep hygiene and some knowledge of how the breath-based tools of mindfulness and yoga can help. to be able to offer the best advice and support.

The first thing to say is that most children experience night-time fears at some point during childhood. Surveys I have seen put the numbers of children aged 4–12 who say they have experienced fear night at, variously, 73% and 64%. Fortunately for the majority of these children their experience doesn't fit the criteria for an anxiety disorder but, as with all concerns over a child's health and wellbeing, if you are in any doubt about this you must seek medical advice from your GP. Further resources are provided in this book.

Regardless of how normal it is to experience night-time fear, parents still need coping strategies and support when dealing with a child who may be afraid of sleeping alone or who suffers from bad dreams. And, of course, children's fears must always be taken seriously. While relaxation techniques and mindfulness will not solve everything, awareness of how the body and mind interact when experiencing fear can offer some practical things to try. Fear is a fundamental response to the need to feel safe. As parents we try to give our children a sense of safety. Using these techniques can help a child to find a space within themselves where they can be calm and secure.

One of the most common fears for young children is that of separation anxiety when sleeping alone. Some experts argue that this practice, most often found in western societies, goes against our long human history as hunter gatherers when children would have been kept safe from predators and the elements by staying physically close to their adult caregivers during the night. Everyone has their own views about this but for many parents, giving their children beds and bedrooms of their own is both practical and desirable. I am not a psychologist but, as a mum, I found my children experienced less anxiety when there was good sleep hygiene and a routine in place.

In other words, the advice about making bedtime as consistent and positive as possible, leads to a child feeling secure, settling well and sleeping better and longer. This includes making a child's bedroom as conducive to sleep as possible, adding whatever comforts are needed, and keeping to a routine that builds in daily habits of bedtime stories, relaxing music or reflections on the day. Lots of cuddles and reassurance are important too—we know that physical affection switches the stress response off and enables the body to relax and rest.

If all the aspects of the bedroom and the routine are in place and children are still upset at being separated, you can try a number of things.

- If the dark is an issue, a nightlight will be a comfort but ensure it is soft, warm hue. We know that LED light and blue light inhibit the body's production of sleep hormone melatonin which will prevent a child from feeling drowsy at bedtime. A nightlight on a dimmer can work well and be slowly reduced over time.
- Make or adapt a special sleep cuddly toy that incorporates aspects of family members. For example, a favourite teddy could wear a scarf created from Dad's old t-shirt or big brother's hoodie. A whole "bedtime bear" can be made reasonably easily with some cast-off clothes, maybe stuffed with some lavender and a bit of the dog's fur! Whatever comfort toy or blanket you can create together will have elements of the people your child wants nearby at night-time and can hold close. Think about how you can enable your child to feel comfort and security once you've said goodnight.

- Staying with your child while they fall asleep can be a rod for your back but understandably many parents do this to avoid causing distress. Reassuring conversations should happen during the day about how nearby you are at night-time, how you can hear them if they call you, how safe the house is, how safe they are. Listen to them and encourage them to share their worries. In the calm light of day, it can be easier to talk about it. Give them plenty of praise for sharing their worries, listen carefully and don't dismiss their fears as silly.
- A white light visualisation goes a long way. As your child is settled into bed and doing some of the breathing exercises mentioned above, you can ask them to imagine a big bubble of white light around their heart or tummy. Feel this white light, how calm and safe it is. Every time they breathe in the light gets a bit larger and a bit brighter. The light expands with every breath to surround their whole body, then their bed, the bedroom, the whole house. This beautiful bright white light is protective and everything in it is safe and peaceful. Every time they breathe in it glows and brightens. The breathing will calm their nervous system down enabling the body to relax and sleep to follow more easily.

For children reluctant to go to bed because they are afraid of having bad dreams, you can use this white light visualisation along with the other *mind calm, body calm* techniques in the later chapters. Often fears of bad dreams outweigh the reality of these disturbances so try to switch the focus on how magical sleep is: repairing our bodies, helping us grow taller and stronger, enabling us to be better the next day at learning or playing sport or being with our friends. While we are sleeping, of course, we might also have amazing, exciting dreams and travel to wonderful places and accomplish impossible feats. Talk with your child, just before sleep, about the dreams they would like to have. Avoid getting excited, but it can be positive for them to imagine themselves visiting distant planets, scoring a winning goal at Wembley or playing in a room full of kittens.

Nightmares and Night Terrors

However well prepared bedtimes are, there will be nights when you are all disturbed. It is horrible to witness your child experiencing bad dreams or waking from a nightmare or night terror; you may well feel shaken up yourself. Cuddles for everyone are essential. The fundamental difference between these two kinds of night-time events are that the night terror is an adrenalin response and the body is flooded with the stress and fear chemical cocktail as discussed above.

A nightmare is more likely to be a mental or emotional disturbance and involves a less extreme response. Nightmares are scary, vivid dreams that usually cause the person to wake. These dreams are often easily remembered, which can be useful. Nightmares occur during the REM stage of sleep you will recall from Chapter 1. A night terror generally happens in NREM (non-REM sleep). The body, fuelled by stress hormones, can thrash around and cry out but people often sleep through them. Certainly it is harder to wake from a night terror but it can be distressing for a parent to watch their child in the grips of one.

One of my children had rarely ever vomited but following a dramatic car sickness incident (think seatbelt, windows, hair...) became really scared about being sick again. He would wake very distressed from a bad dream about it so I know how upsetting it can be, especially in the middle of the night. They may not remember it at all in the morning, but you can still try to help them by looking at the links between daytime worries and night-time fears, as below.

When your child wakes from in the night after experiencing a nightmare, apart from the immediate physical response of comfort, you can try the following:

- When comforting your child, encourage them to take long slow breaths. The 5/7 counting can help (see p.116) and you can do it together, perhaps you doing the counting for them at first. Balancing the breath will quickly reset the autonomic nervous system and help them feel better. If you've practised this, it will be familiar already and easier to apply during any stressful situation.
- Reassure them that everyone has bad dreams sometimes but it is all over now and they are completely safe.
- Change the environment by switching the lights on. Open the curtains. Suggest your child gets out of bed and goes to the loo or has a drink of water. Moving around and changing the feel of the room will "break the spell" of the nightmare and make returning to sleep less frightening. You may need to remake the bed, but just smoothing sheets down and plumping up pillows and restoring any teddies or comforters can help your child move on from their most recent association of bed being a place they have experienced fear.

- Don't talk about the nightmare now but listen to what your child tells you about it so that you can think about it and discuss it later with them in the cold light of day. Instead, once they are calm, talk about something cheerful, look outside at the street or the garden, moon or stars, listen to the night noises outside or notice the quiet.
- Resettle your child by going back to the bedtime routine. Start from the post-bath/shower part and lower the lights, get them comfy, use the relaxing music if that's your normal practice. A few pages read from a favourite book is a great idea, but make sure it is a funny or positive story. Repeating your familiar routine, even if it's the middle of the night, should be comforting and enable the child to settle back to sleep.
- Use any relaxation or body scan exercises you know your child responds to. You can find full details in Chapters 7 and 8. Once the body has been on "high alert" after an adrenalin stress response during sleep, it can take longer to release the tension and return to a state of relaxation conducive to dropping off to sleep.

A useful point to make here about all mindfulness and relaxation practices is that the more they are repeated during a normal day or part of a bedtime routine, the better they will work for everyone during a time of stress, such as waking from a nightmare or an anxiety event such as a panic attack. Remember weaving that parachute? Help your child to learn slow, deep breathing practices and to really be aware of how it makes them feel calmer will be a benefit for life.

Daytime Anxiety/Night-Time Fears

As adults, we know that experiencing anxiety during the day can impact on the quality of our sleep and even lead us to have bad dreams, in fact over 50% of adults report having occasional nightmares. They are more common in people suffering from stress, anxiety or depression. Likewise, children who are frightened or worried about any aspect of their lives can see these play out in their dreams.

Listening to the features of your child's bad dreams will give you clues to their worries. Talk together about these and try and find ways to reassure them during the day. Children's worries can seem trivial but taking them seriously and helping them find solutions will make them feel happier, listened to and, crucially, improve their sleep with all the attendant benefits. During the Covid-

19 global pandemic children experienced fear and a massive disruption to their lives. Research done during this time found alarming increases in nocturnal disturbances for children with a 23.7% increase in vivid nightmares, a 9.9% increase in sleepwalking and night terrors, 28.9% increase in children waking during the night. I share this not to alarm you but to reassure you that you are not alone if your family has been experiencing difficult times.

Discussing worries is an important way you can help reduce your child's bedtime fears. Other things to try include:

- Avoid their exposure to frightening television, stories or images, especially before bedtime. Having the news on in the background may seem harmless but a study has found that 5–6-year-olds exposed to adult TV programmes, including the evening news, slept less well and experienced more sleep disturbances. The link between fears around Covid and children's sleep is quite clear.
- Some children feel things more strongly than others and their stress response is more pronounced. These children can learn to be less fearful but will need the gentle encouragement of parents and teachers. Parents who model calm, confident behaviour will be less likely to inadvertently transmit their own fears to sensitive children.
- It can be empowering for children to hear stories about how their parent (or another family member) overcame fears of their own. Choose something they can relate to with a happy outcome; for example, a fear of dogs that was overcome by looking after a neighbour's dog and realising that most dogs are actually eager to make friends.
- You can counteract fearful thoughts with images of happiness and safety. By working with that interface, that link between the mind and body, you can teach your child how to choose positive, happy thoughts, literally rewiring the brain. During a relaxation session when your child is breathing calmly and their body is relaxed, encourage them to close their eyes and invite them to think a happy thought, perhaps about playing with a pet or running on a beach or laughing with a friend. Imagine that this happy thought is a warm golden light in their chest or belly. Each time they slowly breathe in, this golden light gradually expands, getting bigger and brighter until it fills the whole body. It keeps growing until they are completely enclosed by it, safe and happy.

Afterwards, assure them they can return to their happy thoughts and feelings whenever they choose.

- Writing down or drawing worries can be helpful in letting them go. Encourage a child who is less keen on talking about their fears to express them in one of these ways. Once they have got them down on paper in words or a drawing or a combination of both, you could make a ritual of tearing the paper up into bits or crumpling it into a ball. You could dispose of the paper together in a safe and appropriate way and let go of the worries contained. Some children might not find that this is enough, so you can find a little box or special envelope they can post their worry paper into when they arise. Choose a time to sit down together and open the box taking out just one at a time. Talk about ways to deal with the worry and, once a plan is agreed, the paper can be torn up.
- We know that helping and engaging with other people helps all of us to build feelings of happiness and nurtures a sense of agency and resilience. It stops us getting stuck in our own heads and, as well as helping others, we get a bonus good feeling as well. Focusing our awareness on others, especially the ways we could help them, can have a profoundly positive effect. Encourage children to be kind and helpful to friends, siblings, pets and the wider community maybe by raising money for a charity, visiting an elderly neighbour or relative, making a drawing or card to send someone or lending a hand without being asked. Bringing mindful awareness to this will help it to build—ask how it feels when someone says thank you for helping them. During the end of day reflection chat, you can ask about anything they have done for others or noticed about someone they know. This nurtures positive feelings and helps children to see that they can choose to put their attention on to others in ways that make them feel good too. Kindness is contagious!
- Ask for help. Schools now frequently have pastoral teams with mental health training, or your child's class teacher may have suggestions of ways to help reduce your child's worries. If you are worried about a child's frequent nightmares or night terrors, you must consult your doctor.
- Build a Happiness Toolkit. I do this with whole classes during wellbeing workshops and it works really well. Your child can draw a picture of themselves in the middle of a largish blank sheet of paper. You can draw

the outline for them if they need help getting started. Write their name somewhere. Then start to draw bubbles around the image and fill in the bubbles with things that make them feel happy. This could include games they love to play, places they feel happy, activities they enjoy, favourite food, people, music, stories, memories. They can use pictures or words or both. Lots of coloured pens and stickers always help make this creative and fun. Stick the final work of art somewhere near their bed where they can see it to remind them of the happy things in their life.

Help your child tune in to the way these happy tools make them feel. This paves the way for the gratitude practice that can be so helpful during those less optimistic teenage years. Some interesting research has come out of the National Academy of Sciences in the USA (PNAS) looking at whereabout in the body we experience emotions, and measures this across different age groups. At age 10, we are, on average, able to feel happiness more intensely than we do during the following years of adolescence and beyond. And that brings us neatly to the next chapter, where I consider sleep and how it fits in around our teenagers.

Chapter 5
Teenagers

As I start to write this chapter, the house is strangely silent. This is the first week that schools have reopened their doors to all pupils following the most recent coronavirus lockdown. It is very quiet and the fridge still has food in it, the WI-FI is definitely faster and no one has interrupted my work. Why do I miss my kids then? This is the paradox of the teenager: they drive us to distraction but they fill our hearts with tenderness too; they push us away while needing us. Neither child nor adult, my own teens, plus those I know and work with, seem, in spite of their brashness, self-absorption and indifference to adults, to be unbearably vulnerable at times.

This has never more so than during this pandemic when they have lost and suffered so much. Time away from school has left many of our young people without adequate support from their teachers, pastoral care and essential safeguarding staff; they have missed out of those rites of passage around completing their exams, leaving school. It absolutely broke my heart that both my sons were unable to goodbye to their friends and teachers never mind sit their GCSEs and A-levels. Young people have been asked to bear a huge burden by the rest of society, and they have largely done it willingly. The consequences of their sacrifice will be felt for many years and, as always, will be most pronounced in those adolescents from deprived socioeconomic backgrounds, those with parental mental health issues and where local health support services have been cut back.

The focus here, however, is on sleep and the essential role it plays in the developing adolescent. You will find tools and techniques to help support and guide your teenager to a healthier appreciation of sleep and its place in self-care and their short- and long-term wellbeing. Much of the information in previous chapters is relevant to the teenager as it is to the adults in the home. Good sleep hygiene matters for everyone. Adults modelling a respectful attitude to sleep and wellbeing is important. Teenagers tend to jump on hypocrisy and they will be mightily affronted when you don't practise what you preach. The benefits of practising relaxation and mindfulness are helpful for everyone. There are, however, many things about adolescents that set them apart from the children they used to be and the adults they will become. This will not surprise any parent who has watched the profound changes taking place as their child reaches this stage of development. There are very good reasons for these changes.

The Adolescent Brain

I am wary of writing about teenagers as if they were a homogenous mass, all exhibiting the same behaviours. They are all, of course, completely unique and traverse these years in their own way. I have one very sociable son whose friends mean everything to him. Another son was much more content at home until he learnt to drive and there was no stopping him. However, every human on the planet reaching adolescence will undergo similar changes relating to the brain. There has been a fair bit of discussion about the brain in this book so far. This is because any intervention using mindfulness and relaxation techniques is concerned with the rewiring of neural pathways and its relevance to practices that support improving wellbeing. To understand how to help teenagers, we need to understand what changes take place in the brain during this crucial stage of human development.

In his book, *Brainstorm: the power and purpose of the teenage brain*, Daniel J Siegel has created a brilliant resource for parents and those working with adolescents. I recommend it to everyone. One of the first comments he makes challenges that clichéd perception of the teenager as a roiling mess of hormones and moods:

One of the most powerful myths surrounding adolescence is that raging hormones cause teenagers to "go mad" or "lose their minds". That's simply false. Hormones do increase during this period, but it is not the hormones that determine what goes on during adolescence…what adolescents experience is primarily the result of changes in the development of the brain.

These changes occur along the same evolutionary principles as the stress response. You may recollect that the reason we have such a dramatic reaction to stressful situations is because of the amygdala area of our brain. It enables us to respond rapidly to any threat: to fight, flight or freeze. This ancient part of our brain hasn't yet caught up enough to distinguish the difference between the threat from a predator and the electricity bill. We can experience full blown symptoms of stress from aspects of our lives that put us in no immediate danger at all; we can experience all the symptoms of stress from our *thoughts alone*.

Likewise, the way a child's brain changes as it makes the journey to becoming an adult brain is all about survival. The transition to adulthood involves moving away from relying on parental support to becoming self-sufficient. Relationships with peers become increasingly important. The teenage brain is wired to find safety in a group, to fit in and be accepted by their own generation as they leave the protection of their early caregivers. This explains a lot of adolescent behaviour around friendships, how intense they can be, how they take priority, how devastating it can be for them when things go wrong.

Such behaviours may have led you to utter the immortal parental question you swore as a teenager yourself you'd never say: "If so-and-so told you to jump off a cliff, would you?" From the safety of adulthood, we can be frustrated and hurt by the significance our teenagers put on their relationships with their peers but these are vitally important and they are hardwired into the adolescent brain.

In order to become independent, young people also need to learn how to make their own decisions. Changes take place in the brain to push them towards new experiences and they are "rewarded" for this by the release of dopamine in the body. You may have heard of dopamine, a neurotransmitter sometimes called the "happy" or "feel-good" hormone. It helps us understand what activities make us feel good and it becomes an important part of adolescent function. Teens will not have experienced dopamine levels before in the amounts that the onset of puberty heralds. This explains the risky behaviours teenagers often engage in. They are drawn to exhilarating or thrilling experiences. They are increasingly impulsive. And they are profoundly influenced by the peer group they desperately seek acceptance from. Parents and carers are right to worry about the physical safety of their teenagers: the period from ages 12–24 is the most dangerous of anyone's life.

As well as the time when accidents occur more frequently, adolescence is also a period when the dopamine release can lead to risky experimentation and thereby addiction to drugs, alcohol, sugary foods and self-harm habits. With recent research from the Wellcome Trust (Myriad Study) clearly telling us that approximately 75% of adults suffering poor mental health will first experience difficulties before age 18, supporting young people and teaching them practical ways to keep themselves physically safe and mentally well is absolutely vital.

Another change in the brain of adolescents connected to the increased levels of dopamine is called hyperrationality. It affects the decision-making abilities of teenagers because it seems to prevent them from seeing the big picture, urging them on to experience new things and rewarding them for it. When they make choices, their brains are wired to identify the positive outcomes of the decision, where the biggest dopamine hit lies, and this overwhelms the ability to consider the down-sides. They are programmed to seek thrills and not to engage in risk assessment. This may ring true for you if your teenager has been causing you anxiety with their seemingly reckless behaviour. As they move towards adulthood, this changes and their decision-making becomes more rational.

The Gift of the Teenage Brain

The changes above all sound very negative. From a parent's point of view, it can be frustrating and painful to watch your child hit the onset of puberty and appear to change rapidly both on the outside and the inside. Many adults shudder at memories of the turmoil of their own teenage years and vow they'd never wish to revisit them. They can be excruciating to recall and unbearable to witness in your beloved child. It feels at times like an endurance test, surviving the challenging years until it's safe to emerge into adulthood. Something I have found very difficult is that tiptoeing on eggshells feeling, where everything I say is wrong and someone takes offence regardless of how careful and tactful I think I am being. Arguments can blow up out of nowhere and there is certainly no sound quite like that slamming door. However, it is important to say that there are some absolutely wonderful aspects of the teenage brain that we can celebrate and focus on, especially when times are tough.

Teenagers may appear to put their peer friendships above everything else, neglect their siblings and refuse to be seen in public with their embarrassing parents, but during this time they may well forge friendships that will last them a lifetime. Many adults still enjoy close, supportive relationships with the people they met during their own teenage years. We know that a cornerstone of mental health is strong social connections. The people who have known us the longest, seen us through our various incarnations, are increasingly precious as we grow older. I treasure my contact with the many schoolfriends I've known for over 40 years. When my house feels overcrowded by teenagers leaving their enormous shoes inside the front door and grunting at me, I try to remember that these are the boys who will stand by and support my sons as they become men. The friendships we have in our teenage years can be so much more intense than those in later life when responsibilities, spouses and families of our own need to take centre stage.

It can be alarming, however, when these groups of youngsters engage in risky behaviours and I would never underplay the fears parents experience as they wait up for a child to come home after a party or back from their first festival. It's terrifying and our instinct may be to wrap our children up and keep them safe. Letting children go is a core experience of parenthood and brings with it challenging emotions. On the positive side, we can enjoy their zest for life, and admire their adventurousness. Exploring new things, embracing change and living with passion at this stage in their development can open up their lives to opportunities and ultimately help them to become happy, fulfilled adults. I've known young people who have got into social justice campaigning or volunteering in their communities go on to study at university. Likewise I've seen youngsters get passionate about getting fit, cooking, creating, growing and fixing things—all of which have very transferable skills. The world needs these young people with their vision and energy.

Questioning the status quo often means adolescents challenging their parents or their teachers, which is why it can be such a difficult time for families, full of confrontation, friction and tempers lost. The new levels of emotional intensity teenagers experience during these years is down to the changes in the brain, as discussed. As well as the potential for conflict, however, there is also opportunity for them to begin to think creatively in ways many adults have forgotten. It is frequently young people who come up with great ideas. The hyperrationality that makes them biased towards the positive outcome of any choice can lend itself to thinking in new ways and to exciting ideas.

The world's problems will be theirs next and the capacity for solving them through radical thinking that may overturn the ideas of the previous generation makes evolutionary sense, even if it's hard to be informed of this by your teenager! If you can enjoy engaging with their ideas, it will make life easier. Remember that as the adolescent brain is busy thinking huge creative thoughts, many adult brains have settled into their ways of thinking and lost the habit of challenging themselves or the world.

Neural Pathways

Mindfulness teacher training taught me much about how the brain behaves around issues of stress and cyclical thinking, but learning about the brain's neural pathways was the highlight as it filled me with excitement and optimism. You will be aware from your own experience of the basic process by which we learn. Every parent has been able to observe first-hand how repetitive actions become ingrained as babies absorb everything around them in ways that seem miraculous and ensure they soon become experts at rolling over, sitting up, crawling, etc. Repetition of anything creates circuits in our brains that are described as neural pathways. As well as repetition of actions, this applies to repetitive thoughts.

When explaining this to adults and young people, I ask them to picture a field of long grass. Now imagine walking a particular route across the field. What happens if you never go that way again? The grass has barely been crushed and will quickly grow back up and the field will appear the same. But what happens if you walk that way every day? Soon the squashed grass will be trodden away by your weight and a track will be visible. The more you walk the path, the deeper and longer lasting is the path, until it becomes the normal way to go and it doesn't occur to you to go any other way. In other words, repeating something often enough in our thoughts or actions creates a sort of default setting, a go-to position in our minds with all the advantages and disadvantages that brings.

Our brains physically alter as a result of our experiences and our thoughts—this is called neuroplasticity. Technology such as MRI scanners enables experts to look at the structure of the brain. It has been found that the brains of London's black cab drivers are larger than other people's in the areas corresponding to mapping and memory. This is because the London cabbie, in order to qualify for the job, must learn by heart a complex network of streets and then drive them for many hours a day. Children accept readily that "practise makes perfect" because they see and experience this in themselves and others. In early childhood, the speed and intensity of learning is enormous and new pathways are formed minute by minute.

During adolescence, the rate of learning reduces and the brain makes another clever shift, becoming more integrated. This happens through a process knowns as "pruning" where neural connections that aren't needed are discarded and lost. The pathways not needed are those little-used trips across the field of long grass. The brain holds on to the well-trodden ones.

This has huge significance. Recent research at the University of Oxford has used brain imaging data from the UK Biobank and identified that emotional abuse during childhood is linked with difference in brain structure. The optimism around the use of mindfulness, especially for children and adolescents, is connected to neuroplasticity: the fact that the brain structure can and does change, *depending on how it is used*. And here is the crucial issue. The pathway through the grass is, quite literally, where we choose to put the focus of attention. Remember our superpower?

The focus of attention, for adults and children alike, is fundamental for good mental and physical wellbeing: what we see, what we hear, what we do, what we think. The teenage brain is busy integrating what it has learnt to date, getting rid of the unnecessary and beginning to set itself in ways of thinking and being that can last the rest of life. What this tells us as parents and carers is that, however irrelevant and extraneous our teenagers may consider us to be, the opposite is true, and support and guidance is extremely important during these sometimes stormy years. The changes in the brain lead the teenager towards risky behaviour and the potential for addictions—when you combine that with their natural movement towards their peers and away from the adult carers in their life, it becomes clear how vulnerable they can be.

Your Teenager Needs You!

When my three children were at the toddler and baby stage, I had a dear friend who was older than I and whose offspring were teenagers. We would chat and exchange our parenting experiences. It was a source of laughter that the teenage strops she described seemed to closely mirror the tantrums I was witnessing in my preschoolers. Parallels can definitely be drawn between the huge changes undergone by adolescents and those of the toddler emerging from babyhood. Certainly, these broad periods of development are thrown into contrast by the comparatively placid stretch of years between 5 and 12. Another important similarity is that teenagers need support systems around them to help navigate these years, just as our toddlers needed care and loving attention through that phase of development.

It can be challenging for parents to be there for their teenagers. Demands of work and the prospect of increasing independence move families onto a difference stage once children are established in their secondary schools. Everyone in the house may be coming and going on their own timetables, and times to be together can be rare. Much as the lockdowns during the pandemic have been an undoubted source of stress and loss for many people, for others there has been the unexpected opportunity to spend more time as a family, with many positive stories of families exercising, cooking and creating together. I won't dwell on the negatives here but assure you I am very much aware of and distressed by the rise in domestic violence, child exploitation and abuse, loneliness and mental suffering that many people have experienced. I fear we may not see the true impact for many years to come.

Spending time with teenagers isn't easy when they make it abundantly clear that they would rather be doing other things with their peers, on and offline. And let's face it, they can be prickly, critical, argumentative and selfish. During my past decade of parenting teenagers, they have passed negative judgement on my clothes, hair, teeth, driving, singing, cooking, dancing, work and, especially outrageous, my cleaning. It can be hard at times not to feel hurt and miss the younger version of them. But the changes they are undergoing are not their fault and they have surprisingly little control over themselves. Additionally, those changes can put them at risk of behaviours with severe long-term implications, so we need to find ways to communicate with them and support them in spite of the challenges.

All families are different and you may have clear boundaries around the behaviour you expect from everyone in the house; it may be that these have lapsed over the years; or you may never have had many rules about behaviour and relied on your child to go along with your expectations. This book is about sleep and this chapter is dedicated to teenagers because the advice about routines from Chapter 3 is harder to implement for older children, yet it applies just as strongly. To help your adolescent get the essential sleep hours they need will require clear communication and some boundaries. The primary fact to recognise is that the changes in the adolescent brain mentioned above, also have an effect on the circadian rhythm, or sleep cycle.

Changes to the Sleep Cycle

You will recall that for all humans, the time at which we are ready to sleep is governed by our circadian rhythm and the release of a hormone called melatonin, plus the hormone adenosine which builds up throughout our waking day until it creates enough "sleep pressure" for us to nod off. We know that adolescents throughout the world, regardless of geography or culture, experience a forwards shift in terms of their circadian rhythm and the relevant hormone release. As they reach full maturity this changes again. But, in practical terms this means that, while adults are ready to sleep around 10–11pm, teenagers are not yet beginning to shut down. Asking your teenager to go to sleep at this time can be like trying yourself to fall asleep at 8pm.

The same change, of course, applies in the morning when rousing your teenager at 7.30am is the equivalent of rising yourself at 5.30am. Take a moment to imagine how this might feel. To add to the challenge, we know that people have a tendency to be "owls" or "larks." Owls are the wake late and go to bed late evening types and make up approximately 30% of the population. Larks are morning people and are about 40% of the population. The remaining people are in-between but tend to have a slight leaning towards evening. You may have a lark child who shifts into an owl at the onset of puberty or an owl child who moves even further into owl-ness.

This all becomes problematic when you add the fact that, to function optimally, teenagers require 8–10 hours of sleep every night. We know that worldwide only 30% of adolescents are achieving this. The hours in which to take this sleep and keep in line with their circadian rhythm, however, don't fit with the prescribed hours of a school or working day adopted almost universally in the modern world. This is a source of discussion and controversy among policy makers around the globe with a building movement of thought around shifting the secondary school day to a later start in order to enable adolescents to learn at their best i.e., well-rested. The evidence to support this is strong and it may be accelerated as a consequence of the pandemic when online learning removed the commute to school and often very early starts for many children.

Peri-Menopause and Menopause

For mums and female carers with teenagers in the house, it can be a double whammy when our own hormones changes and symptoms of peri-menopause and menopause get added to the equation. This is happening to approximately 30 million women in the UK. As you can imagine, I have read and studied a great deal of information about sleep, yet find the books don't give much, if any, attention to the changes to sleep that can take place during menopause. Sleep disruption is one of the most commonly reported symptoms and it can come at a time when we are already trying to deal with concerns for our teenagers.

Women who have experienced normal sleep for years can find themselves waking frequently in the night with feelings of anxiety. The hot flushes can be hugely challenging in the night and I've struggled plenty myself trying to stay cool. My husband once told me it was like sleeping next to a slippery dolphin! Supporting yourself during this time of life is essential so seek help from your GP or a specialist menopause nurse. There is a wealth of supplements to look into as well as complementary therapies like acupuncture which can be very helpful.

I swear by my "chillow"—a large gel pack that lives in the freezer by day then gets placed between the pillows at night. When the flushes arrive, flipping the pillow over and feeling cold on your neck is truly bliss. Mindfulness can be a helpful way to manage anxiety and the advice in this book can be applied as equally to you as to your children. It can be a tough time so look after yourself, be gentle with yourself, you are not alone.

In the meantime, we must operate within the requirements of the school timetable and find ways to help our teenagers get sufficient sleep that they can feel at their best even when it goes against their natural rhythm. Having some sympathy for them will go a long way, frustrating and challenging though it can be getting them up and out in the mornings. Going through a school day when you feel tired and bleary is pretty awful. I see so many of these exhausted teenagers in classrooms and I frequently wish I could send them all home for a good long nap. Tiredness makes everything hard, as I am sure we all know.

Perhaps you can recall a time when you were expected to function with insufficient sleep? It feels like wading through treacle. We find ourselves overreacting or not reacting quickly enough, we are emotional and our concentration is all over the place. Our adolescents find their brains and bodies rewired without much warning in ways that make sleeping more difficult than it was when they were younger. This is a time of life when there are already so many pressures academically and socially. Having to navigate through these years while feeling an underlying exhaustion is incredibly tough. Sadly, it can have serious consequences.

Sleep and Adolescent Mental Health

As mentioned above, we know that the vast majority of adult mental health issues begin during childhood. We also know that there is no psychiatric disorder, experienced by adult or child, which does not feature sleep irregularity. Along with nutrition and exercise, good sleep is a cornerstone of health. It is comparatively neglected by the public health agenda. Dedicated sleep advocate Vicki Dawson founded the Sleep Charity in response to the lack of provision. It works tirelessly to help families experiencing sleep issues and the consequences. Details of this vital work can be found in Resources, including the excellent offering for teenagers.

For parents who have established good sleep habits in early childhood, it can come as a shock when those are challenged by the changes that take place for their teenagers. The brain changes listed above demonstrate how susceptible they are to a whole range of issues. In addition, young people are increasingly suffering from mental health disorders in which sleep plays a vital factor.

As well as the physical changes brought on by puberty there is a demanding psychological transition to self-identity, independence, friendship, romantic relationships and the online world. Much of the socialising that teenagers do, in-person or virtually, takes place in the evenings and at night. This is true for teenagers everywhere on the planet. Their later body clock enables this, but many young people struggle to control their online activity and monitor their own sleep needs. They are susceptible to using the socio-cultural drug caffeine to help fuel their late-night activities. The cycle of sleeping inadequate amounts on school nights, leading to severe tiredness during the weekday causes a regular insufficiency, or a sleep deficit. This sleep deficit experienced during the week by many teenagers means that, at the weekend, they take a long lie-in then stay up extra late on Fridays and Saturdays.

The sleep binge may feel good, but it doesn't actually help the problem. No amount of extra sleep can make up for the daily impact of sleep loss on the body and the mind. Teenagers in this cycle experience what is known as social jetlag and the consequent feeling is very similar to the jetlag adults get when moving between time zones and the body being out of sync. Clearly, it makes functioning very difficult and impacts on the ability to concentrate, manage emotions and be at their healthiest mentally and physically.

Crucial work is being done by scientists around the world to look at the links between sleep and mental health disorders. At the University of Sussex, Dr Faith

Orchard is part of a programme researching this link specifically as it occurs in adolescents and looking at ways to intervene effectively and help young people. The findings of her team are unequivocal: sleep quality and quantity during teenage years has a long-term effect on mental health. Dr Orchard was also involved with the Avon Longitudinal Study of Parents and Children (ALSPAC) which ongoing study of child development began back in the 1990s following young people aged 15–24, including their sleep patterns, and which is producing invaluable data. It revealed that young people who were identified at age 15 with poor sleep quantity and quality were more likely to present with depression and anxiety aged 17,21, and 24.

ALSPAC also found that the total amount of sleep time on school nights at this age was a significant predictor of anxiety and depression at those later ages. The intervention programme at the University of Sussex has had real benefits and can give parents hope that improving this single aspect of their child's life can profoundly help them.

We know that 90% of teenagers experiencing depression or anxiety have insomnia or other sleeping disorder. What is not yet clear is whether lack of sleep leads to depression or depression causes insomnia. Certainly the perception of sleep, i.e., how much we worry about not getting enough and feeling awful the next day, has a definite effect. Mindfulness and yoga relaxation techniques can help the mind to relax when the body is weary and the body to relax when the mind is calm. The successful outcome of any of these techniques will be improved by focusing first on the behavioural aspects of sleep—sleep hygiene.

Sleep Hygiene for Teenagers

There are similarities in the sleep hygiene advice for younger children and for adolescents. Here you will find a comprehensive list of the environmental factors that encourage and enable good sleep habits. If you decide changes need to be made to support your teenager with their sleep, it will be much easier if they are in agreement with you. Easier said than done, I know. Refer them to the first chapter of this book about why sleep matters so much, use the resources listed at the end and share honestly with them your concerns about their wellbeing. The Teen Sleep Hub established by the Sleep Charity is hugely helpful and includes an eBook for teenagers to read themselves entitled *You and Your Sleep*. Once they understand the effect that lack of sleep is having on their mind and body, they may feel more open to making changes and you can work through this list together. The focus on how mindfulness and conscious relaxation can help will follow.

- **The bedroom**: Teenagers need their own space and for many of them their bedroom is where they work, play, create, watch, chat, party and chill as well as where they sleep. Making it clean and comfortable is a good ideal to have but may be a challenge in many households. Ensure it is a safe place where their privacy is assured. Add low lighting if possible that will help with sleep and try to find ways they can listen to relaxing music or meditations without using their phones if they want to avoid them before sleep. The priorities are to keep it cool at night (ideally about 18°C) and keep it as dark as possible.
- **Bed:** Understandably, teenagers use their beds for all sorts of activities. It can help form good sleep habits if the bed can be used solely for sleeping. So providing spaces for the other activities is helpful. School work is ideally done at a table or desk, perhaps in another room. A beanbag goes a long way for other activities. Budgets and available space will differ from home to home but if your child associates bed with sleeping and not eating, playing games, doing homework, etc., it can make a positive difference.
- **Shower or bath before bed**: This reduces body temperature and enables sleep to come more easily.
- **Nightclothes** should be light, cotton if possible, no socks, no onesies.
- **Avoid late-night snacking**, especially sugar and carbohydrates. This is a definite challenge for growing, bottomless pit teens who will forage about nightly for cereal or toast. Sugar has a proven detrimental effect on sleep as it overstimulates the body preparing it for activity which is not what we want at bedtime. This is made harder to manage because tiredness leads to a natural craving for sweet things. Wholegrain toast is a far better choice than sugary cereal. Eating sufficient amounts of food during the day will help break the cycle of late-night eating. The neurotransmitter serotonin helps prepare us for sleep and contributing chemical tryptophan can be found in beans, lentils, nuts, whole grain and poultry, so it can help to include these foods. Ideally, avoid eating anything two hours prior to sleep. Share this information with your teenager. See if they notice the difference in the time it takes them to fall

asleep on nights when they've been snacking late and those when they have eaten sufficient during the day.

- **Caffeine:** This should be avoided as much as possible by teenagers but especially in the evenings. Caffeine is an addictive psychoactive stimulant. A doctor recently commented to me that if it arrived in the world now it would be strictly controlled and possibly banned. When I was growing up, Mum would bring a tray into the living room every night with a big pot of tea and cups for everyone, including the dog! I don't think my Irish/Brummie roots are the only reason for this; caffeine consumption has been normalised historically and culturally since the mid-17th century, it's just what we do. Caffeine is not only found in tea and coffee, of course, but in many soft and "energy" drinks specifically marketed at children and young people. It is a drug that shares the same biochemical mechanisms as amphetamines, cocaine and heroin. All these addictive drugs stimulate brain function and can make us feel like our minds are racing, with thoughts coming faster than usual. This can be uncomfortable and exacerbates anxiety in people already struggling with busy minds. Caffeine directly interferes with the sleep process by blocking the sleep-signalling hormone adenosine. Although young people are better able to clear caffeine from their system than older people, it is still a significant sleep inhibitor for them and should be avoided as much as possible. Research measuring the disruptive impact of caffeine on sleep advises limiting it within six hours of going to bed. For the average teenager heading to sleep at 11pm, that is going to mean no caffeinated drinks after 5pm, which may be a challenge if addiction is already established. Try substituting decaf products where possible and strongly discourage the energy drinks that enable them to keep going longer—some of the most hyped products contain more than 150mg of caffeine which is the equivalent of two cups of instant coffee or three cups of tea or six servings of cola! Check the labels and explain to your teenager the impact. If they are resistant, try and bring some mindfulness to the situation by proposing an experiment: cut back gradually on caffeine for a week or so, then eliminate it altogether for a week or two and see whether any differences are noticed around their thought patterns, feelings of anxiety as well as quantity and quality of sleep. Other added benefits to being caffeine-free concern hormone balance which may improve symptoms of PMS for young people having periods, plus better digestion and improved skin for everyone. Before starting any experiment, however, bear in mind that caffeine withdrawal can affect some people quite dramatically hence the advice is to gradually come off it. Initial reactions might be headaches, irritability or fatigue and symptoms can last from 2–9 days. If caffeine consumption is excessive, it would be wise to seek medical advice before coming off it, especially where there are underlying mental health concerns.

- **Alcohol:** Many teenagers may be experimenting with alcohol and it is important they understand the effect of it on their sleep as well as on their overall wellbeing. It is a complete myth that alcohol helps you fall asleep more easily or ensures sound sleep. In fact, alcohol operates on the brain like a sedative, mild form of anaesthetic and does not induce natural sleep. Alcohol fragments sleep, often causing us to wake up throughout the night. It suppresses the REM sleep that enables emotional regulation which is so vital for adolescents. The body has to work very hard to eliminate alcohol from the system so a night's "sleep" following alcohol consumption will be neither restful nor restorative. Young people may not experience the hangovers that older people do, but they are undoubtedly harming their bodies and minds. Like caffeine consumption, there is a normalisation of alcohol in our society but its role in negative and dangerous behaviour is unequivocal. The intake of alcohol by teenagers should be discouraged as much as possible. Experimenting at this stage in development coincides with the cognitive changes related to increased risk-taking and biased decision-making discussed above. Alcohol intake in adolescence can result in addiction with serious long-term implications as well as accidents and terrible tragedy in the short term. The dangers must not be taken lightly. It is hopefully also clear that young people who are sleep-deprived are more at risk from injury to themselves and from others. As always with teenagers, keep communicating with them, explaining the facts and listening to their point of view. Come up with clear rules. Ensure adults in the house model a responsible attitude to alcohol too.
- **Daily exercise** is important for everyone but avoid vigorous exercise right before bedtime. The melatonin released by our bodies that signals sleep forms part of our circadian rhythm or body clock. Melatonin is

stimulated by daylight, especially morning light, so a lack of exposure to natural light can knock the body clock out of sync and contribute to difficulties sleeping at night-time. The school day offers opportunities for exercise and time in the fresh air, but weekends and school holidays can see youngsters sleeping a lot more during the day and getting less time outside. Less light exposure means less melatonin production and increased difficulty falling asleep. If this pattern of sleeping during the day and being awake long hours at night becomes extreme, it could be diagnosed as a parasomnia, a sleep disorder. Seek medical advice if you are concerned about the sleep patterns of any adolescent in your care.

Try to encourage teenagers to get some fresh air and exercise, and ensure they understand the relationship between this, their feelings of wellbeing and the quality of their sleep. Again, bringing mindful awareness to this can be helpful. Ask them what they notice about their sleep on a day when they have been outside playing sport or just hanging out with friends in the park. Do they feel a difference in their alertness? How does the body feel after exercising? I am biased, of course, but yoga is one of the best exercises for creating coherence between the mind and body, switching on the parasympathetic nervous system and turning the stress response off. Some gentle conscious stretches and breath exercises just before bed can really help us relax and settle into sleep. There are specific suggestions in the Chapter 7. Only gentle yoga stetches should be done just before bed. Likewise, do any gym, weightlifting or aerobic workouts earlier in the day.

- **Avoid devices with blue LED light** for at least an hour prior to sleep. The link between the effect of this kind of light and our sleep cycle has been clearly proven. The light emitted by our tablets, laptop screens and smartphones suppresses the production of the melatonin we require for sleep. This is very tricky to implement with the generation of young people who have grown up with devices and are dependent on them for just about everything. Again, your best shot is along the mindfulness route and sharing with them the facts about LED lighting and its effect on melatonin levels. If you can remove your teenager's phone altogether an hour before sleep, I would strongly advise this. If that isn't possible, then you can try turning their focus to more sleep-friendly activities during that important hour before sleep, such as reading, journalling, drawing, listening to music or having a bath. If they can be persuaded to try this for a week or so, you may be able to discuss the differences in how they feel and whether it has been easier to fall asleep. If you are keen to try other experiments relating to eating, exercise or caffeine, you'll need to undertake each one in isolation so you can be sure which effects are making the difference.

- **Establish a bedtime routine** and prioritise sleep in your house. Chapter 3 was devoted to the bedtime routine and had suggestions for everyone in the family. Needless to say, establishing good habits around bedtimes when children are young will also support them into adolescence when sleep is, arguably, even more essential to their wellbeing and development. The fundamental aim is to try and wake up and go to sleep at the same time each day whenever possible. This is much harder at the weekends and during holidays but, if possible, try to limit lie-ins to a maximum of 2 hours. Committing to a wind-down hour before sleep can make a huge difference. This means making a conscious choice to avoid the activities that are barriers to good sleep such as phone use, late-night homework, eating, strenuous exercise and caffeine while opting to prepare the mind and body for a restful sleep. Some activities that promote a good night's sleep are gentle yoga stretching and breathing (see p.193), reading, listening to calming music, mindfulness, a warm shower or bath, drawing, writing in a journal, playing with pets. When we perform these actions, we slow our mind and body down, encouraging the stress response from our busy day to subside and the parasympathetic nervous system to kick in which will promote easier falling asleep and help us stay asleep longer. Some people like to just potter about, maybe getting bags ready for the next day. Remember that for adolescents, this pre-bed hour is likely to occur as you are heading to bed yourself so there will have to be trust involved. Knowing that you care for yourself enough to ensure you get a good night's sleep will set a great example for your teenager as they come to see sleep as the cornerstone of self-care.

When I'm working with teenagers and we're focusing on sleep, I give them this sleep hygiene checklist to complete for themselves. It gives them the opportunity to reflect on what is working for them already, what areas they could make some changes and how they might do that. It makes a good starting point for conversation and for making a plan together. There are plenty of ways parents and carers can support their adolescents with this and the checklist can help everyone focus on making improvements.

Sleep Hygiene Checklist

Look through this list and put an **OK** tick beside aspects you are confident of and a tick under **Needs Work** for the areas you could improve.

Areas to consider	**Needs work**	**OK**
Temperature in bedroom should be cool, ideally about 18°		
Shower or bath before bed		
Keep nightclothes light and cotton. No socks. No onesies		
Keep the room as dark as possible		
Establish a routine—aim to wake and sleep at the same time each day as much as possible		
Keep weekend lie-ins down to 2 hours extra in the morning and 2 hours later at bedtime		
Prioritise sleep		
Ensure you get daily exercise		
Avoid caffeine for 6 hours prior to sleep		
Avoid blue LED lights 1 hour before sleep		
Remove devices from the bedroom		
Keep your bed for just sleep—do other activities elsewhere		
Avoid sugar and carbs several hours before sleep		
Avoid going to bed too full or too hungry		

Don't nap after 5pm and ideally nap for 20–45mins		

Reflect on: On a good sleep day, how many **OK**s do you score…/16? On a bad sleep day…/16? Which aspects most affect you? What could you do to tackle some of these areas? Which aspects involve other people?

Adult Modelling of Good Sleep Hygiene

It's vital to set adolescents a good example if you are trying to support them getting into better habits around bedtime and sleep. Teenagers will leap on hypocrisy and may challenge what they see as double standards. The same facts about the essential role of sleep in mental and physical health apply equally to adults as to children, so there's no defending the position of being the "grown-ups." Adults in the home should try to:

- Avoid falling asleep on the sofa in the evenings
- Consider removing caffeine or replacing it with decaffeinated products
- Prioritise sleep for everyone—aim to get the right amount of sleep yourself
- Create a pro-sleep environment that keeps the noise down and the lights low in the evening
- Establish a calm and relaxing atmosphere
- Assess your own use of phones, tablets, etc. late at night—could you also experiment with an hour off before sleep?
- Assess your alcohol consumption—could it be reducing the quality and quantity of your own sleep? What happens if you make changes

Keeping a Sleep Diary

When issues around sleep are affecting anyone, they need to be taken seriously. Sleep problems are at epidemic levels in the western world and the health implications are vast. When they apply to children, they can be very isolating for families who often find it hard to get help. Parents whose children sleep badly are more prone to depression and anxiety. Poor sleep is very common in children with special educational needs and neurodevelopmental disorders such as autism. Where there is an underlying medical contributing factor, more help is likely to be available but frequently parents are looking for help because it so challenging dealing with the behaviours around bedtime and with the emotional fallout that can include irritability, anxiety, tension, hostility and anger.

Help can be accessed via your GP or one of the sleep charities but it can be dependent on where you live. Often, families are left to find their own way through difficulties. Sleep consultants advise their clients to start keeping a sleep diary in order to begin making positive, effective change. This was covered in Chapter 2 and in relation to establishing a routine for your child, but parents of teenagers struggling with sleep might want to consider it too.

With adolescent sleep issues, a sleep diary can be a helpful place to start because the young person will contribute to it as well. You may recall this was discussed in Chapter 2 and a sample sleep diary template provided. Depending on their age and commitment it can be entirely their project. As with many strategies, the more ownership the young person takes, the more effective it will be. The sleep diary aims to measure the time spent in bed and the time spent sleeping (not the same thing) and to build a picture of sleep over time that can track improvements. It can also be used when trying a new strategy, such as cutting out caffeine, reducing the exposure to blue light before bed or adding in some yoga or mindfulness practices.

The sleep diary can be kept in a notebook or on a chart. Make a note daily of the following:

- What time you get into bed at night
- What time the lights go off
- What time you wake up in the morning
- The total time spent in bed
- The total time spent asleep

This is a good basic level of data to start to gather and it will be easy to see changes if the diary is kept for several weeks or months. It can also be helpful to track other interventions. These might be habits you are trying to cut back, but also new habits you are aiming to introduce. This will depend on whatever you and your teenager have identified as being relevant to their own sleep issues and agreed to experiment with. It could include trying to better manage phone use/gaming, exercise, food, caffeine use, sticking to a routine. Or it could focus on the introduction of relaxation or mindfulness practise, a wind-down hour before sleep, or journalling. Keep a space on the diary page for the relevant factors, noting any changes.

As with any data gathering exercise, it can take a while to see results, so encourage the daily recording of details and be patient. After a few weeks, it will be possible to look at the big picture and talk about what do next. Hopefully, the interventions will have affected the important figure at the bottom of the list: total time spent asleep. If there is no change, this can be discouraging but keep trying different interventions until there is an improvement.

It is important to avoid stressing teenagers about their sleep as they will likely be suffering from sleep deprivation and its many effects. They often worry, as do adults, about falling asleep and about having to face the next day feeling groggy and out of sorts. Once someone asserts a negative belief about themselves and their ability to sleep it creates one of those neural pathways discussed above and, if they repeat it regularly enough to themselves or aloud, before you know it "I can't sleep," "I never drop off easily," "I wake up in the night" becomes a reality.

As with most things in life, the more we worry about it the harder it is to overcome and move on past. The last thing you want is bedtime becoming a flashpoint for stress. So, if your teenager is prone to anxiety, avoid listing the reasons why they need sleep and focus instead on the benefits of good sleep and what barriers they identify, listening very carefully to what they say and how they feel, trying together to find solutions. Making what seem like small changes such as getting the room temperature right and cutting out late-night snacks could significantly improve sleep. Happily, once an improvement is made, the diary project should gather momentum. This is because sleeping more makes us feel better in a multitude of ways that we can easily enjoy as well as measure in the sleep diary. Keeping the diary going once sleep quantity has increased enables even more mindful awareness around subtleties such as mood, concentration and stress levels and can be helpful in many areas of self-care.

Mindfulness and Self-Care for Teens

During the mindfulness course I teach, we spend a session teaching the young people how to do a body scan to relax and enable sleep. It is called Beditation and I absolutely love it because a rowdy room of 15 year-olds transforms into a silent space as they lie on mats and allow themselves to become still, turning their attention inwards, noticing what is going on in the body in the present moment. They have permission to give in to the waves of tiredness many struggle with. Half of them fall asleep. I will share with you how to do this in Chapter 8. Discussion afterwards is always fascinating as the young people become aware of what is often a constant low-level tiredness. Self-care and sleep have already been discussed but it is worth focusing on self-care again in the context of adolescence.

Mindfulness is central to self-care because without it how can we answer questions like: how am I feeling? what do I need? Remember that mindfulness at its simplest is about paying attention, tuning in, noticing what is going on in our mind and our body. With constant external stimulation and the demands made of them off and online, for teenagers it can be a huge challenge to turn that attention inwards and answer those reflective questions. Without knowing how they actually are in a given moment, it is difficult for them to make decisions about how best to care for themselves. It can be difficult to know what they want, who they want to spend time with, what they do and don't want to do, let alone the major decisions about their lives after education and their future.

From the distant shores of adulthood, this might seem trivial, but I can assure you that many young people I have worked with have very little sense of what's going on for them and thereby how to help themselves. Many are in a turmoil about how they feel about themselves, other people and the world in general. Adolescence signals an emerging awareness for young people of themselves as social and sexual beings and these changes take place in a fast-moving, demanding world. Giving them tools to navigate this period enables better mental health and more control over the future.

Mental health is, however, more than a lack of mental illness. All parents want their children to be well in every sense but also to be happy and fulfilled. We want them to experience compassion, gratitude, hope, joy and peace. Compassion is a core wisdom of meditation practice and is taught in the yoga sutras. Self-compassion is vital for young people. Every parent will have heard their child express negative views about themselves: "I'm ugly," "I'm fat," "I'm stupid." I find it painful even to write it because, of course, if breaks our hearts when our children turn on themselves and begin to build a negative self-image. Remember the neural pathway metaphor of walking back and forth through the field of long grass? Tragically the more these messages of self-loathing are repeated the more we begin to believe them. Mindfulness will help young people learn to manage their negative thoughts but negative speak is something parents and carers can help with.

How we speak about ourselves, and others affects how we feel, how we relate to other people; it has consequences for our wellbeing and happiness. Teen-speak in our house gave me the charming term "chatting shit" for putting other people down. By the time you read this, it will no doubt be obsolete and have been overtaken by another phrase, but I think it expresses very well what my generation called "bitching". It's social currency to "chat shit," criticise your peers, parents and teachers often to get a laugh or to establish yourself in a social group. At one level, it can be harmless banter (I don't suppose anyone says "banter" any more either); certainly, I've taken criticism from my kids to heart at times and been told it's "just a joke".

Bringing mindful awareness to how it feels to both "chat shit" about other people but also to be spoken to negatively can be a helpful place to start a conversation. When a child expresses negativity about someone else, it isn't always a good time to intervene and suggest they consider that their grumpy maths teacher might be ill or stressed or that their thoughtless friend could be experiencing problems; but when they are calmer it could be beneficial to focus on how it feels to rant about someone. Yes, it might feel better in the short term but if we are honest, it can leave a bad taste in our mouth and make us feel a bit "icky." I don't ban ranting in our house as it does sometimes help us all feel better to have a good moan about someone else, but a short purgative rant is far healthier than a constant low-level grumbling of negativity.

Turning that awareness onto ourselves can be harder. It is easier to think compassionately about other people than it is about ourself. Encourage your teenager to be kind to themself in every way, not to dwell on their mistakes but to see failure as opportunity and that there is something positive to be found in every situation, even if it is a minuscule crumb. There is a lot of research about the power of gratitude to change the way the brain works, and this is covered in Chapter 8. In the meantime, you will positively influence a child of any age by mirroring positive speak about yourself and other people. Everyone benefits when they let go of complaining or "chatting shit"—so stop ranting about colleagues, relatives, celebrities and politicians. As my gran used to say, if you can't say something nice, don't say anything at all.

Try the self-compassion exercise below with your teenager—do it yourself as well, it feels great. It's a well-known practice that you may have come across before so it should be possible to memorise the gist and then do it with them. If they are not keen to do it with you, talk them through it or copy the text for them to read themselves. Ask later how they got on, what they noticed in their mind and body? It can be very powerful. If it's done at bedtime, it can be a really helpful sleep aid as the body will be flooded with feel-good hormones, the stress response will reduce and a physical coherence established, all of which supports a good night's sleep.

Self-Compassion Meditation

Find a warm comfortable place to sit or lie where you won't be disturbed for a few minutes. Close your eyes. Find the sensation of the breath coming in and out of the nostrils. Notice the gentle rise and fall of the chest and belly. As you breathe out allow the body to settle into stillness.

Now imagine a bench in the sunshine. The bench might be in a beautiful flower-filled garden, or beside a calm lake or a sparkling sea. Visualise yourself sitting down on the bench. It is warm and you feel peaceful and safe. Now call to mind a person that you love. If a person doesn't spring to mind, a pet works too. Choose someone for whom you have uncomplicated feelings of love and positivity. Imagine them sitting beside you on the bench or, if it's a pet, on your lap or tucked by your legs.

As you breathe in, feel love for your companion in your heart. Smile if you want! Now wish for them a life of peace and happiness. In your mind, say "May you be happy. May you be peaceful. May you be full of joy." Imagine your positive wishes landing on the person beside you, filling them up. You might imagine them glowing with a warm light or smiling at you or putting their arm around you.

Feel the closeness of the person beside you, maybe the touch of their hand or a warm doggy head on your lap. Next ask blessings for you both: "May we be happy. May we be peaceful. May we be full of joy." Allow the sensation of shared wellbeing to build around the two of you. You can imagine that bubble of warm light glowing wider to include you too. Sit with this feeling for a while.

Your companion now rises from the bench, gives you a final smile or wag of the tail and walks/dances/skips off into the beautiful landscape around you. Become aware of yourself, still sitting on the bench, still warm and safe. Use the breath in to keep your heart wide open, keep the smile. Say to yourself: "May I be happy. May I be peaceful. May I be full of joy." Feel the sunshine on your face. Allow yourself to accept this blessing. Let it fill you until you are glowing too.

You can stop there and open your eyes slowly when you are ready but the traditional Buddhist practice can be extended a little further. Continuing to follow the gentle movement of breath in the body, allow the warm glow you feel in your heart to expand outwards to take in the park, then the world beyond it and all the people in that world. Say: "May everyone be happy. May everyone be peaceful. May everyone by full of joy." Sit with this sensation until you are ready to open your eyes. This meditation can be adapted so feel free to change the words to more appropriate ones. Some examples are: may we be healthy, may we be strong, may we be contented, may we be loving, may we be wise, may we be inspired. It is not easy for some young people to show themselves kindness or compassion, they can be fiercely self-critical of everything about themselves. They can lack confidence, and they turn on themselves with a frightening harshness. This meditation is about first wishing the best for someone you care about, which should be easy. The next step to wishing the best for yourself and others happens more reliably once the focus has been on someone else. Practised regularly, this compassion meditation can profoundly improve wellbeing and relationships.

Establishing a Mindfulness Practice

The superpower of attention has been much mentioned. If you can discuss this with your teenager, they may be able to relate to experiences they have had. Try asking open questions such as:

- What is it like when you give your full attention to an activity (such as a sport, singing, playing an instrument, skateboarding, painting or drawing, etc.)?
- What is it like when you are juggling lots of activities at the same time, (such as homework/music/messaging/eating etc.)?
- What is it like when your head feels full of thoughts?

- When do you feel really "in the moment" or "in the flow" or "in your body"?
- What it is like when you are worried or anxious?
- How does it feel when you are tired, and how do you function?

Listen carefully to the replies. When I ask these sorts of questions in groups, the responses can be hesitant at first, but once someone has the courage to share that they sometimes feel their head is going to explode, or that they messed up a test or performance because they were worrying about something that happened before or will happen later, a good discussion always takes place. It turns out that everyone worries about things; that everyone struggles sometimes with too much going on in their minds. Most young people can relate to that flow state when they get lost in an activity and have no sense of time passing. They also tend to be excellent multi taskers but will admit that trying to do lots of things at the same time generally leads to nothing getting done to its best.

Suggesting that sitting quietly for 5 minutes a day can help with all this appeals to most people but can also seem preposterous to others. It would not be wise to advocate a mindfulness practice for everyone, it isn't right for some people and a general resistance to it won't lead to results. To support an adolescent trying to start a practice, encourage them to see it as an experiment and to have a friendly curiosity about what might or might not happen when they try. Do it with them maybe? Perhaps do it as a family to start with. However much you might urge them to give it a go, be aware of any opposition. There are other ways to introduce mindful awareness that don't involve formal sitting. If they have agreed to give it a try, turn to Chapter 8 where you will find instructions along with other ways to develop mindfulness.

Repetitive, cyclical thoughts are a very common reason that people of any age find dropping off to sleep difficult. Teenagers with busy, pressurised lives often feel the stresses follow them home. With their smartphones and social media, they can be plugged in full time to what is going on in the minds and lives of other people. This can be a kind of non-stop chatter as the phones ping and ding. Any message coming in could detonate their mood and this makes them incredibly vulnerable in my opinion.

When the young people I teach first practice simply sitting mindfully for a few minutes, what often blows them away is the *silence.* In a busy school, you can imagine how rare this is. Not only is no one speaking but no one is moving either. We tune in the sounds coming in from outside the room which could be voices, traffic noises or birdsong but through calm, steady breathing the body becomes very still. The mind follows. The sounds inside the room might be a clock ticking or the gentle breathing of others.

Even though thoughts pop up, as they always do—the blank mind is a myth—it is possible to watch them arise and remain anchored, remain in the present moment. This creates in the mind a silence that can be extraordinary for some people whose minds are usually non-stop chatterboxes. The space created in this silence can be enlarged through regular practice. It has profound benefits, not least that a quiet mind enables an easier descent into sleep. That good night's sleep, as I'm sure you don't need reminding, is vital for our young people's physical health, immune system, emotional regulation, ability to concentrate, their memory, the quality of their relationships—how they learn, how they feel, how they behave.

Chapter 6
Technology

Technology has been steadily transforming our lives for well over a century now. Radical changes seem to be coming even more rapidly nowadays with developments in artificial intelligence, quantum mechanics, nanotechnology, etc. When I see a young child watching a movie on a tiny phone screen, it strikes me as astonishing that technology has changed so dramatically during my lifetime. As a teenager I used to drag the clunky phone from its sacred spot on The Telephone Table in the hall, stretching the curly wire out so I could shut us both in another room and talk privately to a friend until my dad hammered on the door about the cost of my phone call. Many older people sometimes feel they are in *Back to the Future* as the handheld equivalent of the hoverboard glides past. Almost every aspect of modern life has been transformed by technology and its role in relation to sleep needs to be considered.

This chapter will consider the way modern life has changed sleep patterns and the challenges that parents and their children face around the use of technology. It's not all doom and gloom, however. You will find plenty of suggestions about ways in which technology can be harnessed for the good, and used to support the sleep habits of your children. One thing we know for sure, is there's no going backwards so I've aimed to find the most helpful ways to make technology work for us.

How Technology Has Changed Our Sleep

Our ancestors would have lived in tune with the seasons, rising with the sun and going to bed when it got dark. Life revolved around daylight hours and evening light would have been fuelled by candles and firelight as they could be afforded. The arrival of electric lighting in the late nineteenth century utterly transformed how humans live and work. And it profoundly altered how we sleep. As Matthew Walker says in his brilliant book *Why We Sleep*:

At one time, we went to bed in the hours after dusk and woke with the chickens. Now many of us are still waking up with the chickens, but dusk is simply the time we are finishing up at the office, with much of the waking night to go.

We work and socialise long into the evening and night when our ancestors would have been getting lengthy recuperative rest. Sunset holds no significance for the way we spend our time, and the hours of darkness are no longer governed by the seasons. The prehistoric biological cues linked to daylight and melatonin production are knocked out of kilter by artificial light, altering our circadian rhythm. Melatonin is released as it becomes dark—and you will recall that it functions best when we have been exposed to daylight—but evening electric light effectively fools the body into thinking it is still daytime when it is dark outside. This enables us to enjoy a huge variety of evening activity but pushing forward the onset of sleep can eventually make it harder to fall asleep: a problem we know is experienced nightly by millions of people across the industrialised nations.

Historically, once electric lighting was available, shift-working became possible and the factories of the industrialised countries were able to run all day and all night, locking millions of people into a nocturnal existence with very serious health consequences. Clearly, the reality of electric lighting affects the majority of the population on earth, and it is no coincidence that the World Health Organisation has identified sleep deprivation to be an increasingly dangerous issue. They have classified night-time shift-working as a "probable carcinogen" so clear is the evidence about the effects of such disrupted sleep patterns on the health of those workers around the globe.

Interestingly, cultures who still exist without electricity and who are able to live more in tune with their circadian rhythm have a biphasic pattern of sleep where they have a long period at night of 7–8 hours but also nap during the afternoon for 30–60 minutes. The nap has great restorative powers, I am a massive fan and take one whenever life permits. And there's the issue: modern life often fails to acknowledge even the basic value of sleep, and it certainly isn't going to be a champion of the nap. Or is it?

Fascinating research undertaken by the Harvard University School of Public Health concluded that a daily nap had a measurable effect on reducing the likelihood of death from heart disease. Some of the world's most successful companies have recognised that a well-rested workforce is also a more productive workforce. People who have had sufficient sleep have better concentration, memory recall, emotional balance, creative ability and immune systems than those suffering a sleep deficit and they contribute more and better to the bottom line of their employers.

As Arianna Huffington, author of *The Sleep Revolution*, says: "The idea that sleep is somehow a sign of weakness and that burnout and sleep deprivation are macho signs of strength is particularly destructive." This has been recognised by some businesses who have enabled sleepy employees to take a power nap and return to their desks replenished for the rest of the day! Now so many of us work from home, perhaps we can finally give ourselves permission to take a strategic snooze, knowing that our productivity will be enhanced?

However rested we are following our nap, it is likely the desk we return to will have on it a laptop or PC and be lit using LED lighting. This has a profound effect on our circadian rhythm. The blue light emitted by these bulbs and devices is twice as capable of suppressing melatonin production as was the old warm yellow light, due to receptors in the eyes being more sensitive to short wave-length blue light. With many people, including children, using laptops, tablets and smartphones in the evenings it is important to realise how much havoc the LED lighting is playing with natural sleep rhythms.

We live in the modern world, however, and for most of us returning to candlelit evenings and waking to the local rooster isn't a desirable or possible option. I wouldn't recommend the rooster either as we were woken for many years by Alan the enthusiastic chicken I mistook for a female when he was tiny. So, it's alarm clocks for most of us in the mornings but bringing mindful awareness to the sleep rhythm of everyone in the household matters hugely because of the health implications repeated throughout this book.

The sleep hygiene advice in Chapters 3 and 5 includes recommendations about exposure to LED lighting prior to bedtime. It's worth repeating here that efforts made to reduce or avoid using phones, laptops and tablets will have a positive effect on the ability to fall asleep. This is a challenge with our phone-dependent children, and you will need to work together as a family to come up with boundaries and undo any habits that have built up around phones and screens being used late in the day by everyone. Screens have become, in many households, a default way to spend the time. How often do you see people in queues or waiting rooms glued to their phones?

The ability to sit quietly and not automatically drop into a screen is being lost, at great peril to us all. Spending time doing things that are NOT screen-based may be hard to start with as the habit is so entrenched in most of us. Some of the suggestions below may be helpful.

Tips to Reduce Screen Time

- Set a time limit on pre-bedtime screen time—aim for 1 hour minimum if possible. So, if bedtime is 9pm, ask for phones, etc. to be off 8pm or earlier. For an 8pm bedtime, I would suggest no gadgets after dinner.
- Promote alternative evening activities such as art, listening to music, journalling, reading, audiobooks, model-making, Lego.
- Lengthy baths or showers will aid sleep and help the body relax.
- Yoga stretches or mindfulness practice prepare the body for sleep.
- Playing with siblings, pets or playing board games, card games, puzzles or jigsaws can all be fun.
- Spend time outside during the summer months. An after-dinner walk can be very restorative.
- Bring mindful awareness to how it feels to do these alternative activities. Ask children what they notice about their alertness, energy levels, feelings of happiness.
- Notice how feelings of sleepiness change—it should happen earlier, quite naturally. Keep talking about how it feels and how falling asleep is different after non-screen time.

You will need to be honest about your own use of screens too and reflect on how that may impact on your child's attitude to their own usage. If you are always tapping away on your phone or checking emails on your laptop into the evening, this sends the message of total normality. Now many more of us are working from home since the global pandemic, we are not leaving our work at the office but, unless you are lucky enough to have a nice home office in the garden, you are likely to be working from a table somewhere or, in my case, squashed into a corner of a family room.

It's hard to stop sometimes when you have a lot on and switching off physically and mentally can happen later and later in the day. Possibly your own sleep is impacted by late-night exposure to screens. If you suspect that this may the case, it is worth experimenting with consciously turning off the tech an hour before you head to bed. Pay attention to whatever differences it makes to your enjoyment of your evening and to how you later fall asleep. Notice the quality of that sleep.

As ever with our children, modelling positive behaviour is vital. This is especially important around teenagers who will take no prisoners over any double standards. Try to practice what you preach and make a pre-bedtime rule about screen use that everyone can understand and buy into. Trying out new non-tech evening activities may be much more rewarding than you think. Perhaps you have been using screen time as a kind of babysitter? We have all done this, so don't beat yourself up.

Of course, it's simpler to hand over a tablet than come up with a game, especially after a long day and when you may well still have multiple tasks to complete before you can fall into bed yourself. But I would urge you to give it a try because the time you invest in some non-tech time before bed will pay off later as your child, whose melatonin levels are now much more suited to sleep, will drift off more easily and will be likely to stay asleep longer.

Smartphones, Social Media and Young People's Mental Health

Everyone's addicted to their phones—at least that's how it appears when we see them in apparent constant use whether at home, work, in restaurants, gyms, bars and walking down the street. A 2020 report by Childwise found that the majority of children owned a mobile phone by the age of 7. By age 11, the survey found 90% of children had their own device and by the time they start secondary school ownership was "almost universal". The same report asked children and young people about their attitude to their phones and found that 39% said they could not live without them. 57% sleep with their phones beside them. 44% said they would feel uncomfortable if somewhere without phone signal, and 42% admitted to being "constantly worried" about running out of charge.

The NHS has collected data showing that UK children aged 5–16 years spend an average of 2–3 hours per day watching television, 1–3 hours on the internet, 1–2 hours playing video games and over an hour on their mobiles (not talking)—this makes an astonishing 6.3 hours a day. How are they fitting this in when they have school for 6 hours a day plus the travel time and after-school activities? The answer, of course, is that they are spending the majority of their waking free time in front of or engaged with some kind of screen. And they frequently don't even realise their time is disappearing this way, it is an utterly normal and, to them, desirable way to spend their time.

Questioning one of my teenage sons about his phone use was not easy: his phone time is his downtime, it is about relaxing, being lazy, chatting and having fun with friends online. During the 2020/21 lockdowns, I think most parents and carers would agree that our children would have been horribly isolated and lonely without the ability to contact their friends online. Connection is the major benefit of smartphone technology and its potential for positive interaction and enrichment is enormous and is here to stay. Likewise, it's completely unrealistic to think we can undo the habits our children have around their phone use, especially the behaviours that make them "normal" and socially accepted by their peers—but parents will want to ensure their children are safe and that their health is not under threat.

As a mindfulness teacher, the key issue for me around social media use is the manipulation of attention. Attention, you will recall, is our superpower: where we focus it is vital and taking control of it is fundamental to our wellbeing. The business model of the social media company is not the sale of its users' data but the *sale of their attention*. Algorithms are continuously nudging social media users in certain directions, hijacking attention in increasingly subtle and manipulative ways.

Ex-Google employee Tristan Harris, now co-founder of the Center for Humane Technology, is one of the contributors to the 2020 Netflix docudrama *The Social Dilemma* which exposes the strategy behind the business model of social media companies. Harris and colleagues reveal how we are being manipulated into deliberately addictive loops and Harris confirms that this business model "does not have our best interests at heart". The main benefit of social media is to connect people, but it works at the same time deliberately to divide and polarise. It also degrades democracy and reduces, because of the culture of division, our collective ability to solve the problems that face humanity—primarily that of climate change. Environmentally-minded young people might be interested in this argument.

Explaining all that to your TikTok-ing ten-year-old might be a tricky task. You could, however, sit together as a family and watch *The Social Dilemma*. Have a discussion about it afterwards and keep the conversation going. With my own teens, I have found that they definitely object to being manipulated. This has been the way in to getting them to look at their own use of social media and consider how happy they are to be "sheeple", steered along rabbit holes by tech billionaires, being fed targeted information in multiple ways that can affect their mental and physical health.

Technology companies are competing for our attention and the attention, in particular, of our children. When our attention is elsewhere and we are occupied in sports, activities, books, crafts, etc. we are depriving them. The CEO of Netflix has said that their biggest competitor is sleep. The vital sleeping hours of our children are being actively competed for by these tech companies and they will ruthlessly encroach on them without impunity. Parents will hopefully want to be part of the resistance. Helping children to take control of their attention will liberate them from the manipulation of tech companies, educate them to make the best choices and enable them to have those vital hours of sleep they need.

Phone addiction is a real thing. It even has a name: *nomophobia*—the fear of being without your phone. Another term, *textiety*, describes the anxiety caused by feeling that you need to immediately respond to every message. Textiety becomes worse if you don't have your phone with you. Like all forms of anxiety this can be a very uncomfortable, even distressing, feeling as the body's sympathetic nervous system kicks in. Try the quiz below for an honest look at your relationship with your phone. Treat it as a mindfulness exercise as you reflect on your feelings, do it without judgement or expectation. Get everyone in the family to take it—discuss the results together. You may be surprised: I have come across several families where the adults display much worse dependence on their phones than their tech-savvy kids.

How's your Nomophobia?

1. When sitting on a train or bus or waiting somewhere, do you…?
   a) People-watch or use the time to look round or daydream
   b) Read or listen to music through my phone
   c) Look at something on my phone

2. When your phone rings, buzzes or vibrates, do you feel an intense urge to check it for updates and messages?
   a) No, I'll deal with it when I am ready to
   b) Sometimes, if I am waiting to hear back about something particular
   c) Er…of course, I might miss something!

3. If you are out of range of a phone signal or there is no WI-FI, how do you feel?
   a) Fine, it will come back on again later
   b) Mildly irritated especially if I need to do something
   c) Enraged—how can I run my life without a decent connection, I thought this was the 21st century?

4. Do you ever use your phone while cycling, skateboarding, scooting, etc.?
   a) No never, I'm busy
   b) Only if it repeatedly alerts me
   c) Of course, no big deal

5. Where is your smartphone while you are asleep?
   a) Charging in another room or maybe in a bag or pocket, not sure
   b) Charging on the other side of the bedroom
   c) Right beside me, of course, either on the pillow or bedside table

6. Do you find yourself looking at and answering messages at all hours of day or night, even if doing so interrupts other things?
   a) No, I'll look at it when I have time
   b) Sometimes, it's hard to focus otherwise

c) Definitely, it's my lifeline and I don't want to miss something important

7. Do you lose track of time when you are on your phone?
   a) No. I decide how I spend my time
   b) Sometimes I look up and a chunk of time has gone by, but I try not to let that happen
   c) Duh—that's what it's for!

8. How do you feel when you don't have your phone with you?
   a) Fine as long as I know I haven't lost it
   b) A bit weird to be honest. I am OK as long as it's not for long
   c) Freaked out and stressed, hate not having it near

9. Do you worry about your phone battery running out?
   a) Not really, there are always other ways around any problem
   b) Yes, in case I needed to contact someone in an emergency or if someone needed to get hold of me
   c) Yes, I would be scared and distressed without the means to keep in touch with family and friends or to keep up to date with everything

10. Do you prefer your real-life or online identity?
   a) My what? Real-life me is fine
   b) I like both, depends on what I am doing
   c) My online identity is definitely better in loads of ways

Result: if you scored **mostly a's**, you are pretty unusual and to be applauded for making the choice to live your life foremost and use your phone as and when it suits you. People scoring **mostly b's** are reasonably well balanced about their phone use and show only fleeting signs of nomophobia. Use the other answers to help you make the best choices for yourself going forward. **Mostly c's** suggests you are showing some signs of being hooked on your smartphone. Keep an open mind about other ways to manage your phone use and experiment with different behaviours (for example, not sleeping right next to it or switching alerts off to focus on something in real life).

When doing any experiment, bring full mindful awareness and notice how it makes you feel before during and afterwards. Anyone with serious concerns about themselves or other people in their care should seek advice from a family doctor, of course.

The impact on mental health for young people of excessive use of social media has been well-documented and I urge anyone interested to look at some or all of these reports: *Social Media and Young People's Mental Health* by Jonathan Glazzard and Samuel Stones (2019), *Social Media, Young People and Mental Health*: briefing 53 by the Centre for Mental Health (2018) and *#StatusofMind* by the Royal Society for Public Health and Young Health Movement (2017). The chief executive of the RSPH Shirley Cramer says:

Social media has become a space in which we form and build relationships, shape self-identity, express ourselves and learn about the world around us; it is intrinsically linked to mental health.

The power social media has over our young people is mixed. It has, as we know, the major benefit of enabling connection between people, ideas and creative ventures. Users can express themselves, as Ms Cramer states above, in diverse positive ways. The harms, however, are also far-reaching and can have devastating effects. The major threats to mental health include: cyber-bullying which has been experienced by 7 out of 10 children and young people; ideation around self-harm and suicide, proven by tragic suicides of young people; body image concerns affect both young men and young women and can lead to dangerous behaviours; easy access to violent or pornographic images can have a profound effect on relationships and lead to potentially dangerous attitudes around consent, respect, sexual equality and violence.

We know that most 16–17-year-olds will have recently viewed adult content via social media platforms. There has been a woeful effort by governments to protect children from these images. Viewing pornography or violence online can change the behaviour of children and cause anxiety and fear especially for young children. It fuels a culture of sexual violence and, at the very least, objectifies largely women and girls which distorts sexual behaviour and attitudes. Pressure is increasing on governments to legislate properly for robust age verification checks. It can't come fast enough in my opinion.

Sleep loss is also flagged up in multiple reports as a dangerous consequence of excessive social media use. As well as the time spent using their phones, young people frequently experience difficulty sleeping in the remaining hours of the night due to the anxiety and distress they feel after engaging in social media.

It's a shocking list and, if you read the reports I can guarantee you a sleepless night of your own worrying. There is help out there and there are things that parents and carers can do to support young people. Adult mental health is also at risk from tech use. It's hard to drop off when newsfeeds have filled our mind with images of the world's ills. Social media rows and images of other people's "perfect" lives impact on adults as well. Most schools and colleges now include in their timetable lessons about online safety, cyber-bullying and healthy use of social media. Secondary schools will discuss healthy relationships with their pupils and cover issues around consent and equality.

Schools are required to address the mental wellbeing of their pupils and staff, and will all have policies and interventions you can ask about if you want to know more. Mindfulness is being recognised by more and more schools as an invaluable resource to support young people. Thousands of research projects have evaluated the effects of mindfulness training in many contexts and find consistent benefits to psychological health including feeling calmer and more positive, coping better with stress and anxiety, improving concentration and focus and getting on better with others.

Mindfulness and Healthy Tech Use

Introducing a child or adolescent to mindfulness practices empowers them in ways that can help them flourish in the short and long term. One of the benefits I focus on when teaching these skills is the issue of choice. We reflect as a class on the choices we make each day, frequently without noticing what we are choosing, just doing the same old things. This is sometimes called being on autopilot and you will have experienced it many times yourself. It happens when our minds are occupied with something other than what we are doing right here, right now. You may well have found yourself driving while mulling over an issue in your mind and, lo and behold, you arrive at your destination with very little awareness of how you got there.

When we look closely at the choices we make daily, we find that some of them are those *autopilot choices* ("I always have toast for breakfast"), some are driven by what's going on in our *bodies* ("I'm tired, so I'm having this energy drink") and some are made based on what's happening in our *minds* ("I'm worrying about my day and don't want anything for breakfast"). Generally, people aren't aware of what is prompting the many small decisions they make each day. Mindfulness can bring greater clarity and, ultimately, help us to make better choices for our wellbeing. The next step with students is then to bring mindfulness to the situation: pupils are encouraged to take a few moments (see My Minute p.205) perhaps when they first wake up or before an activity or choice, to stop, tune in to what's going on in the mind and body, asking perhaps "What do I really want to do/eat/play? What is best for me right now?"

Honestly, this can be revelatory for young people, and I absolutely love hearing how they experiment using mindfulness in their everyday lives and how their decision-making improves as a result. Some benefits I have heard over the years include greater honesty about doing what they feel best for themselves rather than going along with the crowd; choosing to do activities they love even when they aren't "cool"; choosing the healthier option in terms of food and drink or exercise and noticing how much better that feels; a greater awareness of other's needs as they have space to reflect on the impact of their choices.

Importantly for me, of course, is that the awareness of how tired they are helps them to appreciate the value of sleep and make better decisions about bedtime. Much of the focus of those who advocate mindfulness is on the aspects of our lives that can be improved such as concentration, wellness and stress management, but the single most important benefit in my view, especially when it comes to children, is happiness. When we bring mindfulness to our daily lives, we can better notice the small, often simple things that make us happy and we can "grow" them, helping ourselves to be happier people. Tuning in to the awareness of feeling good sounds like such a simple thing, but for some young people and, in particular, for adolescents hardwired to make socially acceptable choices it can sometimes be impossible. Technology certainly hasn't made their lives any easier.

Reaching for their smartphones and opening those social media apps is an autopilot activity for the majority of young people. If your youngsters have shared the results of the above nomophobia quiz with you, it might have opened a conversation with them. No one wants to be called a "boomer" (it has frequently happened to me) so we need to try and understand the role social media plays in the lives of our children and how they feel about it. Guiding them towards a mindful awareness of the impact their tech use might be having on their wellbeing can be a positive experience for the whole family, especially if you include your own honest views. Keeping the conversation non-judgemental is vital; you are asking questions with curiosity and interest. There are no right or wrong answers, you are aiming to encourage your child to reflect and review their behaviour, to notice what is going on for them, to bring awareness to what they are doing around their tech use.

Questions to Encourage Mindful Awareness of Tech Use

- Do you use your phone on "autopilot"? How do you know you are on autopilot? What does it feel like?
- How do you feel after you have been on your phone for, say, over an hour? What do you notice about how your body is? How your mind is?
- How do you feel after time away from your phone, doing activities or schoolwork or playing? How is your mind after this? How is your body?
- What do you notice about other people, your family or friends, when they have been on phones for ages? What's it like interacting with someone who has been busy on their phone for a while?
- Have you ever tried to cut back on your phone use? Why? What happened when you did?
- Do you ever talk to your friends or a teacher or family member about phone usage? Have you helped anyone else talk about their worries? What advice would you offer?
- Are there ways your phone can help with relaxation, stress or sleep? How do you know it has helped?

Talking to your child or adolescent about their phone/tech use can be really helpful if you try to unpick what exactly they are getting out of it. Clinical psychologist Dr Jenna Vyas-Lee works with families and health services and recognises the essential role sleep has in health. She describes how she "crowbars" sleep interventions into aspects of her work with adults and children. She recommends this unpicking process and says it can be very revealing and, vitally, it attaches value to what they are doing. Remember they have grown up with this tech and it's totally normal, so we won't get very far as parents and carers if we hold the "your phone is rotting your brain" attitude.

You will likely find that your teenager is getting some or all of the following from their smartphone/tech use: gaming, learning, socialising, being creative, campaigning, entertainment. They may be engaged in social justice or looking good. Help them to identify which aspects matter most to them and whether or not those are active (socialising) or passive (entertainment). It may be much easier to experiment with substituting an activity late at night when you recognise and value their priorities. The alternative activity delivers a similar result and aligns with their values. So instead of watching beauty tip videos, suggest a home facial. Instead of tweeting about causes they are passionate about, try writing articles or letters. Instead of sitting in their bedroom chatting, enable them to meet in person—we've all got out of the habit of doing that in recent years. See if they can bring awareness to the difference between those passive and active uses then, in that pre-sleep hour, see if they can choose the passive ones that are less likely to stimulate them or engage them in potentially stressful debates.

In Chapter 5, I focused on the changes that take place in the adolescent brain. Hopefully, you will recall that one of those changes is a drive to be accepted by their peers—social media plays directly into this new brain activity making peer interaction and approval a high priority. This makes it important to keep communicating with your teenager about their use of it and how it might be affecting them.

The focus of this chapter so far has been around the harmful impact of technology on our young people and a look at ways we can support them. It is important to balance this out now and consider some of the ways in which technology can help in terms of sleep and wellbeing.

Technology and Gadgets that Can Support Good Sleep

Depending on budget, it is now possible to buy gadgets that monitor a variety of biological functions from your blood pressure to your blood oxygen saturation, heart rate to brainwave pattern. I track my runs on an app that tells me my pace, distance and calorie consumption. Millions of people, including children, use wearables to help them feel more in control of their health and wellbeing. Technology has changed in extraordinary ways over the past decades and the rate of this change is accelerating. When you consider buying any sort of gadget or tech to support your own sleep habits or those of your children, you need to carefully consider the benefits and the pitfalls and how relevant the tech on offer is to the specific sleep problem. Beware of the eternal promise technology waves before us: that it will magically resolve difficulties on our behalf. Below you will find a list of items that can be purchased, including a consideration of the pros and cons.

- **Sleep masks**—our circadian rhythm is linked to daylight and darkness contributes to a good night's sleep. Once the baby stage is over, children may not to be happy about blackout blinds rendering their bedrooms pitch black. They often wish for a nightlight or other source of electric light. This is a sleep inhibitor and a sleep mask can therefore be helpful. It creates darkness behind the eyes but can be removed for bathroom trips or if the child wakes in the night. During lighter summer months, wearing a sleep mask can help keep bedtimes where they need to be. There are many to choose from including the inexpensive fun ones with furry features or superhero characters. You can buy weighted ones which gently rest on the eyelids. There are scented ones with soothing lavender, known for its use in aromatherapy to aid relaxation. Some masks block out not only light but sound so, for a noisy household, this might be very helpful. At the high-tech end of the shopping list, there is a full blackout mask on the market that has extremely lightweight memory foam around the individual eyepieces. You can buy masks that use sound and light therapy and include sleep coaching audio tracks that can be downloaded onto a phone. As well as considering your budget, you'll need to think long-term about whether introducing a sleep mask will create a dependence for your child. Most of the high-tech masks on the market are aimed at adults travelling on planes or trains or for shift-working adults who need to sleep during daytime hours. For children, sleep masks can be useful for establishing better sleep patterns, especially for adolescents who have been struggling to get enough sleep for some time. For younger children, the simplest ones can help darken a room and help them get off to sleep faster. In practical terms, the position in which someone sleeps can make certain masks less useful, for example weighted masks work much better for back sleepers. Read the reviews online and ask around for tips. At my daughter's early sleepovers, all her friends got their various sleep masks out—they didn't do much to stop the giggling though!

- **Weighted blankets**—difficulty falling asleep is usually due to either the mind or the body being overactive and this is where the weighted blanket can be helpful. It is exactly what it sounds like: a blanket that has small weights inside. The purpose of the blanket is to apply a firm consistent pressure to the body, and they come in a variety of sizes and textures. They can help the body to release tension, relax and prepare for sleep. Some parents report their children go off to sleep quicker with one of these blankets but also that they stay asleep for longer. An important advantage they have is around sensory processing. Sensory experience is part of child development, but some children are more sensitive than others and will respond to the proprioceptive input from a cosy heavy cover at night that helps them to relax prior to sleep. If your child shows signs of sensory sensitivity such as dislike of waistbands or rough fabrics, it may be that a weighted blanket will appeal to them. There are a multitude on the market, and you can find instructions to make your own as well. I would caution against anything that makes the child hot as we know that cool temperatures are important for healthy sleep, so choose breathable lightweight fabric and adjust the temperature in the room if necessary, especially during warm summer nights. It is also vital not to put too much weight on, of course, so make sure the size and weight of the blanket is appropriate for your child by reading the instructions or seeking advice from a doctor or health visitor. Introduce it slowly to your child, start with it over their feet and ask how it feels, whether they like the sensation of gentle weight. Never force a child of any age to use a weighted blanket. It is also advisable to just use the blanket for bedtimes and not encourage it to be hauled around the house or taken out in the car—this will keep the association with bedtime. If your child's sleep habits improve after using a weighted blanket, beware not to put all the credit onto the blanket when you are talking with your child. Make sure to give them lots of praise and encouragement for being a good sleeper, focusing on the extra energy they will now have for playing and doing well at school. Try to avoid creating a dependence where your child becomes convinced they cannot sleep without the blanket. The purpose of any sleep aid is to put better habits in place and enable the mind and body to wire in, in neurological terms, the healthy sleep routine.

- **Sleep tracker**—the technology around wearables that track aspects of our lives with a high degree of accuracy is advancing by the day. I can see it becoming more and more normal to have a detailed knowledge of your own circadian rhythm, including the various phases of sleep throughout the night. If your wearable device also tracks what you have eaten that day, what exercise you have done, whether you have practised mindfulness meditation and how much time spent using apps, messaging, etc., then you could build up the sort of detailed picture that we only aim at when starting a sleep diary. You would be able to make links between the quantity and quality of your sleep and your diet and exercise, for example, and improve your sleep hygiene in multiple ways. There are multiple sleep trackers on the market that are able to measure heartbeat, skin temperature, brain activity, movement and breathing rate. They include ones that you wear on your wrist, sensing pads that you put under your mattress, some you wear like a headband. Coming onto the market shortly as this is written, is a home hub device that will track you as you sleep and answer questions the following day about whether or not you snored! If these all sound very adult, it is because they are. Some are directly marketed at adults suffering from insomnia which, as we know, is a growing problem globally. Some are marketed as fitness and recovery tools for athletes. I would not encourage the use of any tracking device for young children. It could create an anxiety around sleep that will be difficult to undo later. For adolescents, perhaps those training for sports, it might be suitable but again it is vital not to make sleep into a more stressful issue than it already may be. Constantly checking stats and measuring "performance" will not help on its own. Using a tracker alongside positive changes to diet, exercise and screen use can be helpful to see which changes promote better sleep but I would suggest it is used in the short term only. Your aim is to help your child or young adult to learn to sleep naturally and learn for themselves what works best to help them achieve this. Adults experiencing insomnia might try a sleep tracker if it helps to reveal any patterns that may be contributing to poor sleep.

- **Mobile phone radiation shield**—the evidence around damaging effects of radiation emitted by mobile phones is far from conclusive. There are and have been many research projects looking into the ways electromagnetic radiation causes harm. I would encourage you to do some research if you would like to know more. In terms of sleep and whether the electromagnetic waves interrupt the sleep cycle, there is some evidence that sleeping next to your phone can change the structure of sleep, but it is by no means conclusive. No government nor health advisory organisation has identified it as a high enough risk to advise against, but some scientists have voiced concerns that risks are higher for children. Anecdotally, we know that some people seem to be more sensitive to electromagnetic activity—it is *not* recognised as a medical diagnosis, but enough people have reported adverse reactions to electromagnetic fields to have coined the term Electromagnetic Hypersensitivity (EHS or microwave syndrome). Symptoms of this typically include sleep disturbance but also headaches, tiredness and fatigue, depression, prickly skin, rashes and pain and aches. These are quite broad symptoms, of course, and several of them are linked directly to insufficient sleep. With teenagers more likely to have their phones with them at night, many admitting their phones are actually in bed with them, a device that can block most of the radiation could be a useful experiment if your child seems to be displaying symptoms of hypersensitivity. Testimonials published by the manufacturers of these blocking devices are exuberant in praise of improved sleep quality and quantity. You will have to make up your own mind and try it out, carefully noticing and recording any changes.
- **Blue-light glasses**—the evidence connecting exposure to blue LED light and the impact on melatonin production is incontrovertible. The advice in this book is to avoid using digital devices for at least 60 minutes prior to sleep and, ideally, longer for children. You can now, however, buy specially manufactured glasses that may help some people. The lenses are coated with blue-light blocking technology and can be combined with an optical prescription. For people using screens all day, the benefits to sleep are clear but users also report fewer

headaches and eye strain. For adolescents using laptops or PCs for schoolwork, then switching to their phones for downtime chatting and social media use, these glasses may be helpful. There are many on the market, so do your research with your teen and then try them out with mindful awareness, noting any differences in sleep quality and quantity as a result. Most smartphones also have the option to reduce the brightness or even the blue light, so check the settings or speak to your phone provider for advice.

- **Lock boxes for tech**—if you are trying to reduce the amount of time your child spends engaged on a smartphone or tablet, a timed lock box could be a good way to enforce rules and remove the endless negotiation. When my kids were young, I spent a lot of time haggling over their gaming time—the 30 minutes after-school rule would be changed one day to 40 minutes with the agreement of only 20 minutes the next day. It had to change when friends came over; it was longer at the weekends; it had to enable fair access for all the children. It was such a total headache that their dad and I struggled to remember what the latest terms and conditions were and argued between ourselves. In the middle of one of the regular and predictable battles, I had a moment of clarity, reminded myself I was the grown-up here and just banned all gaming from Monday through Thursday. Fridays and weekends would be relaxed. It was a success for many years and our post-teenage son now admits it worked well and that he would have been swallowed up without the boundaries. This, however, was before child smartphone ownership became ubiquitous. Current challenges for parents are around time spent on social media, allowing the phone in bedrooms, age-appropriate restrictions and overall hours absorbed by phone/tablet use. A simple solution is to purchase a lock box with built-in timer. They generally resemble a mini safe inside which all tech gets placed, and an agreed release time is keyed in. Once the door closes, there is no way to release the contents. If you hadn't diagnosed nomophobia by then, this should answer some of the quiz questions (see p.163)! While this is a fantastically clear solution to the issue of taking regular tech breaks, it can lead to conflict and anxiety if not handled appropriately. Discuss the issues with your child. Agree the terms. Join in yourself. Try to avoid using it as a punishment. Enabling young people to recognise for themselves the way they feel after long periods of phone use is the ultimate aim because it enables them to make better choices for themselves. Ask those mindful questions about noticing how they feel; share how you feel yourself without your phone; try to resist judgement.

- **Gentle wake alarm clocks**—we know that the adolescent body clock shifts onwards from where it was during the pre-teen years. This makes it harder for our teenagers to wake up early in the morning, particularly for those with long journeys to school or college, or those with chores, training or clubs before school. An alarm clock is necessary for almost all adolescents and the standard alarm clock will probably be loud, jolting them out of what is likely to be a phase of deep sleep. This is a deeply unpleasant way to wake up, of course, and does nothing for their mood or enthusiasm for the day ahead. I often teach groggy, grumpy teenagers for the first lesson of the day and have a massive urge to pack them off back to bed for a few hours. Perhaps it is not so bad for some of them if they are woken less abruptly. We know that daylight suppresses melatonin and enhances wakefulness. You can buy alarm clocks that use LED light to imitate sunrise, gradually brightening the room over a period of time and making waking up more biologically natural. Some of these gentle wake alarm clocks also incorporate sound effects such as chirping birds or waves lapping the shore. Vibrating alarm clocks can be placed under the pillow and may suit people who are more sensitive to sound and prefer to be woken this way. It may be worth trying out some of this tech with your child if they have trouble waking in the mornings. Remember that only 40% of the population are defined as "larks" who naturally prefer to go to bed early and rise early. Abrupt wakings never put me in the best of moods during my teenage years, and definitely ensures I'm sympathetic now to the sleep patterns of adolescents whose brains are undergoing dramatic change that simply require more kip. A gentle wake alarm clock may not transform teenager's sleep, but it might make them considerably less grumpy over breakfast.
- **Cool air purifier**—the temperature of the bedroom is an important part of sleep hygiene. Our bodies need to be a few degrees lower than usual, and this can be difficult to achieve on hot summer nights. Homes may have windows that do not open very far or are not big enough to allow

cool night air to circulate in the room. A fan may be helpful or a mini air conditioning unit—the latter may not be as pricey as you think and the portable ones requiring just water can be easily moved around the house. If your child's bedroom overlooks a busy road, you may not be keen on the air pollutants from vehicle exhaust making their way in through an open window. It may be worth considering investing in one of the air purifiers on the market that are able to capture gases, pollutants and allergens. Check to see whether they include air conditioning or just have a fan that circulates the air. Air purifiers can help hay-fever suffers too.

- **Aromatherapy diffusers**—with insomnia rates going through the roof during the global pandemic, I notice it is now possible to buy aromatherapy products in my local petrol station. This is quite a change from its old hippy reputation, and I am delighted at the rising awareness of the benefits of aromatherapy. There has been much research linking natural essential oils to improvements in feelings of stress and with difficulty sleeping. Aromatherapy takes oils from plant flowers, berries and leaves. The scents work by balancing the very oldest part of our brain. Oils helpful for stress management include lemon balm, marigold, bergamot, ylang ylang. Lavender is the most well-known oil to support sleep. There is plenty of information about how to use essential oils and how they can help with sleep and anxiety. You can buy a huge variety of roll-ons, pillow sprays, body lotions and bath products and using these can be a low-cost way to experiment. Not everyone is affected by aromatherapy, but if your child responds well to one of the oils it might be worth investing in a diffuser that can be plugged in at night and gently release the scent throughout the sleeping hours. Using oils can also be a pleasant way to support the bedtime routine—include them in the bath or on the pillow as your child settles down for sleep.
- **Apps**—there are apps galore to support mindfulness, mental health, sleep and healthy use of technology. New ones are being added all the time to the app stores and it is not possible to review or rate them accurately here in this book. Anecdotally, the young people I work with report finding helpful those apps with guided meditations; timers and reminders to take a few minutes to practice mindfulness; blue-light

desaturation; sleep trackers; relaxing sounds or music; and those social networks that share tips and support for mental health issues.

- **Noise-cancelling earplugs**—for adults sharing a bed with a snorer, investing in a pair of noise-cancelling earplugs can transform the ability to sleep and are more effective than the disposable foam ones. Beware, they can be expensive, and it took me decades of elbowing my husband before I took the financial plunge. But they were worth every penny. Look around and see what's on the market to suit you. They are frequently marketed at travellers who want to snooze on the plane, so check that they will be suitable for your ears if you sleep on your side.

I hope this chapter has gone some way to removing the demonisation of technology that many parents feel, and that it has perhaps bought some mindful perspective to a hot issue in many households. I completely relate to that instinctive sense of enmity. Watching your child choose to spend a sunny weekend afternoon shut away in their bedroom, often with curtains shut, tapping away at their screen can be very difficult. We all experience doubts about whether we are doing enough to protect their young minds.

Befriending tech seems the wisest way forward to me, resisting the knee-jerk response that it is evil and frying the brains of our beloved children. This involves keeping the discussion going in your family, being prepared to be open and challenged about your own tech habits and ultimately noticing the effects of the various aspects of tech use on the wellbeing and happiness of everyone. Mindfulness is a vital tool in recognising what is going on in our minds and our bodies and will help us make better choices around our tech and our sleep.

Chapter 7
Body Calm: Mindfulness and Relaxation Techniques for the Body

A regular part of the work I do with young people is to ask them to assess how tired they are feeling in a given moment. Every hand in the room generally goes up in response to the question: "Who's tired right now?" The teachers and teaching assistants in the room invariably raise theirs as well. We discuss how they know they are tired, what tiredness feels like. Even young primary school children can identify that being tired makes their body heavy and sluggish, their mind fuzzy, it means they get angry quickly, they feel tearful. Everything feels hard and it is difficult to be positive and happy. I then get them to calculate the amount of hours they spent sleeping (not time spent in bed) the previous night. This is known as *sleep efficiency.*

I tell them the recommended hours of sleep they need to be functioning at their best and never once has more than a handful of children in the room achieved that amount of sleep. Yet they are able to recognise that feeling rested is *much better*. They can describe the opposite of tiredness: feeling zingy, energised, full of beans, alert, engaged, alive. They recognise that when they are well-rested they cope better with challenges, are less volatile, less likely to be "triggered" by everyday events. They are aware of greater feelings of optimism and positivity. But night after night the vast majority of young people miss vital hours of rest and end up paying a high price the following day.

When we talk about why this is the case, they generally cite procrastination, homework pressures, wanting to enjoy their free time and, most frequently, that their body or their mind is unable to settle and enable them to fall asleep. This chapter is about the ways in which relaxation and mindfulness techniques can be used to help the body to release tension and make sleep easier. There are a selection of exercises and visualisations to choose from. With younger children, you can read them aloud or just try talking your child through the instructions. For older children, share the relevant exercises and discuss how they could try them for themselves.

These are aimed at children and adolescents because I have used them, and I know that they work. Adults can do all of these with great effect as well, but Chapter 9 has a series of suggestions for use by adults experiencing sleep challenges. Combine these with the mind calm exercises in the following chapter and you will have a full arsenal of strategies for the whole family to experiment with.

The Body/Mind Connection

It is acknowledged by most of us that the mind and body are closely linked; that what is happening in one affects the other. I have found yoga and mindfulness to be some of the best ways to explore the relationship, in fact the word "yoga" is Sanskrit for *union*—meaning the union of the mind and body and spirit. Plenty of people who've never done a downward dog in their lives can relate to the way that physical activities help to clear the mind and relieve stress—also that mental focus and concentration make a difference to the success of those activities. With children, it is helpful to nurture their awareness of the relationship between their mind and body. And it starts with the very basics of identifying the difference between them.

When working with groups of young people, I start to introduce them to the experience of stopping, turning their attention inwards and asking themselves "how am I right now?" Young children are easily able identify their emotions: they feel happy, excited, sad, angry. Adolescents are able to recognise more complex feelings: confusion, anger, desire. Once they have become accustomed to doing this, it splits into a more precise self-assessment: "how is my body right now?" and then, "how is my mind?" Generally, they write down one word for each and I am used to seeing responses such as: my body is….restless, hungry, jittery, heavy, achy and, of course, tired; my mind is….jumpy, fuzzy, clear, busy, crazy.

Working through a mindfulness course with the children moves them gradually along the path to noticing the changes to their mind and body brought about by regular moments of stillness. Many of them begin to appreciate that taking the time to stop and pay attention in the moment, even for short two-minute sessions, can have a positive effect on how they feel and function. They then choose to do this more often or for longer.

Awareness of the ways in which thoughts (the language of the mind), emotions (the language of the body), the body itself and the mind all constantly interact can be really liberating for young people. They can see that a thought such as "my homework is late" or "my friend just ignored me" can cause a cascade of emotions and these can be felt in the body in a tense stomach, a tight chest or throat, rapid breathing, feeling hot. The brain does not know the difference between a thought and an actual event. When this sinks in, an entire class can feel like they are taking a breath of relief. When they understand that we all experience this, all the time, it empowers them to get better at noticing when it happens and to use interventions to help them feel better.

The autonomic nervous system was discussed earlier in this book. To remind you, it is the part of our nervous system that regulates the body's involuntary processes. These include the heart rate, blood pressure and respiration rate which will increase when we are in a stressful situation or have a stressful thought. The breath is the only part of the ANS that we can actively control which is why it is such a fundamental part of all mind/body practices. This means that when we use the breath consciously, we are able to create *physical coherence*. When the body is balanced and coherent, over 1,000 positive, subtle changes take place. We feel better. Children are brilliant at recognising this and almost always respond positively to the statement "mindfulness and/or yoga helps me feel calmer".

The exercises below are all ways in which to increase greater awareness of how the mind and body interact and the ways we can all influence the relationship to our benefit. Some of the exercises are based on mindfulness techniques that are tried and tested. Others are based on the ancient tradition of yoga nidra, sometimes called yogic sleep. It takes the body into the place between waking and sleep and can be deeply relaxing. I have used these for many years with children aged 4 upwards. The connection means that some exercises overlap between mind and body, of course. I have attempted to sort them into those most suited to calming the body in this chapter and those for calming the mind in the next, but I suggest reading through them all then selecting those you feel most appropriate for your family.

Beside each exercise, you will find a **C** and/or **A** to indicate the suitability for **c**hildren (5–12) or **a**dolescents (13+). Greater awareness of our inner world and the subtle ways our thoughts, emotions, feelings and actions inter-relate is incredibly empowering. Not least, is that understanding and knowing how to deal with worries and how to consciously relax will enable and improve sleep.

A Word of Caution

Not all children will respond to that switch of attention from their outer world to the inner and it is vital that children are *never* put under pressure. People of all ages who have experienced trauma can find that high levels of discomfort in the body become more extreme when focused on. This can be very distressing and we should never expose children or adolescents to unnecessary distress. Anyone who has experienced trauma should be supported by professionals. Another sign that these exercises may be unsuitable would be a child reporting feeling nothing or feeling numb. Discomfort is normal and mindfulness enables us to safely explore and sit with sometimes difficult feelings but if young people express *extreme discomfort* or *numbness* when engaging in these exercises, it should be a red flag to stop and seek help via a GP or school pastoral team or mental health helpline.

1. Checking In C, **A**

This simple exercise is a great way to start supporting your child to build awareness of how they are feeling; developing a language of emotion which will empower them and build self-regulation. It will also help them learn to recognise the difference between their mind and their body. This can be done with multiple children and they might enjoy doing it with siblings or friends. Do it yourself too! Teenagers enjoy this too but may be less forthcoming about what they recognise. If your teenager isn't keen to share what they notice, encourage them to write down their findings somewhere, perhaps in a journal. Again, the carrot for them is that Checking In enables greater awareness and understanding of their feelings.

- Choose a moment in the day when it is possible for your child to turn their focus inwards. Ideally, find a quiet place where they feel safe.

- Ask them first to focus outwards and tell you what they notice around them. Encourage them to use their senses: what they can hear, see, smell, feel, taste.
- Then explain you would like them to try turning their brilliant powers of observation inside for a moment or two. Suggest they close their eyes.
- Invite them to ask themselves the question: "how am I right now?" Allow them time to explore their inner world, encourage them to notice what's going on, to be curious.
- Once you've heard their response, explain you're going to invite more difficult questions now, do they feel up to the challenge? If they agree, ask them to return to closed eyes and check in again, this time asking "how is my body?" then "how is my mind?" Explain you just want one or two words for each. If they need some suggestions, you could offer words like heavy, bouncy, twitchy, clear, busy, achy.
- When they are ready to give feedback, have fun sharing the findings. How amazing it is that our body can be feeling one thing while our mind feels completely different!
- Repeat this often, make a game of it.

If your child frequently identifies that they feel *tired* in their mind or body, use the opportunity for a chat about how tiredness feels. Likewise, on a day they seem full of beans, ask them to Check In and see whether they can connect feeling energetic with feeling good. Try to enable them to make the link themselves and resist all urges to point out that their tiredness is linked to bedtime procrastination!

The same principle applies to adolescents. Ask your teenager open questions about tiredness and how it feels, what they notice in their mind and body. As with younger children, remove your judgement and approbation even when it is glaringly obvious that the reason they are yawning and have shadows under their eyes is they were thumping about the house far too late the night before and keeping everyone else awake. The aim is for them to work out *for themselves* that feeling tired is actually awful and that being well-rested feels a lot better. This enables them to make better choices and care better for themselves.

2. Body Scan: Tense and Relax **C, A**

A body scan is a really great way to calm the body before sleep and is best done lying in bed. There are several versions, and this is often the easiest for younger children to understand and enjoy although teenagers can find it very helpful too. To give it the best chance of success, run though the sleep hygiene tips in Chapters 3 and 5 (for teenagers) and make sure the bedroom and your child are completely ready. There's no point getting halfway through this and them leaping up remembering their maths homework isn't finished. The instructions are for an adult to lead a child through, but they can easily learn it for themselves once they know it works. Teens will be able to do it by themselves or using one of the many meditation apps (see Resources).

- Get comfortable lying down in bed, ideally on your back, and allow the eyes to softly close. Notice any twitchy feelings or whether the body is reluctant to lie still and wants to move about. Have a little wriggle then choose to stay still and see what happens next!
- Now tense all the muscles in your feet, feel the toes curl up, scrunch them together as tightly as you can, hold your feet and toes as stiff and tight as possible for a moment or two then RELAX them.
- Feel the feet and toes let go of all that tension. Notice how it feels now to let the muscles and the tendons become heavy and soft. You can make a soft "siggghhh" on your out-breath if you feel like it.
- Next, tense up all the muscles in both your legs from the ankles all the way up. Tighten those calves, shins, knees, the big strong thigh muscles, hold them all in as hard as you possibly can, hold it, hold it…and RELAX. Breathe out, ahhhh!
- Let go of your legs, all the way down to include the feet and toes. Everything feels heavy and relaxed and soft. Enjoy the sensation of the legs spreading out and resting after a long day of carrying you around.
- Move the focus upwards now to the tummy, bottom and lower back. Clench all those muscles as hard as possible, notice if your body rises up a little bit as you do this because you are squeezing so much. Hold it. Hold it tight. Then LET GO. Sigh as you release. Breathe out.
- Feel all the tension in the lower half of the body drain out now, downwards into the bed. Especially notice how the tummy feels as it

gets soft and heavy. We often hold worries there and it can feel really good to relax the whole area, letting it release and rest.

- Now, it's time to squeeze the chest, the upper back, the shoulders. Hunch those shoulders up as hard as you can, so they almost touch your ears. Suck in the ribs around the front and back of the chest. Notice if your breath changes as your lungs are compressed. Hold it for a moment, hold it...then let go and RELAX. Take a big, long breath in and an even longer sigh out again, letting everything soften.
- Feel the body from the neck down become very heavy and still and relaxed. Enjoy letting those hard-working muscles rest and release.
- Time to make fists from the hands now, screwing the fingers and thumbs as tightly as you can. Tense the muscles in the forearms, elbows, biceps and triceps. They have been working hard all day, make them do a little bit more now and hold everything in both arms as tightly and firmly as you can. Keep going. Then RELAX. Breathe out, feeling very heavy now.
- Let the fingers gently uncurl after that super-tight scrunch. Feel them floppy and heavy beside the body. Let all the muscles in the arms and tops of the shoulders become soft as they let go. They feel like they are melting into the bed.
- Finally, we move to the neck, face and head. Keeping the eyes tightly shut, screw up all the other muscles in the forehead, cheeks, nose, even the ears. See if you can tense up your scalp. Tighten the neck muscles. Hold this as hard as you can. Maybe your breath will change here too as the nose and throat get tight. Hold it.... hold it...then let go with a big breath out and a gentle sigh.
- As the head completely lets go of all tension, notice how heavy it is. Like a watermelon! Notice how soft and heavy the eyes feel, how even the ears are relaxed. The whole of the body now feels heavy, melting into the bed, feeling ready to rest after a long busy day. How nice it is not to have to do anything now, to be lazy, every out-breath making you a little bit heavier, a little bit sleepier.

It's quite likely your child will have dropped off before you finish! This happens when I have fully grown year 10s lying on a hard school floor, so a comfy bed should make it even easier. If they reach the whole of the body relaxing stage, you can encourage them to let each out-breath, make the muscles even heavier, even more relaxed.

3. Balloon Belly C

This is a repetition of the exercise recommended in Chapter 4 where we discussed ways to introduce mindfulness to your child. It is especially good for young children and is simple to learn and repeat. A few elements have been added to make it useful for doing in bed before sleep.

- Lie down and get the body really comfortable. It might take a few moments to find the best position so take whatever time it needs.
- Close the eyes and place the hands on the tummy. Take a big deep breath in, imagining the tummy is a balloon that is filling up with air. Notice what happens to the hands as you do this. Breathe out again steadily, letting the balloon empty. See where the hands are now.
- Let the breath come in and out softly, gently, without forcing or controlling it. The hands rise and fall quietly as the balloon fills up then becomes floppy and empty.
- Each time the balloon empties notice that the whole of the tummy and chest is feeling very heavy and sinking down into the bed.
- The whole of the body gradually becomes heavier and more still with every breath. Enjoy the feeling of resting, not doing anything, just gently drifting like waves lapping on the beach.
- If the hands or tummy feel very tired now, they can rest beside the body instead and the attention can move to wherever the breath can be most easily felt. It might be in the chest, rising and falling softly. It might be in the nose, cool on the way in and warm on the way out. It might be in the throat. Wherever the breath is, just stay there and enjoy the rhythm. Our breath is like a friend, always there with us and keeping us company as we gently drift into lovely peaceful sleep.

Visualisation Game

Lots of the exercises in these final chapters ask children to imagine or visualise things. This is a powerful tool, and children are often much better at it than adults. The following game is fun to try with all the family and enables the participants to see just how powerful their imagination can be—that it actually influences what the body does. One person sits comfortably in a supportive chair while the person reading the instructions sits near them and talks them through the game. The instructions are for the person reading to say aloud:

- Close your eyes and see if you can become nice and still.
- Breathe in and out gently, noticing how the body rises and falls with the breath. See if you can feel the rhythm.
- Now stretch both your arms out straight in front of you at shoulder level, without opening the eyes. The palms can face downwards and the hands can be loose and relaxed.
- Now imagine that there is a very heavy shopping bag on one wrist. It might have potatoes in it or a big bag of flour. Try and visualise the heavy bag.
- Now imagine attached to the other wrist is a big shiny balloon, light and floating straight up in the air.
- Open your eyes now and look at your arms!

What almost always happens is that one of the arms has moved downwards while the other has drifted upwards. It should amaze the person whose eyes have been closed as they will not have noticed the tiny movements, but you can assure them that the simple power of their imagination, their visualisation has made this change. They can use this power in lots of the exercises to help them relax, feel good and sleep well.

4. Petal Breathing C, A

This exercise was also covered in Chapter 4 but it is useful before sleep as a way of making that connection between the mind and the body. When the little acupressure points in the fingertips meet, a feeling of calmness can be induced.

It is sometimes used with adults and children in Cognitive Behavioural Therapy (CBT). It can be done before getting into bed or when lying down but you may find the sitting version works as a precursor to getting into bed, especially if the child is reluctant to go to bed yet, there is some procrastination going on or claims of being "not tired".

- Sit comfortably or lie back in bed with the hands resting loosely on your lap or thighs or on the bed beside you. Turn the palms upwards.
- Now, imagine the fingers of each hand are like the petals of a flower. As you breathe in, open the petals up to the light and spread the fingers wide. Keep them soft!
- As the breath goes out again, slowly bring the fingertips together softly, like the petals of the flower closing for the night.
- Keep breathing gently in and out and match the movement of the fingers to the breath, open and closed. See if you can get the fingertips to meet exactly at the moment the breath is fully in or fully out. See if both hands can move exactly at the same time. See if you can feel that the whole body is breathing, working together. Feeling calm and relaxed with every breath.

5. Grow the Happy Feeling C, A

This exercise links in with Checking In and starts with finding a positive thought, which is then deliberately extended throughout the body and can lead to feelings of wellbeing and peace. It is particularly good for children who worry about having bad dreams. It is natural for worries and fears to surface at bedtime, as discussed in Chapter 4, so setting the intention to sleep well and have good dreams can really help. If you do this regularly with your child, you might even notice that they start "collecting" good memories to use for this bedtime exercise. It is a powerful tool for enhancing wellbeing and looking for the good things that happen to us that might just slip by without us noticing.

Teenagers can seem to have an in-built resistance to positive thinking. This can be expressed by their scathing dismissal of any suggestion that they focus on the good things in life! As we know from Chapter 5, their brains are wired during adolescence to grab hold of negative thoughts, while the good thoughts can slip off. Helping them understand that this is normal and not their fault can be empowering for them. In fact, it is a tendency of many adults too and goes back to the ancient parts of our brain that are wired to ensure our survival, always looking for danger and threats. This means that we all, including our teenagers, need to make that little bit of extra effort to encourage the good thoughts and, especially before sleep, to nurture and grow them. So, this exercise may need to be adjusted depending on the age of your child. Try sharing with your teenager that scientific research has been done linking positive thinking with increased levels of happiness and wellbeing. They should be able to do this exercise for themselves. At its heart is the connection between happy thoughts and good feelings and how to consciously maintain this, rather than allow the thoughts to do what they tend to: slip away to get replaced by a worry.

- Once comfortable in bed, close the eyes and turn the attention inwards, away from the busy day you've had. See if you can connect to your breathing, letting the chest and tummy slowly rise and fall.
- See if you can find a really happy memory! Remember a time when you felt contented, felt a warm glow inside. Maybe a time you had fun with friends or when you did something you were super proud of. Maybe a time when you did something nice with your family and you felt happy and safe and loved. Maybe cuddling a pet or a grandparent. It might be a very simple memory of watching a movie with people you love or opening a wonderful present at Christmas or on your birthday. [Be careful your child doesn't get carried away with excitement at the memory—we're looking for a contented, happy, calm memory!]
- Remember as much as you can about the special time. Try and see it in your mind. Notice where you were, what the people around you were doing, maybe what the weather was like. See if you can remember again how happy you felt. Find that happy feeling in your body, notice what it's like and where you can sense it.
- Now tune into where that happy feeling is and imagine that it is a warm, bright light. The light is glowing and you can feel it in your body, maybe it is in your heart or in your tummy. Notice how light and bright it is, maybe it is yellow or orange.
- Every time you breathe in, you can make that light glow a little bit brighter, a little bit warmer. See if you can feel it gently getting bigger and brighter. Notice how nice it feels.

- Now see if you can make your warm golden light get a little bit bigger so that it fills the whole of your chest and tummy. Notice how warm it feels, perhaps like golden syrup swirling around you or warm soft sand beneath you.
- See if you can breathe in again and allow the light to get even bigger and brighter and warmer so that it expands to fill up your legs, your shoulders, all the way down to your fingers and your toes.
- The next time you breathe in you can let the light run upwards into your head, into your face and eyes and even your ears. The happy memory is everywhere now, filling you up, lighting up your whole body. Every tiny cell in your body is bright and light and glowing.
- You can decide now to have lovely dreams, take this happy peaceful feeling with you into your sleep, knowing when you wake up in the morning you will feel great.

6. Antar Mouna C, A

This is an ancient yoga practice, meaning Inner Silence, and is a technique that harnesses the power of the sense organs. In adult yoga, it is a complex practice forming part of the core aspects of yoga philosophy. I have adapted it for use with children because it's a quick and effective way to draw their attention inwards and enable their bodies to calm and relax, but adults will be able to enjoy this too. For children who don't enjoy the more physical processes of relaxation in the Body Scan or Tense and Relax exercises, this achieves the same end, but the mind has a specific sense-related task to keep busy with while the body comes to a natural still point. As much of the focus is on what can be heard, it doesn't work so well when there is a lot of noise either in the house or environment so I wouldn't suggest choosing this if you live beside a busy road or next door has their music on full volume.

The version below is to be read to younger children but you can share it with older children who might be interested to learn more about it online or follow a guided version on an app. Teenagers will be able to apply the same sequence of moving through the senses by themselves and may want to experiment with doing them in a different order—make sure the practice always ends up with hearing though as that links through to listening to the sounds in the body and heart.

- Once ready for bed get as comfy as you can and prepare to use your super sensory powers. Start off with some gentle breathing to find a still place so you can focus while relaxing.
- With the eyes open gently notice what is around you. Look closely at parts of the room you might normally not bother with. Any cracks or marks on the walls. The corners. Where the walls meet the ceiling. Notice any shadows. What colours can you see? Notice if any object grabs your attention but choose to just stay looking carefully without needing to do anything or say anything. Turn your eyes up to the ceiling now and try to keep them open for a few more moments. Notice that they are feeling very heavy now and it's time to give them a rest. Softly close the eyes. Notice any shapes or lights you can see behind the eyelids. Let the sense of looking go.
- Allow your sense of taste to go to work. Are there any flavours in your mouth? Toothpaste? Perhaps you can feel its mintiness in your nose too, or on your tongue, behind your teeth. Allow the sense of taste to get bigger. Then let it rest as well.
- Smell power next. Imagine your nose is like a dog's, super-sensed to pick up everything. What can you smell? Soap or shower gel maybe? Washing powder on your sheets or nightclothes? Perhaps an outside smell if the window is open or food smells coming in from other parts of the house. Where is the smelling happening? Is it in your nose or your throat, what does it feel like? Let that go now.
- Time now to notice all the things you can feel against your body. So, maybe the pillow under your head or the duvet resting on you. How heavy is it? Can you feel your nightclothes anywhere on your body, maybe around the ankles or wrists or neck? Notice all the points of contact between your body and the bed. Are there places that aren't touching the bed? What can your toes feel? The soles of your feet. Perhaps you can feel a soft movement of air on your face, your lips, your ears, nose? Notice any tiny feelings of touch. Then let them go.
- Last super-sense power—hearing. See if you can stretch your hearing like a bat or an owl so you can hear all the sounds that are coming from *outside* the room. Listen for them as they arise and then fall away. Is there silence between noises or is there always a buzzy noise? Are there voices? Barks? Music? Cars? Birds? Listen to them all, for as far as your

hearing can stretch. Then let that go and bring your attention to the sounds you can hear *inside* the room. Perhaps a light bulb quietly fizzing or a clock ticking. Can you hear any sounds caused by a breeze in the room or by anyone else? Finally, bring that hearing down to just notice the sounds inside your own body. You will have to listen really carefully now. Can you hear your breathing in your nose or throat or your chest? Can you hear a pulse anywhere, gently ticking away? Can you hear your heartbeat?

- Even if you can't hear your heartbeat, you might be able to feel it, so see if you can tune into it. Clever heart, beating away all day and all night. Your heart. Perhaps you can feel that heartbeat now growing a bit wider, taking up more space in your body, in your room. It is warm and comforting and you can rest in it, keeping you company while you drift off to sleep.

7. Yoga Nidra — C, A

This is another ancient yogic practice and it enables the body to get to that lovely drifty place in-between sleep and waking and works by giving the mind something to do while the body settles into a deep place of relaxation. When adults are guided through it by an experienced teacher, they are encouraged to keep the mind alert, as my dear yoga teacher says, "I am awake, I am alert, I am practising yoga nidra." For children, however, we are encouraging sleep, and this makes an effective precursor which many will enjoy and find helpful. It is suitable for children of all ages. Once adolescents have learnt how to do this and are finding it useful, they will be able to do it by themselves. If you are reading this aloud to your child while they lie in bed, read through the named parts of the body reasonably quickly. Unlike the body scan, we don't want to dwell on the areas named but allow the mind to hop lightly from one to the next. Adults will be able to find a guided version online and give it a go too.

- Lie back in bed and get comfy and gently close the eyes. Know that yoga nidra is a friend to relaxation and rest. Ask yourself, "can I be a little more comfy?" Make any adjustments so the body feels as comfortable as possible.

- Start by opening up the senses. See what you can taste, perhaps the toothpaste still in your mouth. What can you hear? Listening with superpower ears to the sounds outside the bedroom then to the sounds inside the room. Can you smell anything? Notice the touch of the bedclothes on the body and feel the bed underneath you. Maybe you can feel the air temperature on your skin. Switch to internal vision and rest the eyes.
- Notice the breath, not controlling it, see if you can feel the whole body breathing. Notice the rhythm, like the tide gently coming in and out. Every time you breathe out, count backwards from 10 down to zero. On each out-breath notice that you are easily able to feel more relaxed and more still, more quiet.
- I am going to name parts of the body now. When I do, gently touch your attention to the area, like the light of a star softly resting on it for a moment. Starting with the right hand, palm, back of the hand, wrist, elbow, shoulder, the soft space at the throat, right side of the chest, tummy, hip, right thigh, knee, ankle, top of the right foot, sole, toes. Then up to the left hand palm, back of the hand, wrist, elbow, shoulder, the soft space at the throat, left side of the chest, tummy, hip, left thigh, knee, ankle, top of the left foot, sole, toes. Both legs together. The whole of the tummy, whole of the chest, soft space at the throat. Neck, chin, lips, nose, tip of the nose, right cheek, ear, right eye, eyebrow, space between the eyebrows, left cheek, ear, left eye, eyebrow, space between the eyebrows, the hair. Whole of the head. Whole of the body.
- The whole of the body feels heavy now. Can you feel how heavy the whole body is? The bones, muscles, tendons, organs feel so heavy. The whole body supported by the bed. Let the feeling go.
- The whole of the body now feels light. Can you feel lightness, like you might float upwards? Let the light feeling go.
- Can you notice that when you breathe out now the body feels heavy, limbs floppy and weighed down? When you breathe in, the body feels light and floaty. Move between sensations of heaviness and lightness as you gently breathe. Then let go of that.
- See if you can feel your heartbeat, slow and steady, the whole body resting and welcoming sleep. Perhaps you feel a bit like water is gently lapping through the whole body like waves coming in on the beach,

notice the rhythm. Just being. Nothing to do, nowhere to go, nothing to want.

- Find that little star again and let its soft light move into the heart space behind the breastbone. Feel it light up, know that you can fall into it, safe and warm and comfortable, resting the whole body, ready for a wonderful peaceful sleep.

8. Stretch and Relax C, A

All parents and carers know that when children and adolescents have been physically inactive during the day, they are less able to drop off to sleep at night so it's a no-brainer to try and ensure that their bodies get a good dose of exercise at some point in the day. Weekends and school holidays can be a challenge, especially if your teenager only emerges at lunchtime and or when children plead tiredness after a busy week. Sleep needs to be prioritised for everyone's mental, physical and emotional wellbeing and much has been said already about shifts in the circadian rhythm of adolescents that cause them to sleep later whenever they can. So, I am not advocating hoofing everyone out of bed on a Saturday morning for a bootcamp. Some gentle yoga at the end of the day, however, can be a perfect preparation for a good night's sleep and you can sell it to your footballer or rugby player child by sharing with them that many national and international teams have a yoga coach. Any gym bunnies will feel the benefit of stretching newly-created muscles, and aligning the body. Yoga restores the mind/body balance bringing coherence, while stretching out the body enables it to better relax and rest at the end of the day.

Try the following stretches together before bed. Refer back to the bedtime routine in Chapter 3 to see where this might fit in best for your family. Doing the stretches together in a communal room in the house as a family might be great fun or it might work better to do them one-to-one in your child's bedroom if there is space.

Anyone with disabilities may need adaptations of these stretches, such as using a wall for support during any balances, so make adjustments or just choose the ones that seem to work best.

Adolescents may have learnt some yoga at school or college and be willing to try a short routine before bed. Many of them spend their evenings hunched over homework or over their phones which is not great for the back, shoulder and neck—all places where tension is often stored in the body. If you can encourage them to experiment with these stretches, they may notice that it is easier to sleep following a release of this tension and be encouraged to learn a bit more yoga themselves in a class or online. Adult body tension is almost always in the neck, shoulders and lower back, so these exercises will help release those areas. These stretches are all simple ones designed to move the spine in different directions, increasing flexibility and gently building strength.

Yoga goes really well with most other sports and can improve performance for dancers, gymnasts, footballers, tennis players and surfers. As with all mindful movement, never over-stretch the body or ask it to do more than it is ready to at the given moment, and ease off or stop if anything hurts. The list below may look quite time-consuming but I have done it hundreds of times with children of all ages and it takes about 10 minutes. Adults and older children may want to do a longer version on their own once they have got the hang of it and can adapt it to the demands of their day and how they are feeling in the moment—learning to understand that we are always changing and that our needs vary from day to day is a great lesson in self-care.

- Ensure there is enough space to stretch without bumping into any furniture. You don't need a special mat although that can be quite nice to create a focus and intention. Wear loose clothes, nightwear is ideal as we're not going to get sweaty, just stretchy! And bed can follow on easily.
- *Mountain Pose to full body stretch*—start with feeling the feet, hip-width apart, on the floor, connecting downwards. Breathing in deeply bring the body into alignment, feeling like a string is pulling the crown of the head gently upwards. Allow the chest to rise and the lungs to expand with every in-breath. Notice the ribs lift and fall. Drop the shoulders and relax them. Check the face is soft and relaxed. Stand tall like a mountain. Take a few breaths then sweep the arms out to the sides and up over the head. Stretch the fingertips up to the ceiling. Stretch another millimetre taller. Hold it…then bring the arms down and relax.
- *Floppy Monkey*—move the feet slightly wider apart, keeping them steady and connected to the ground, arms loose at the sides. Fold slowly over at the waist until the whole upper body is floppy while the legs remain strong. If the hands reach the floor, hold the elbows and release

all tension in the head, neck and shoulders. You can gently swing from side to side to loosen up the hips and back of the legs. Older children may want to place their hands on the floor or hold onto the ankles or feet—hold this stretch for a few breaths then relax, taking the elbows in each hand, and swaying gently if not already done. Come up out of this very slowly, uncurling and building the spine up again vertebrae by vertebrae, chin to chest, until the last thing to come up is the head. Stand tall again for a few breaths.

- *Spaghetti Swing*—with the feet slightly wider than hip-width keep the lower body still while rotating slowly from side to side, the feet connected to the ground. The movement here is all in the waist/hips as you look over each shoulder. The arms and hands are soft, like cooked spaghetti, and float gently out from the body as you swing. This rotation of the spine is one of the most effective ways to release tension in the hips, waist, shoulders and neck. Keep it gentle and discourage any wild flailing!
- *Rainbow Arms*—standing still with feet still hip-width stretch one arm straight up in the air, palm facing inwards, fingertips gently stretched. Slowly bend in the direction of the palm, making a long straight curve up the side of the body. Don't stretch too far or too hard, just a gentle movement. Try to keep the hips and lower body still. You can do this a few times or some children might like to hold each stretch for a breath or two. Repeat on the other side then relax.
- *Gentle Back Bend*—keeping feet as above, place the palms on the back of the hips or lower back. Gently draw the elbows together which will push the chest forward and out and move the shoulder blades closer to each other. Tuck the chin down towards the chest to avoid any strain at all on the neck and arch the back, keeping the hands in place to support the back as it gently bends. If your child has any problem with their back or neck, do this with great care and watch out for any balance issues. Keeping the movement small and soft and slow should be enjoyable and allow tension in the shoulders and back to release. Don't hold it for more than a breath or two then slowly come back to the mountain pose.
- *Cat Stretches*—these feel fantastic, especially after the standing exercises above and should make a welcome move downwards now onto the carpet, rug or mat. Come onto all-fours with the hands underneath

the shoulders and the knees under the hips. Let the feet be flat and floppy. Take a moment to settle the body into this neutral position and check the elbows aren't hyperextended (some children have a natural tendency to do this, but it puts pressure on the elbows and should be avoided; they can slightly bend the elbows if this is happening). On the next in-breath drop the spine by moving the tummy down towards the floor, lift the chin upwards. Think of a happy cat arching its back. Breathing out turns us into an angry cat as the back arches upwards now, tummy lifting up and away from the ground and the chin rolls down into the chest. Follow the breath in and out, curving the spine downwards and upwards, from happy cat to angry cat. Younger children might enjoy a little "miaow." You can add in a favourite in my classes: disco cat. This is where we move from neutral to gently swinging the head and hips one way then the other. It's quite tricky to explain but children instinctively seem to know how to do this and it can be fun. Don't do too many!

- *Downward Dog*—older children will enjoy this but younger ones might have had enough by now so you can skip this and move to Child's Pose below. For the keen beans, they can move from their neutral cat position into downward dog by spreading their fingers wide, ideally pointing forwards and flat on the floor, tucking their toes under and pushing the hips upwards straightening the legs. Push away with the hands and allow the head and neck to be floppy and relaxed. This will give the shoulders, hamstrings and calves a lovely deep stretch but don't overdo it or hold for long. If you've had success with this posture and your child is looking for an extra challenge, you can add in the ever-popular "dog doing a wee" where they lift one leg up, bend at the knee and open out the hip like a dog cocking a leg on a tree. Repeat the other side. For less frivolous teenagers, you can call it a hip-opener.
- *Child's Pose*—finish by returning to the neutral cat posture and, on an out-breath bend the knees and allow the bottom to rest down on the back of the legs. Sweep the arms round to the sides, turn the palms upward, allow the forehead to rest on the ground and relax. Staying in this quiet posture, tune into the breath. Notice how this feels. Allow each breath to bring the mind and body together, calming and resting. Ready for sleep.

Sport and Exercise

All schools and colleges have a PE curriculum that is hopefully varied and engaging. This will vary from school to school. Not all children are "sporty", and it is common for primary school children to feel less enthusiastic about sports as they move upwards through the system. Schools that promote a competitive culture can bring out the best in some children but this can be a major turn-off for others. Competitive sports bring pressures too and children can get anxious about upcoming races or matches—keep an eye on this and judge whether competing is causing your child more stress than enjoyment. Young people have enough pressures on them as it is without taking something as potentially life-affirming and enjoyable as exercise and turning it into an ordeal. Speak to their teacher or coach if you have concerns and be honest about any pressure you may be inadvertently applying. Talk to your child and listen carefully to their responses.

As a parent, it can be a challenge to keep your child participating in exercise as they get older and move through the school system, but the key is to find something they enjoy doing and to look for ways to build in exercise that can keep them fit and healthy as well as improve the quality of their sleep. It sounds obvious but if you take a moment to think about simple enjoyment of exercise you might recall pleasure you have taken yourself in running or cycling or swimming or whatever exercise you took that made your heart beat faster and filled you with exhilaration and delight in your own body and what it could do. Connecting to this, feeling good in our bodies is a basic in-road to happiness and wellbeing.

So, when our kids tell us they love the feeling of skateboarding or whacking a ball as hard as they can, we need to listen and honour that. Exercise comes with a great freebie too—the sense of wellbeing lasts beyond the exercise itself as our bodies are flooded with post-exercise endorphins. Research shows that exercise boosts our mood because it fundamentally changes the brain both in the moment and over time.

You will recall there is a connection between daylight and the production of melatonin—the hormone that signals we are ready for sleep. Melatonin levels need to build during the daytime, and we know exposure to sunlight plays an important role. To give you an idea of how much this matters, we can compare sunlight with electric light using lux, the unit employed in the measurement of light. On a sunny day, light can be measured at 100,000 lux. By comparison, even with all the electric lights on indoors, levels are only likely to read 300–500 lux. Getting children and adolescents outdoors really makes a difference when building healthy sleep patterns.

As with all things parenting, modelling positive attitudes to exercise yourself will really help, maybe examining your own activity levels. If you are not someone who joined Joe Wickes during lockdown or did a couch to 5k challenge, consider ways you can exercise with your child in a fun way. A simple walk rather than taking the bus or driving might do the job. When looking for the right activity for you or your child, look around your local area and talk to other parents or school staff about suitable activities in the community. It doesn't have to be conventional or costly—a drama group generally involves fun movement with others; a community choir has people on their feet and breathing deeply to create a beautiful sound. Joining an environmental group might be the way in for teenagers interested in helping preserve nature and will get them outdoors and feeling useful. Keep it regular and simple and aim for a dose of fresh air and exercise each day while not beating yourself up over the odd duvet day.

9. Grounding and Centring C, A

This set of yoga exercises is less about releasing tension in the body through movement of the spine, and more about grounding adults and children whose difficulty sleeping may be to do with having excess energy and who struggle to be still. I come across children like this all the time and always aim for very small improvements while accepting how difficult it might be for them. For many children, their attention is always focused outwards; they are stimulated by noise and activity all day long at school, possibly having long days and a hectic schedule. For some neurodiverse children, a lot of noise and stimulation can cause a sensory overload as they struggle to process everything. Adults will be focused outwards too for much of the day with demands of work and family so, if you find yourself jittery and over-scheduled, these grounding exercises will help you too. Finding time before bed to clear that overload, come into a still place and calm the body down will help with falling asleep and getting that much-needed good night's sleep.

You can fit these exercises into the bedtime routine in the same way as for the stretch routine above, but the focus is on connecting the body and mind to the ground and turning the attention inwards. It should feel comforting and, when used regularly, support emotional regulation and self-care. For adults and older children, learning to ground yourself is an invaluable skill that can help us cope with the emotional rollercoaster of adult and teenage life and get familiar with the feeling of returning to the self, to the centre, in spite of all the ups and downs.

- Choose the best time and location for this routine, experiment if necessary to find what works best. If an after-school meltdown is common in your house, you could try doing these when you are all home together rather than wait until bedtime.
- Start by sitting down, ideally with bare feet or just socks on. Locate the K1 acupressure points in the feet. You will find these in the centre of the foot, just down from the ball of the foot. Give them a gentle massage. You can do this for your child if they are not too ticklish, or help them find the points them rub them themselves. Explain these are the grounding points in the body that enable them to connect with the earth below. See if you can breathe calmly while doing this and notice any sensations in the toes as you rub the K1s.
- Standing up next, start in *mountain pose* (above), standing tall with the shoulder blades sliding down the back and the upper body soft. Take some breaths. See if you can still feel those K1 points in your feet. Imagine that you are breathing in and out through them, downwards through the body, through the feet and deep into the ground below. Perhaps imagine they are like magnets, keeping the body steady and drawn to the earth.
- Start to gently sway from side to side, keeping the breathing going through the feet and not allowing the sides of the feet to lift up. Come back to centre and notice how easy it is now to stay still and tall.
- *Toe-ga* when breathing in next move gently up onto tiptoe. See if you can hold it there before slowly lowering the feet on the out-breath. Try lifting all the toes up and moving the balance backwards onto the heels. Return to centre, each time noticing that connection with the ground. Notice all the tiny adjustments your body and feet make to keep you steady and upright—our clever proprioceptors are sending messages to

the brain whenever we move. Lift all the toes up again, trying spreading them as wide as you can before placing them down again. Lift just the big toes, leaving the others on the ground. Now leave the big toes on the ground and see if you can lift the other toes. For the ultimate toe-ga challenge, trying lifting all the toes up, spread them, then place the big and littlest toe down while leaving the others up. Warning—this can make your brain hurt!

- *Tree Pose*—start with both feet flat, then slowly shift the balance across to one of the feet. Feel the breath go down through that foot, like the roots of a tree holding on firmly to the ground. Gently lift the other foot up and turn the knee slightly out to the side. If the foot only rests on the other foot, that is totally fine, but some children will be able to place the foot above or below the knee. Others might be able to bring it up to their thigh. The key is to find the balance point and try to keep steady. It helps to find a *drishti,* or focus for the eyes, such as a point on the floor to look at and avoid looking around the room. Once steady, the hands can come upwards and either move outwards like the branches of a tree or keep the palms softly pressed together at the heart centre or up above the crown of the head. Hold this for a few breaths then come out of it steadily rather than falling out of it. Repeat on the other side. Notice if one side was easier than the other side. If you do this regularly, notice if some days are "good balancing days" while other days it seems much harder. Anyone finding balancing tricky can do this while using a wall or chair for support.

10. Dream Buster C

This exercise is for children worried about having bad dreams and it sets the intention for a good night's sleep and happy dreams. Whether or not you are a fan of the law of attraction, it is clear to most people that what we expect to happen frequently does. A child fearing they will have bad dreams can easily become upset and worried at bedtime. So, it is no surprise when they appear later that night needing comfort after a bad dream and upsetting their own and their parents' sleep. A cycle of interrupted sleep and reluctance to go to bed can wreak havoc in families and seem impossible to break. This exercise is worth a try if you have found yourself in a situation like this.

For children who have experienced trauma, a more complex response is required and professional help may be needed. Use some of the tools in the following chapter designed to calm the mind alongside this one. The first few times you do this, have an empty loo roll insert and a handful of tissues or loo paper as a useful prop. After they have got the hang of it, you probably won't need it but it's a really helpful visual aid. I have indicated that this is more suitable for younger children because a more sophisticated version for adolescents can be found in the next chapter, but you can adapt it to suit.

- A good positive bedtime routine is a prerequisite here: a wind-down period from the day, preferably without screentime, followed by a warm bath or shower, a story and a transfer to a comfy sleeping place where the lights are low and the atmosphere calm.
- Without bringing up the subject of sleep yet, get comfy with your child for a few minutes, chatting together. Ask them to think of three things that happened that day they feel good about or grateful for. This might be a fun playtime with a friend, scoring a goal, drawing a picture or getting a compliment from a teacher or friend. If they struggle to come up with three, you can help by praising them for something they may have done at home such as being kind to a sibling or pet, helping you or doing something you asked them to do. Explain how grateful you are to them for making you laugh or giving you a hand. If the list is going on a bit don't worry, watch them carefully for signs of positivity and happiness. Ask how it feels. Show your own pleasure and happiness too. Good time for a hug.
- Then switch the focus onto other people. Regardless of what religion you practice as a family, if any, we can send the focus of our good wishes, our blessings, to other people. See if they can identify three people or groups of people they would like to bless or thank. Your child might choose to bless a friend or teacher or family member who is poorly at the moment. You can wish them well together. They might send a blessing to all the dogs in the world, all the fish in the sea or the birds in the sky. They might bless all the people who care for the gardens, woods and beaches. Or the people who keep the streets clean or cook their favourite take-out. One of my sons loved this when he was little and once blew me away by blessing all the people in the world who create

and make music. They could bless their favourite author or YouTuber or sportsperson. You can listen and add your good wishes, or you can choose your own recipients. Never underestimate the power of blessing. Ask how it feels to do this.

- Hopefully, your child will be feeling good now. Take your cardboard loo roll inner and loosely push some crumpled loo paper down into it. Explain that this loo roll is like their brain and inside are any worries about bad dreams. Turn it so it's vertical and start to push extra bits of tissue up inside it, explaining that these are all the positive thoughts about themselves and the other people that they've just had. Every time they think a happy thought, it fills up their brain. As you add more from the bottom some of the original tissue will start to pop up out of the top. Explain that the positive happy thoughts push all the worries out of the way until there is no more room for them and the only thoughts in the loo roll/brain are good ones. There's lots of room for creativity with this—using different coloured tissues to represent the negative and positive thoughts or using newspaper (pre-prepared) for the negative thoughts that get forced out by the white or coloured tissues. You are showing your child how to displace negativity and worry with positivity and good feelings.
- Now that their brains are full of positive thoughts and feelings, it's a good time to reassure them that they will have happy dreams tonight and wake up feeling great. Talk about the dreams they would like to have—flying over the sea, playing under a rainbow, meeting a mermaid or a superhero, scoring the winning touchdown at Twickenham. Ask them for details of whatever dream they come up with—what are you wearing? What's it like there? How does that feel?
- Congratulate them for the wonderful night's sleep they are going to have now and the magical dreams that are just waiting for them to fall asleep. If a child persists in believing their dreams are going to be bad, show them the loo roll again and find another positive thought to push that one out. Explain that there is no room for anything negative now and they've done a brilliant job resetting their brain. If the middle of the night or the morning bring tales of a bad dream, continue to offer comfort, of course, and just try again the next night until you have a breakthrough.

Chapter 8
Mind Calm: Mindfulness and Relaxation Techniques for the Mind

The reasons many young people give for not having had sufficient sleep can include procrastination and having too much to fit in before they are able to get to bed, but commonly reported are a restless body and a busy mind. Chapter 7 offered a selection of exercises to help the body come into a still place prior to sleep. We know that the mind and body are linked in the most extraordinary ways across neural, hormonal and sensory circuits, meaning one is always affecting the other. The set of exercises in this chapter is more angled to the "mind" side of the equation and aims to help children and adolescents who find their mind still whirring away at the end of the day. It offers ways to help the mind release worry, process events of the day and become calm. Adults can use them too, of course.

If a child has had a very busy day, and this is most days for the average child, sometimes it is not until they actually stop at bedtime that worries arise. This makes bedtime frustrating in many households; knowing your child needs to go to sleep but that they need to get things off their chest first. As I have said, my teenagers always seemed to want to engage in a heart-to-heart round about midnight on a Sunday. It's not just children, however: emotional issues for all of us frequently pop up when the busy day is over, the phone's on charge, the washing up done and the cat put out. Perhaps we all have too much to do in our modern lives? Perhaps there are not enough moments in the day to quietly reflect and process what's going on for us?

For many of us, our commitments and responsibilities demand the majority of our waking hours. How precious do those activity-free moments sometimes feel—waiting for the kettle to boil or queuing up to pay for something? A core aspect of mindfulness is understanding *non-doing*: that when we are still and quiet even for a few minutes, we are not *doing*, we are *being*. Crucially for tired children, it is during moments of being, and not doing, that emotions and thoughts arise that need processing before the day is over. When I have a day of running from one commitment to the next with no downtime or even time to grab more than a sandwich on the hoof, I find I collapse at the end of the day and feel utterly drained. The thought of repeating the same the next day can fill me with dread. So, I try to avoid days like that as much as I can and value each precious minute of non-doing I can ringfence for myself.

Yes, my ideal way to relax and have some "me time" is a luxurious hot bubble bath with candles but there's fat chance of that some days and I have to grab it while sitting in traffic or even staying in the loo for an extra few moments! Luckily, with a bit of practice, a minute is all it needs to reset—as you will see in exercise 1 below.

Tips for Families on Less Doing, More Being

In today's rush, we all think too much seek too much—want too much—and forget about the joy of just being.

Eckhart Tolle

Families who play together stay together, says the old adage which may or may not have any truth to it. I am more likely to advocate that families who relax together find life easier and more enjoyable, so the following tips are about doing nothing as a deliberate choice—and noticing what happens when you do.

- Squash your urge to fill time with activities and stimulation for your children—try building into the day empty times that contrast with those planned activities.
- A bored child is (eventually) a creative child—you are not an entertainment machine. Giving children free time to fill on their own helps them connect with their creative side and they will soon find something, often quite random, to play with. Let them be.
- Allow silence into your house by resisting the need to talk and fill the gaps. Home is a safe place where polite (or not) conversation isn't required. We can resist silence by having background noise from TV

or radio. Turn it all off now and again. Children who learn to be comfortable with their own and others' silence are being given a gift that will stand them in good stead as they grow. Silence is where we connect with ourselves. Adolescents in my mindfulness sessions frequently share how surprised they are to find they actually enjoy the "strong silence" created. Strong silence is a silence we choose rather than one imposed on us, it can be empowering and pleasurable.

- Try not to label non-doing as a "waste of time". The teenager who lounges about for hours seemingly doing nothing is comfortable in their own space and head, which is a precious thing, to be valued and not judged or dismissed as laziness.
- If you are someone who "can't be doing nothing" or likes to be "always busy", reflect on why that is. Were you taught this way of being by your parents? Experiment yourself with some of the practices below. Non-doing is a gift you can give yourself too and enables you to model that healthy behaviour for your children. "Mummy/Daddy, what are you doing?" "Nothing! I am just being," is a great conversation to have. Many societies across the globe value "busyness" above all else because of its links to productivity. It can seem like a virtue—to be bustling about all day long completing tasks from the to-do list, contributing to the world and lives of others. This is all vitally important, of course, and things would grind to a sorry halt if we all stopped our doing but, like everything in our lives, it needs balancing with resting, refreshing, replenishing. Check your being-doing balance and take care of yourself.
- Give yourselves permission, as a family, to loaf about together doing nothing and be comfortable with this non-doing. Resist the urge to relax only when the last dish has been put away or the place is tidy. Flopping onto the sofa when there are still jobs to do isn't a dereliction of duty or a disaster: teaching your kids the value of rest and relaxation is vital for their health and wellbeing as well as your own.

1. My Minute **C, A**

All mindfulness techniques have at their heart this regular practice in one form or another. I find that asking children whether they reckon they can sit still for a whole minute provokes a chorus of "yeeeesss, of course I can!" but if I wait a little longer after asking, the odd doubt arises. They glance at each other. It's not something they are often asked to try. Hmmm...perhaps it might be more difficult after all? Together we think about what might make it easier: being comfortable first, being away from distractions, including each other, turning the lights down. And then we give it a go. When we choose to sit in silence, tune into our breath and our body, we quickly bring our brains into coherence. This rewires our neural networks, bringing our heart and mind into harmony. Even if it's just a single minute, the change takes place.

Whatever the situation in your family, building in time during a day for a minute of silence is preventative in terms of bedtime dramas; like letting steam out slowly rather than it building up and exploding out later. Helping children learn to do a My Minute is a tool they can later build on and is not, crucially, a punishment like a "time-out" for poor behaviour so make sure it's always a positive and enjoyable experience. This way they will choose to do it by themselves at the time and place they most need it. Adolescents can be encouraged to sit for longer but a simple My Minute at the right moment is a surprisingly powerful tool for emotional regulation and resilience. Adults should love this, make it a positive choice several times a day.

- Have a chat about the benefits of taking a minute to stop and just BE with nothing to achieve, nothing to do. Explain this is best when we are sitting or standing and ask what barriers your child can see to prevent them doing this. Remove those barriers if possible (shut the door, turn off any noises, ask others not to disturb you).
- Sit or stand and take a few deep breaths slowly in and out. The eyes can be closed or part-closed but, if standing, just lower them a little so no one falls over. Start a timer if you are using one or glance at a clock. Drop your attention down through the body and into the feet. Feel the connection between the feet and the floor. Notice all the points of contact between the feet and the floor. Notice any places the shoes or socks are touching the body. Notice any tingling feelings in the feet. Find the breath and notice the soft lift and fall of the chest or belly. Can you feel the warmth of the breath as it leaves the nose? Can you notice it is cooler on the way in, perhaps you can feel that in the throat or the nose?

- Keep the attention on the breath and the feet on the floor, noticing if any thoughts pop up in the mind but choose to think about them later and to stay in this moment for a little longer.
- Once the minute is up, move slowly out of the position. Ask how that feels? Ask what they were able to notice? Ask if they found it easy or hard? Ask if any thoughts came up that might be worries? If a worry has popped up, talk about that now rather than wait until they are tired later on.
- Encourage your child to do this for themselves as much as they want to. See if they can notice the best moments in the day for doing this practice—before a test at school or a big match or a performance. They can try it if they have an argument with someone or if they are feeling upset. Giving space to emotions allows them to be processed and released. Learning to notice that we feel calmer after taking a My Minute means children choose to use this invaluable tool for themselves when they need it.

2. 5/7 Breathing C, A

This is a repetition of the mindfulness introduction exercise from Chapter 4 but has been extended to use pre-sleep. It is very simple, but it helps to still and calm a busy mind by giving it a simple job to do while the body comes into a place of relaxation. This is particularly helpful for teenagers experiencing anxiety. Remember that the teenage brain is a complex and changeable place and the ability to manage these emotions must be learnt. This exercise gives young people a sense of control over their feelings and, once tried and tested, confidence that they can use it as a tool when they feel unable to quiet their minds.

- Sitting or lying comfortably, close the eyes and find the breath. Breathe normally and notice what the mind is up to. Are thoughts arising? Are any emotions coming up? Choose to allow those to just be for the moment and turn your attention back to the breath.
- As you next breathe in, count in your head up to 5. As you breathe out, count up to 7. Notice how this feels. Rather than count faster on the out-breath, try to slow the out-breath down, just enough so you can get to 7.

See if you can continue counting 5 in, 7 out, for a few breaths. Stay with this breathing even when thoughts come up, choosing to keep counting, in and out.

- After a while, drop the counting, breathe normally and open the eyes. What was it like? How does it feel now?

3. Worry Pebbles C, A

This is a visualisation exercise to help with worries. If you haven't done anything like this before with your child, you can try the Visualisation Game on page 186 first for a fun way to demonstrate to them the power of their imagination. This works for adolescents too who can use it when they are feeling like they are carrying a weight of worries on their shoulders. It can be difficult sometimes, with our adult worries about paying the bills and holding everything together, to recall that an insignificant, easily-resolved worry can, for a child seem enormous.

As parents and carers, we must try to let them have their own worries and resist the urge to fix or solve everything for them. As they grow, children will need to learn to solve their own problems, not have them magically whisked away by the "snowplough" parent. Sometimes it is enough just to bring that worry up to the surface, to let it be seen and heard without judgement. Learning ways to deal with the *feeling* of worry without necessarily solving the problem is a vital tool for wellbeing. And, as we all know, lying awake worrying is a major source of sleep difficulties. This exercise helps young people tune into a worry, while grounded, and learn a way to let go of it.

- Lying down somewhere comfortable, warm and safe, allow the eyes to softly close and the body to become still.
- Find the breath and notice it coming in and out of the body, lifting the chest and belly, enabling the body to feel heavier and softer with every out-breath. Allow the feet and legs to let go and relax. Let the hips and tummy release and relax, feeling heavy and soft. The chest and shoulders let go now, relaxing deeper and deeper. The arms and hands let go next, feeling floppy and heavy. The head and neck can let go too, the eyes feel so heavy, the forehead relaxes, the jaw and tongue and ears. The whole body now is relaxing more and more, deeper and deeper.

- Imagine now that you are walking along a beach. Feel the sun warm on your body and face. Feel the sand soft under your bare feet, sinking a little with each step. Beside you, you can see the sea, gentle waves lapping up onto the sand and over your toes. You can hear the rushing sound of the water; you can hear seagulls calling overhead but everything else is peaceful and calm. You feel safe and relaxed and happy.
- Put your hand into your pocket now. You can feel a smooth white pebble there and you take it out and roll it around your hand. This pebble represents something that is worrying you. Look down at the pebble and name the worry. As you look at the pebble you see writing appear on it, the words you have used to name your worry. Allow your feelings about the worry to pour through your hands now and into the pebble. It becomes a little bit heavier in your hands. You stop now and face the sea. Take in a deep breath then throw the pebble as far as you can into the sea. Your throw is much better and goes further than normal because you are powerful here on this beach and your arm is strong and your aim is true. Watch the pebble fly out over the water then hear it plop or splash down. The sea takes your worry away with all the other pebbles, all the other worries and you can turn and carry on walking along the beach. You feel lighter than you did before, maybe you skip a bit or run.
- Check your pocket again and see if there is another worry pebble in there. If there is, repeat the action and then watch it sink into the beautiful blue waves. Keep doing this until your pockets are empty and you feel so light you are practically floating above the sand. Stay on the beach playing as long as you want to, happy and free.
- This might be a perfect time to drift off into a lovely sleep and dream about your magical beach but if you want to come back into the room, take in an extra deep breath and give your fingers and toes a little wriggle. Move your head gently from side to side while breathing in. Notice how your mind feels now. Choose to let yourself sleep deeply and to wake up feeling light and rested.

4. Thought Buses A

This exercise is a visualisation suited to teenagers and comes from the brilliantly developed .b course created by the charity, The Mindfulness in Schools Project, with whom I trained years ago. I cannot praise their work enough and it is a privilege to count myself among the many thousands of teachers they have trained around the world to deliver their robust and scientifically supported curricula. Hundreds of thousands of young people have benefitted from the courses they offer. If your child(ren)'s school has not offered this, you can apply a bit of parent power and ask the mental health coordinator or other school leader to look at the courses on offer.

The mind is an incalculably amazing place, and we will all spend a lifetime learning to understand and utilise our own, sometimes conquering its more disruptive habits but ultimately harnessing it to enable it to serve our best purpose. A fascinating and helpful fact is that, while the mind is occupied largely with *thinking* and *sensing*, we can learn to shift the balance between those two activities by using mindfulness. By choosing to focus more on what we can *sense*, we can reduce the amount of thinking that takes place. For someone who finds their head full of thoughts, whizzing about sparking off emotional responses in the body and creating impulses to act, just recognising that this is what's going on and then making the choice to shift the focus onto sensing instead can reduce that volume of thought traffic. Hence the imagery of the buses that travel around the roads of our mind, clogging it up and creating unpleasant traffic fumes.

Thoughts are just thoughts; they are not real. Yet, because of the emotions they bring up, they have the power to transport us to completely unwelcome places. Practising mindfulness enables us to recognise that this is what's going on—"ah, a thought!" and another one, coming along like buses. A study of psychologically normal people found that they had about 4,000 distinct thoughts every day. The Cleveland Clinic's Wellness Programme found that 95% of our thoughts are repetitive and 80% of them are negative. This study was done on adults and it's my dearest hope that by building metacognition (awareness of how our minds and thoughts work) in young people they might experience fewer negative thoughts as they grow to adulthood.

Talk this exercise through with your older child or teenager and help them understand the theory of it before giving it a try. This works well with any of the exercises that focus on grounding and staying in the present moment by using the breath. Adults can find this practice liberating as well, as it sinks in that thoughts are just thoughts that come and go, and we can find a still place in the mind to watch that happen.

- Find a quiet place to sit or lie where you won't be disturbed and can turn your attention inwards.
- Allow the body to become still and relaxed and focus on the connection between the feet and the floor, if sitting, or the body and the bed if lying down. Feel all those places of contact and let the body relax downwards. This is your bus stop: the body on the chair or bed, still and grounded.
- Find the breath and notice the chest or belly rising and falling. Feel the sensations of the breath in the throat or nose and choose to stay with them. Imagine that you are standing at a bus stop. You are quite contented here, not needing to go anywhere or be anywhere. You are choosing to stay at this bus stop which requires tuning in to what can be felt and sensed so use all your senses to help imagine yourself there. Perhaps feel the sun on your face and body, standing tall and steady.
- As a blank mind is largely a myth, at some point a thought or worry will pop into your head. Imagine this as a bus. Make the bus as big as you want it to be, see what colour it is and which direction it is driving. Notice the worry or thought is written on the side or front of the bus. This bus contains all your feelings and thoughts about that worry and, if you climbed on board, it would take you off on a long circuitous route. You might end up somewhere completely different, somewhere you don't want to go right now. You choose not to get on. Stay at the bus stop by watching the breath, feeling the feet or body. The bus drives by and you are aware as it passes you and travels out of sight. You are still and steady at the bus stop. Your mind is clear again, just sensing, breathing, connecting to the ground.
- Another bus might appear with a different sign on it, representing the next thought. There will always be more buses. Make the choice not to board this one either, to remain where you are, in the present moment, not transported away. Stay steady.
- Each time a bus goes by without you onboard, allow your confidence to quietly grow: you are doing this, controlling your own mind traffic, you

can choose where you put your focus, where you decide to keep your attention. This is an amazing skill to learn and is incalculably powerful. Enjoy the stillness. Keep feeling the sun on you, maybe some birds singing. Notice how calm you are with nowhere to go, nothing to do, just making the time to be. Notice if the traffic is changing, are there fewer buses perhaps, or is there more time between them?

- This can be practised any time but works well prior to sleep as it helps clear the mind enabling it to drift off into a peaceful sleep.

5. Trigger Figure A

This exercise is more suitable for older children and adolescents and is a good one for adults to try too. It is about recognising the link between our thoughts and emotions and noticing where they appear in the body. The mind will always be busy, and bedtime, as we know, is when difficult thoughts can pop up. Enabling teenagers to recognise that this is happening and how certain thoughts will trigger them and what to do when this happens can be a powerful and liberating tool for them. The Thought Bus exercise above strengthens the ability to notice thoughts passing by and choose not to engage with them. However, sometimes the emotional pull of a thought is very strong and, sticking with the metaphor, we find ourselves dragged on board the bus and taken off on a journey that may throw up some difficult feelings.

Adults practising mindfulness and people undergoing CBT will learn the challenging concept of sitting with discomfort. What the Trigger Figure exercise does is, firstly, establishes a place of mindful stillness, then allows any difficult thoughts or emotions to arise. Our instinct is almost always, when confronted by painful or uncomfortable thoughts and emotions, to seek to distract ourselves from them. We resist our own mental pain. Of course we do. However, the fear of the emotion is often considerably worse than the reality of just feeling it. This exercise gently encourages us to allow the feeling to be, from within the safe space of mindful awareness. As with the Word of Caution above (p. 181) however, if a young person is experiencing distress or is in danger of becoming overwhelmed by their feelings, it would be wise to consult a mental health practitioner and seek advice about whether further support would be appropriate.

Read through this exercise before deciding whether it would be useful for your teenager. Explain to them first that it is an empowering practice, and that the intention is to liberate them from difficult thoughts and feelings, but that this will involve not fighting or resisting the feeling, instead allowing it to be without getting caught up in the whys and what ifs. As with any practice, it gets easier every time it is done and, crucially, it builds emotional resilience and confidence that they *can* cope with difficulty.

- Find a safe, quiet place to sit or lie. Using gentle relaxing music or low lighting can be helpful to achieve the right mood in the room. Aromatherapy scents such as lavender can encourage the body to relax. Begin to tune in to the breath, allowing it to rise and fall naturally, noticing the gentle lift of the chest and belly, softening the body on the out-breath, enabling tension to release and noticing any sensations of heaviness and calmness.
- If tension persists in the body, try taking a deeper breath in, then sigh on the out-breath, sending those tense feelings away. You can try saying a mantra to yourself such as "I am calm, I am still" or "breathe in, let go" or "peace, calm" whatever seems to work best. Or just remain focused on the sensations of the breath, the body breathing itself.
- Minds will do what they do, and will throw us some thoughts. Notice when a thought arises, like a cloud crossing a clear blue sky. Keeping the attention fixed on the breath, see if you can take a mental step back from the thought and resist following it. You can say "ah, I am thinking about food/homework/something someone said earlier…but I am choosing to stay with my breath." This is challenging stuff and takes practice, but I find that young people are often fascinated by the way their mind works and bringing this gentle curiosity to the practice is a helpful way of creating that distance between the thought and the thinker. As with clouds on a clear sky, the thought will pass by. Try saying to yourself, "This thought will pass." Once someone has experienced this themselves and noticed that their mind has returned to the breath and to the stillness in the body, they will be encouraged to keep doing it. It isn't easy! Like training a puppy not to pull on its lead or jump up, the mind needs training with firmness and repetition but also, always, with *kindness* and *patience*, acknowledging that we are learning something difficult here, that will get easier, but we need to keep being friendly and gentle with ourselves in spite of any frustrations.

- As you watch your thoughts arise and pass, it is likely one of them will trigger an emotion and it will be harder to allow it to drift away. Thinking about an argument or a worry can cause the body to join in too. Notice that this is happening. Bring that curiosity to the experience. How amazing that a single, simple thought can cause such a cascade of emotions and feelings in our body! What exactly does it feel like? Where in the body can you feel the tension? Perhaps it is in the belly or around the chest. Notice there might be a strong reaction to get away from this feeling. Has your breathing changed? Is there an urge to move the body, to open the eyes and find something to distract you? Try, if you can, to keep that sense of distance. You could say to yourself, "Ah, this is a trigger for me right now. I am going to watch it. I am not getting sucked into it."
- Without following the thought path of that trigger, picking apart the argument or running through scenarios, try to stick with the breath in the present moment. Stay grounded while keeping an awareness of any change in the feeling. Sit with it. It's *just a thought* making you feel this way, yes the feeling might be uncomfortable but it will pass. You may notice the feeling building, like a wave. See if you can allow it to build without getting overwhelmed. Know you are safe; you are not your thoughts or your feelings. You are breathing. Stay with the breath. Like a wave it eventually breaks, it washes over you, it releases, it subsides.
- Once the feeling has built up then down again, notice how the body feels. Sometimes it can feel quite drained, but congratulate yourself on doing something mentally empowering. You have not been overwhelmed by your thoughts, you have stayed grounded, you are OK. This is a powerful tool you can keep building like a muscle in the gym that gets stronger and more reliable with every lift. Be proud of your strength and this achievement.
- That might have taken some time, or it may have taken place in a matter of seconds. Depending on how you are now feeling, you could bring the practice to an end with a few more gentle centring breaths, noticing any new feelings of calmness in the body, preparing for sleep.

6. Name It and Tame It C

This is an exercise for younger children similar to the Trigger Figure for adolescents. It builds emotional intelligence and helps children understand their feelings as they come up, by giving them a name. As the title suggests, the process of acknowledging a feeling, describing or naming it, removes some of its power to overwhelm. Doing this encourages a mindful awareness of emotions, giving them a space to be. It's important to bring your attitude of non-judgement to this practice. As parents, we can't help but want our children to be happy. But is it reasonable to want them to be happy *all the time*? Is this a fair thing to ask of anyone? If our children feel a pressure to be happy in order to make us happy it can set in place a very painful set of consequences which could see them suppressing or denying their emotions and putting the need of the parent to be reassured of their happiness before being true to how they actually feel.

I'd like to quote from the brilliant Caitlin Moran's book, *More Than a Woman*. This book made me shriek with laughter and cry my eyes out. She describes the unreasonable pressure parents place on their children by telling them, "We just want you to be happy." It can over-burden them with responsibility when they already have enough on their plates. As she writes:

If you are not allowed day-to-day sadness—if your wholly natural bouts of pessimism and hopelessness are something you feel your parents try, immediately, to jolly you out of—or else, you must conceal from them completely—then is it any wonder that small amounts of suppressed, daily sadness and anxiety start to metastasise into something darker, and harder to shift?

I can't concur more fervently. I once overheard a mum say to her young daughter: "Stop crying now, you're making Mummy sad." We need to try to honour our children's feelings, even if they make us feel sad or uncomfortable or guilty or keep up awake worrying. We are the grown-ups, and our job is to listen and to be present.

- Unlike the majority of the exercises in this book, this one doesn't have to take place in a formal way although you might like to suggest to your child that you sit down together to talk about how they are feeling. If you do this, employ the active listening skills from exercise 8 below, and give them your full attention, eye contact, empathy and care. If, instead, you prefer a less formal approach, it will require some mindfulness around what you hear from them and how you respond.

- When your child behaves in a way, that suggests a strong emotion behind it—for example, losing their temper, being unkind or rude—ask them to stop for a moment. Don't engage with whatever the behaviour has been but try to move beyond it to the emotions behind their actions. Ask open questions "I can see you are not very happy right now, can you tell me about that?" and try to avoid naming it for them "You seem angry" or "You seem sad." You are trying to help them learn to identify and recognise their own feelings. They may need some guidance: "You are crying/shouting—can you tell me why?" and you may need to keep going until they reach the point of owning their feelings "I am angry" or "I am frustrated."
- Once a feeling is named, immediately mirror it back to them, making it clear that you see them. "I can see that you are sad." You can gently ask them how they know that they are feeling sad/angry/jealous? How does it feel? "I can see how annoyed you are and that it feels horrible." Depending on the nature of the behaviour you might be able to skip the whole thing and go straight for the reassuring hug, saying how proud you are that they recognise how they feel but that it isn't kind to break someone else's toy.
- After naming the feeling, a child will often feel calmer. You can sit quietly with them for a few minutes then ask if they still feel upset. Do they know what might help them to feel better?
- The part of the brain we use to identify our own emotions is called the insula and it also does the job of recognising other people's emotions. If your child has recognised their own feeling of sadness/frustration/anger, they are better able to notice them in others, to empathise and make better choices about how they express their feelings.
- Teaching your child to use any aspect of mindfulness such as 5/7 Breathing, Petal Breathing or My Minute gives them a tool to use at times when they would like to calm down, creates some space for the emotion to subside and for them to let it go and move on.

- A child who hasn't demonstrated any emotional outbursts during the day can find bedtime is when they come up. This is a great opportunity to do a mindfulness exercise with them and leave space for them to tell you how they are feeling. Common bedtime issues are fears about bad dreams, worries about something that has happened or anxieties about the next day's events. Rather than get bogged down in the detail of the worry, try to get past and to the emotion behind it. Mirror it back. Help them name the feeling. Comfort them and stay present. As always, praise them for any leap of understanding they make, and reassure them that you are always there to listen.

7. Journalling A

This is a Reflect and Review tool that can be used by adolescents but may be suitable for some older children. A parent-led exercise for younger children follows below.

In other cultures, and in times gone by, a day of the week was often put aside for leisure and, in some cases, for prayer or reflection. Before the advent of 24-hour television, social media, almost universal phone ownership and the bedroom TV, people prepared for bed more gradually. Broadcast TV used to go off for the night and there were fewer late-night external distractions for the mind. Reading before sleep is rarer now than ever but provides a welcome period of wind-down. A wind-down gives us the chance to reflect on the day—maybe asking what went well? what did I enjoy? what am I grateful for? how would I like tomorrow to go?

It is much harder to achieve when there is an abrupt switch from screentime, via exhaustion, to sleep. Sometimes sleep is less like a gradual drift and more like passing out. Teenagers have frequently told me that this is a regular experience for them. As we sleep, our brain processes the day's events for us, but less time to wind down and less time actually asleep can hinder this and, thus, we wake in the morning with a sort of hangover from yesterday's worries. That overnight therapy reset hasn't fully occurred.

Our fast-paced modern world means that, for many people nowadays, a day off or a weekend is often crammed catching up on the jobs we didn't have time for during the week or for continued busyness and scheduled activity. Without time and space to reflect on what's going on for us, the positive as well as the negative, is it any wonder that worries can build, like a snowball rolling down a hill gathering in size and momentum until it feels like it will crush us in its path? Part of processing our experiences is letting them go so we don't find ourselves carrying the great weight of accumulated stress and worry. A lovely teaching of the Buddha's is that: "Each morning we are born again. What we do today is what matters most." It is easier to feel the truth of this when we have let go of the day's pressures and writing them down in a journal is a helpful way to do this.

Adolescent life is full of change and pressures lurk everywhere. Finding a safe place to express emotions and thoughts can make a huge difference. And a journal is safer and more private than social media options. I am aware that online forums offer a place where teenagers who feel isolated in their families or communities can find sympathetic and like-minded people to engage with and this helps them feel less alone. But learning how to be alone—not lonely—is a fundamental part of life. Many relationship problems that occur during the teenage years and beyond start from an inability to be comfortable alone in our own headspace. Needing to *not* be alone can distort over time into full blown co-dependency and a host of poor decisions taken out of fear of facing ourselves and the way we feel. As French philosopher Blaise Pascal wrote, "The sole cause of man's unhappiness is that he does not know how to stay quietly in his room."

Journalling, or keeping a diary as it was called in my day, is very straightforward. Discuss some or all of this with your teenager and encourage them to give it a go for their mental wellbeing and, of course, as a great way to calm the mind before bed, leading to a healthier and longer sleep. If your child is keeping a sleep diary as part of building better sleep habits, they can use the book to record the relevant sleep hygiene aspects covered above.

- Find a suitable notebook to write out your thoughts and feelings at the end of each day. Ensure it is respected by the rest of the family—hide it in a safe place if necessary. (Parents—*never ever* snoop in your child's journal.) Commit a short time at the end of each day to reviewing and reflecting what's going on for you.
- Write yourself a note at the beginning that you will not judge yourself for anything you say, do, or write. Reflection is quite different from self-condemnation. Commit to writing facts and feelings and not to criticising or finding fault with yourself. Curiosity and kindness are key

aspects of mindfulness and can be consciously developed as you catch yourself heaping on any blame or guilt. You're just a person, doing their best, living on this confusing planet, finding your own path. Be kind to yourself. If you find this difficult, imagine that it is your friend confessing something that they feel bad about. Notice how you would comfort and reassure your friend. Then apply the exact same advice to yourself. Humour is a mighty tool, so use plenty of it if you can. Learning to laugh at ourselves is incredibly liberating and rescues us from the dismal state of taking ourselves too seriously. We're all pretty ridiculous at the end of the day.

- Journalling can be used alongside many mindfulness practices and works very well in conjunction because of that commitment to turning the attention inwards to whatever is there, without judgement, sometimes tackling a difficult or uncomfortable feeling. Notice how it feels to let it all out on paper. Rip it out after and scrunch it up if you want. How does that feel? Note that our most uncomfortable and unpleasant feelings are around shame, fear and self-loathing. Sadly, these are part of being human and expressing them in a safe place can go some way to releasing them. Feeding ourselves the opposite, positive emotions of confidence, courage and gratitude is covered below so make sure there is place in your journal for these as well.
- The Trigger Figure offers the opportunity for some wisdom when it is completed regularly and combined with a reflection tool: identifying our own triggers. Notice whether certain people or situations crop up regularly causing you emotional discomfort. Perhaps there are ways of managing those? Encourage your teenager to brainstorm solutions to reducing these trigger moments. Let them know you're happy to listen and to help. Sometimes we can all get so tangled in our own thoughts and feelings that we can't see a simple answer. Remain available to your child or direct them towards another trusted adult who can help them shed light on any dilemmas.

Journalling is about the process itself and not about reading it back, but it can be fascinating to read a diary after some time has passed and perspective gained. Adolescents are changing all the time and can look back at the intensity of their feelings a few short months later and be astonished they ever felt that way. This can be empowering as they appreciate empirically that they will not always feel the way they do right now, that this too shall pass.

8. Reflect and Review C

This is a daily practice that involves *active listening* by the parent or carer and can become a rich source of closeness and understanding between you and your child. It can be so rewarding that, when your child swaps you for a journal in their teenage years, you can feel properly rejected and surplus to requirement. Joking aside, establishing open lines of communication while your child is young can be a lifeline for you both during a stormy adolescence. This exercise essentially builds trust between you. The release of worries and fears will make for a better night's sleep.

At the heart of it is mindful parenting which involves showing up and being present for your child. Much of what we do as parents is, by necessity, practical and material but the emotional side requires us to give of our time, attention and energy. Buddhist teacher Thich Nhat Hanh offers this wisdom: "The most precious gift we can give others is our presence. When mindfulness embraces those we love, they will bloom like flowers."

Most of us are poor listeners, but active listening is a skill that anyone can learn—some workplaces train their staff in it. It means making a conscious effort to hear and understand what the other person is saying. *Hearing* is an accidental brain response to sound and involves no effort whatsoever. By contrast, *listening* is focused and intentional. Unlike many of the exercises in this book that take place at or around bedtime, this can fit in around family life and makes sense to have earlier in the afternoon or evening especially if bedtimes are a flashpoint and your child is very tired after a long day. Your child may not want to come straight in from school and give you a blow-by-blow report on the day, so allow them time to wind down and relax before you begin.

- Find a suitable time and place to sit with your child and reflect and review their day with them. In general, avoid doing this in the car as it needs your full attention. Older children often talk more openly while sitting beside a parent so, if you have established good practice, you could occasionally do it, but it will have less impact when you aren't trying to do something else at the same time.

- Active listening starts with asking open questions. An open question is one to which there is more than a one-word answer. This is more than "how was your day?" Asking "how have you been feeling today?" or "what things have you done today?" is more open and requires more than an "ok" in response. Explain you are interested to hear whatever they tell you.
- Try not to interrupt your child. This is challenging as they may go right round the houses telling you about something that could be summarised quickly. Listen to the language they use. Look at them, make eye contact, smile and show you are relaxed and listening. Remember any key words they use so you can ask a bit more when they have finished, especially those that suggest judgement—these might include "good" or "bad," "right" or "wrong."
- You can use affirmations like "I know" or "I see" to show you're listening carefully and, when they have finished one part, you can reflect it back at them "It sounds like you really enjoyed playtime" or "It sounds like lunch today wasn't so good."
- Ask for clarification and details. Why? How? Your child may tell you how they felt after a particular interaction or activity, or you may need to prompt that: "how did you feel then?" Don't interrupt them but you can reflect their words back at them and help them build a vocabulary for describing their emotions. "That sounds quite scary, did you feel frightened then?"; "That sounds fun, did you feel proud of your drawing/test result?"; "It sounds like you were really kind and helpful, how did that feel?"
- For a bit of variety, you can try asking some fun questions such as: what was the funniest moment of your day? Best sound you heard? Best thing you saw? Best thing you ate? Best smell? Nicest thing someone else did? Kindest thing you did today? These answers, while not full of emotional detail, are all slanted towards identifying the most positive aspects of the day.
- Listening actively with your full attention helps your child develop emotional intelligence as well as their own problem-solving skills. It helps them identify and manage their emotions, builds empathy between you and engenders trust. Avoid any conflict and remain patient and present.

- If your child expresses feelings of worry or fear, you can offer comfort but resist the urge to solve the problem for them. Ask open questions that will make them think for themselves "Could you ask to join in that game next time?"; "Is there anything you could do to prepare for the match/test?" Rather than handing them the help you think they need, ask "Is there anything I can do to help you with that?"
- Bring the review to an end by thanking them for sharing with you, make it clear you have enjoyed and appreciated all the details. Praise them for all the noticing they have done about how they feel, and for any ways they have solved their own problems. If it's not been a good day, reassure them that tomorrow is another day and that you are confident they will bring their energy, good humour and positive outlook to it. It will be an easier day for them, too, after a nice long sleep!

9. Gratitude Practice C, A

Piglet noticed that even though he had a Very Small Heart, it could hold a rather large amount of Gratitude.

A.A. Milne

I wonder whether, since the pandemic, we are all a little better at practising gratitude and feeling appreciation for the simple things in life that give us pleasure? The collective experience of losing much of our freedom and the opportunity to interact with one another does seem to have generated an increasing sense of priority among us for our green spaces and the touch of a friendly hand. The practice of gratitude has always been a part of mindfulness. Whether we are tuning in to the taste and texture of our food during a mindful eating practice, or appreciating the movement of our body during exercise, we all have the capacity to tune into the good things in life, to how they make us feel.

You will have read earlier how neural pathways form in the brain. Neurons that fire together, wire together—in other words, creating positive habits of thinking about the world and ourselves, forms a pathway in our brain that we are more likely to take, especially when times are tough. Gratitude practice is all about building this, and it is particularly important for adolescents. During this period of brain development, a process known as pruning takes place. The neurons that are no longer used or needed are pruned away to make room for the forthcoming challenges of adulthood.

However much work I do with children and teenagers, it always breaks my heart a little when I see the change from those year 5 children, bubbling over with enthusiasm about everything, full of questions and curiosity about themselves and the world, to the sometimes sullen, reluctant-to-engage year 8s. When you are in year 8, most things are "boring" or other less acceptable adjectives. Seeing a year 8's face light up when their mate has made them laugh is like seeing the sun come out from behind the clouds. It's a joy and too often a rare one. It is not their fault, as discussed above at length. But we must not give up on them and we must take whatever opportunity we have to remind them of the good things in life and help them to keep alive, and regularly used, those pathways of love, respect, self-compassion, peace, hope, joy and gratitude. These are not the pathways we want to get pruned away during the great adolescent brain clean-up.

This practice can be used with your child and talked through with your teenager. Explain about the neural pathways and that every time they have a positive feeling or thought and consciously hold it for a few breaths, it is helping create that pathway to feeling good about themselves and the world. The object of our gratitude in this exercise can be as simple and as small as you like: the sun on your face, a cold glass of water, those freshly cooked French fries, it's the feeling that matters. And it's potentially life-changing.

My own gratitude practice goes back more than a decade to a time when I became seriously ill. My children were very young and it was horrendous to leave them during hospital treatments. At times, I was unable to walk, was constantly nauseous and in a great deal of pain. An old schoolfriend came to visit me. In her kind and honest way, she said she couldn't offer much but that she had read about a refugee woman who had endured unimaginable suffering in a war-torn country and had lost her family, home and health. This woman had eventually woken one day and decided, in spite of the horror she had witnessed and a bleak and uncertain future, to find something to feel grateful for. There wasn't a great deal for her to choose from, so she went with being glad that there was air to breathe. The next day, she looked for another thing, the same the day after and so on. It enabled her to rebuild her life and to survive her ordeal.

After my friend had gone, I felt humbled by the story and decided that I could surely manage that. I started that day and wrote down my grateful thing (it was seeing my dear old friend). I have continued the practice ever since and have thousands and thousands written down in notebooks. Over the years, the focus of my gratitude has remained largely unchanged. I am grateful for my body and that it now works again. For my family, friends and pets. For trees and birdsong. A hot bath. Clean sheets. A cup of tea. I share this story with you because I truly believe it was a vital part of my recovery from illness and that it enabled me to become stronger after hitting such a desperate low. I have found that it helps, especially on those difficult days when it's hard to find anything to feel glad about and I want to kick things (thank you, menopause), but the nightly practice of picking up my notebook and casting about for something good has never failed me, I promise. There's always something.

- Begin a discussion with your child about gratitude. Ask what they think it means. Is it being glad? Feeling blessed? Appreciating what we have? I have been bowled over by some children's responses to this question in the classroom and humbled by their heartfelt instinctive understanding of what it means to feel thankful.
- Suggest you play a game before bed and try to come up with three things to feel grateful for that day. Let them lead the way on this and only prompt if necessary. You could share your own if they are finding it hard to get going. Take a moment to focus on each thing. Ask how it feels to do this? Can they describe the feeling?
- Older children might like to write down their three things. Adolescents can add it to their journalling. For the latter, on days when they aren't inclined to write much it can be simpler to just write their three things ("music, no homework, fishfingers") the important part is feeling it, allowing the sense of gratitude to be present in the body as well as in the mind.
- Practising gratitude strengthens our resilience to cope with the challenges of life, building those pathways in the brain that can lead us out of difficult times. It also develops emotional intelligence and can help us regulate our emotions by knowing that we have the power to change our mood when we need to. This may be a practice that makes up part of your bedtime routine or it may become a lifelong tool, just

exposing your child to it will give them a great deal. We know that people who experience gratitude are happier individuals than those who don't. Those moments before sleep are more likely to lead to a peaceful night when the mind has deliberately chosen to rest on things we appreciate and that make us feel good.

10. Affirmations **C, A**

The work of the late, great Louise Hay brought us the power of the affirmation. Regularly repeating positive messages to ourselves can be extremely empowering and can make real change in our lives. We all know the phrase "fake it 'til you make it"; affirming to ourselves that we are brave, strong, smart and kind, even when we don't fully feel it, gets to work on our subconscious and enables a gradual shift away from the negative stories we tell ourselves to actually feeling braver, stronger, smarter and kinder. You can use these with your children, giving them messages of your belief in their good qualities but it's even better to help them to identify the aspects of themselves they would like to nurture and grow. Becoming a great sleeper can just be part of the mix.

Creating affirmations with your child can come out of your active listening. If you notice the language they use about themselves, "I'm rubbish at maths", "I'm always last" you can help them create short phrases to repeat regularly, then check in to see how it's working for them: "I'm getting better at maths all the time", "I'm trying my best and enjoying the race." This doesn't have to be done at bedtime but, if you are trying to improve your child's sleep, it can make a nice part of any bedtime routine or fit in around the Review tool.

- Find the appropriate time to discuss what an affirmation is: that it helps us to rewrite any negative stories we have been telling ourselves. These stories are not *facts*—they are just messages we give ourselves and we can change them whenever we want. Think of it like reprogramming a computer that has been working on the wrong settings. If you want your computer or tablet to run at its best possible capacity, you would go in and change the code to make it work better for you. Our brains are similar, and we can choose the "software" we download.

- Ask your child if there is anything they would like to be better at or to find easier? Create a positive and simple affirmation. Be careful not to make it a conditional statement such as "I would like to be…" or "I hope I can…" instead firmly state it as a fact, something that has already been achieved and is set into reality. "I am good at making friends", "I understand what the teacher says." If they choose something seemingly impossible, don't immediately dismiss it but try to find a way to modify it so it allows for a move in the right direction. "I find writing stories easier every day" or "I am getting better at catching the ball." See if they would like to write this down, or if they'd like you to do this. Written affirmations can be decorated with drawings or patterns by your child and can be put up somewhere in the house where they will see them every day. Make it a game to say them out loud. If there is a major setback and an affirmation seems to be irrelevant, find a new one that suits the circumstances, rewrite it and replace the old one. Adaptation and creativity are the key!
- If you would like to bring the topic around to sleeping, open a dialogue with your child, finding an aspect of what is not working that can be improved. "I get ready for bed quickly" or "I feel happy and safe in my bedroom" or "I look forward to bed and having lovely dreams." Be careful not to wave this at them when you are in the middle of a bedtime wrangle; just be clear that you still believe in it, and you are confident it can be achieved. Saying affirmations about sleeping well during the day rather than just before bed can sow those positive seeds in advance.
- Teenagers are often interested in affirmations when they understand more about the workings of the brain. Reprogramming themselves not to hate their bodies, find school boring or their friendships challenging can be appealing. You can help them with some wording or just leave them to try and create their own. Be clear you support them and that things can and will get better—but they have more agency than they think to make the changes they want to see. Teenagers are always wiser, stronger, more resourceful and more beautiful than they think they are. Bringing mindfulness to the issue of sleep can enable them to focus on how much better they feel when rested and how much easier life's challenges are to manage after a decent amount of sleep: "I choose to rest and be ready for tomorrow" is simple but effective, giving them

permission to stop procrastinating at bedtime and give in to tiredness. As with younger children, encourage teens to write their affirmations down and put them somewhere they can regularly see or refer to. As always with teenagers, respect their privacy and wait for them to share any details with you.

Chapter 9
Mind and Body Calm Techniques for Adults

The majority of the mind and body techniques for children and adolescents in the preceding chapters can also be done by adults. Doing them with your child is a great bonding opportunity that will enrich the bedtime routine. Talking with your teenager about what you have each been doing around relaxation and reflection can also be rewarding. However, there are practices particularly aimed at supporting adult sleep and you will find a selection below to experiment with.

Adults tend to cite stress as being the main cause of their insomnia. Sometimes sleeplessness can be caused by interruptions from children and by physical barriers when someone is experiencing pain or illness. As with children, the reasons adults cannot sleep are often when the body is unable to relax and when the mind is too busy. The busy mind goes over the day's events, tomorrow's challenges and all our worries about our family, work, relationships, finances, etc. which, as we know, tend to surface once we stop for the day. Most of us are carrying a huge amount of responsibility with all its incipient worry. Stress is experienced by everyone, but we must attend to our experience of it and develop ways to manage it—our health depends on it.

Research at Harvard University has found:

Too much stress for too long creates what is known as "chronic stress" which has been linked to heart disease, stroke, and may also influence cancer and chronic respiratory diseases. And illness is just the tip of the iceberg. Stress affects you emotionally, as well, marring the joy you gain from life and loved ones.

The highly renowned and respected cell biologist Dr Bruce Lipton states that stress is the cause of at least 95% of all illness and disease.

With this in mind, my biggest message to busy parents and carers is to give yourself permission to stop. Ideally, take some time every day to nurture yourself. When we are stressed, a host of hormones build up in the body, including cortisol, and these trigger those parts of our DNA that can turn into disease. We can't always eliminate the stressors in our lives, but we can find ways to cope that keep us mentally and physically safer from that toxic build-up of biochemical messages. Taking care of yourself can be as simple as a daily 5-minute mindfulness practice, just stop doing and take the chance to be. Lie on the sofa. Take a bath. Stop running about from task to task and cut yourself a big chunk of slack. Your health will benefit and your sleep will improve. It is only when we rest that the parasympathetic nervous system can kick in, releasing stress and enabling the body to mentally, emotionally and physically repair. Here are some ways to do this.

1. Take Five

We all know that we can rely on the wonderful Delia Smith to ensure our cakes come out perfectly every time, but she has also written a profound and inspirational book about the inner life and how tuning into our deepest selves offers the opportunity to tackle problems small and large. In *You Matter: the Human Solution*, she writes:

Giving time and space in everyday life to be still, silent and initially just to daydream will allow this sometimes neglected, but natural, capacity to expand into something deeper, which can open up new perspectives on things.

This practice just requires five minutes of your time. Ideally you will be able to sit alone somewhere quiet, but it can be done while waiting at the dentist or outside your child's school. Like me you may feel you spend a fair bit of your day waiting for someone to finish football or drama, so instead of scrolling through your phone or drumming your fingers on the steering wheel, give yourself the gift of five minutes stillness while tuning in to the present moment.

- Wherever you are, make a conscious choice to take the next five minutes for yourself. You can note the time or set the timer on your phone if you like.

- Sit comfortably, with the spine straight if you can. Uncross the legs so both feet touch the ground. Allow your eyes to gently close or, if open, soften the gaze downward. Take a big breath in, then let it out slowly through your nose. Notice the body release any tension as you breathe out. Repeat this.
- Drop your attention into your feet. Feel the connection with the ground below. Can you feel your shoes touching your toes and heels? Move your focus up to the ankles. What do they feel like right now? Then the shins and calves, letting the breath help any tension to drain out downwards through the feet. Slide your attention to the knees, the back of the knees. Maybe noticing the areas of the body that are touching the chair. Feel into the buttocks and the contact with the chair. Release any tension in the lower back by breathing out long and slow.
- Holding the focus of the mind on the lower body, feel yourself grounded and centred. The breath lifts the chest up and down, slowly, peacefully. Maybe notice the belly moving gently too.
- If the mind wanders or becomes distracted, don't worry it's natural, just choose to bring it back to the breath, the feet on the floor, the body in the chair, the release of tension.
- Stay in this peaceful place beyond the five minutes if you have the opportunity, otherwise open your eyes and draw in a fresh breath to energise yourself for whatever happens next.
- Do this every day. It can be done as often as you like, and you may find yourself able to do it while standing up after a while. It's a fraction of your day but has a power to transform how you feel when practised over time.

2. Change Your Sleep Mindset

I have spoken to many adults about their sleep and regularly find they have an entrenched mindset about it—and this can be a barrier to making improvements. It can mean that however much you attempt to improve your sleep hygiene or your phone use, your sleep issues remain the same. This can be discouraging and create further anxiety on top of the tiredness you may be struggling with. The solution could be as simple as reprogramming your mind to think differently about the way you sleep.

- First identify what your belief about your sleep currently is. Take the first answer that pops into your head when you imagine someone asking, "How's your sleep?" Write it down. Over the years, I've heard statements such as: "I always wake up in the middle of the night", "I toss and turn all night" and "I wake really early and can't get back to sleep."
- Look at the written statement and give it a score out of 100 as to how much you really believe this to be true. Notice if this takes a while and you dither about the right number. Maybe it's not always true? Maybe it happens a bit less often than you think? Settle on what you reckon is a fair and accurate figure.
- Now reflect on what you'd like to be true about your sleep. Make it more specific than "I sleep well"—so add in details that describe your sleep as you want it to be. This could be, "I drop off easily and sleep all night", "I wake feeling refreshed and rested", "I fall back to sleep quickly and easily." Write it down. Give it a score for how true it currently is. It might be 0!
- Take the first sleep statement and destroy the paper however you want, rip it up, chuck it in the recylcling or the fire and decide as you do that it no longer describes you. Every time you catch yourself thinking that negative thought, setting off along the well-trodden path of "I'm a terrible sleeper"—stop! Remember destroying the statement. It is no longer true. You'll have to be vigilant for a while to stop yourself thinking or speaking this, but it will soon be replaced by your second statement—the way you choose to sleep from now on.
- Put your positive sleep statement somewhere you can see it easily or write Post-Its and stick them by your bed, on the bathroom mirror. Repeat it to yourself as many times a day as you can with a feeling of complete confidence: "I sleep well every night."
- This neural pathway reprogramming practice is used in hypnosis and some cognitive behavioural therapy. To work best, it should be done in a relaxed and positive frame of mind. Even if you think it will never work for you, allow yourself a few weeks to experiment with it in the spirit of curiosity and fun. Don't focus on your sleep too much, park any worries about that and find out whether you are one of the people that this works for.

- It's not a guarantee because some people are less susceptible to hypnosis, self or otherwise, but stick with it for a few weeks, repeating your affirmation throughout the day. If anyone asks about your sleep, tell them your new mindset and smile. Fake it before you make it. After a month, look back at the score you gave this statement and see whether anything has changed.

3. Bedtime Yoga Routine

Tension in the body is a common reason for sleeplessness, especially if you are experiencing pain. If you have regular pain anywhere, talk to your GP about the options around pain management. Being kept awake by pain should not just be put up with, so ask for some help. During my period of serious illness I would be woken most nights in terrible pain and I know how isolating and frightening that feels.

As we age, aches and pains in the joints, neck, shoulders and back are extremely common. A short yoga routine before you get into bed can really help to ease tension and encourage the body to relax. If you sit at a desk all day or perform physical work, you'll be carrying tension somewhere in the body. Releasing this regularly can help prevent that tension turning into something more chronic. You might even fancy joining an online or in-person yoga class.

A strong predictor of a healthy old age is having a flexible spine, and yoga is a great way to increase this as well as to help sleep come more easily. This routine can be done in less than 10 minutes. Wear anything comfortable that allows movement. Have a cushion or pillow nearby in case you need a support. You don't need a mat, just a rug or carpet will do, although a mat can be a nice part of the ritual. In yoga, we come to our mat without judgement or expectation, just allowing the body to bc, as it is in the present moment.

- *Cat stretches*. Start on all-fours with the hands below the shoulders and the knees below the hips. Breathe in and drop the belly to the floor, allowing the spine to curve. Look up. Breathe out, drop the chin to the chest and raise the middle of the back up to the ceiling. Continue moving with the breath, allow the movement to ripple through the spine and enjoy the release in the shoulders, neck and hips.

- *Thread the needle.* In the same all-fours position, lift one hand off the floor and "thread" it through the space between the other hand and knee. Slide the arm along the floor and gently lower the shoulder and head to the mat, turning to face the direction of the arm. Rest and relax in this position, bottom high. Take a few breaths here then push back up to all-fours and repeat on the other side. This is great for the shoulders, neck and lower back.
- *Floppy fish.* Lie on your back and stretch the arms out to a T-shape in line with the shoulders. Palms down. Rest for a breath here then, on an in-breath, draw the knees up onto the chest as far as they feel like going. Let the legs become heavy on the chest then, on the out-breath, lower them gently over to one side. If they don't reach the floor, pop a cushion below the knees. If this isn't comfortable, put the feet back on the floor and lower the knees from here. Turn the head in the opposite direction from the knees. Take a few breaths here, releasing any tension in the lower back, neck and shoulders. On an in-breath, draw the knees back onto the chest and the head back to neutral, give the knees a little hug then repeat on the other side. Finish with the knees hugged in tight, maybe lift the nose to the knees to give the neck an extra stretch then rock lengthways until you come up to sitting.
- *Cosmic egg.* Keep the knees hugged in tight and rest your head down. You can lift your feet up too for a gentle balance. Tune in to your breathing which will be quite audible. Feel the ribs at the back expand and the shoulders curve forwards and round.
- *Leg elevation.* The final posture involves the upper half of the body resting while the legs are elevated. This can be done by placing the heels and lower legs on a bed or few firm pillows. Arms can be by the side or out in that T-shape or just resting on the belly. Breathe in and out gently through the nose for a few minutes allowing any remaining tension to drain away. This asana really helps with any swelling in the ankles, feet or legs. It improves blood circulation and reduces inflammation.

4. Three-Part-Breath

This is a formal yoga practice known as *Dirgha Pranayama* that some people respond really well to. There are many benefits to learning this deep diaphragmatic breathing. It calms the mind, soothes the nervous system and increases awareness of lung capacity. Most people don't use their full lung capacity, taking short shallow breaths—this is called ineffective breathing and places strain on the heart and lungs. Consciously choosing to breathe deeply is effective for stress reduction and increasing oxygen supply which nourishes every cell in the body. It also strengthens the diaphragm and surrounding abdominal muscles. After regular practice, it will be easy to do this profoundly beneficial deep breathing as part of everyday life.

- This can be practised sitting but, if you're new to this, it is definitely easier lying down. You can do it in bed or on a mat or floor if you prefer. Put a pillow under the knees if the lower back feels tight. Allow the body to settle and become still.
- Close the eyes and soften the face, shoulders, neck and chest. Breathe in and out slowly through the nose, then place the hands or fingers on the lower belly. Notice where you feel the natural movement of the breath—the chest? Belly? Ribs?
- Direct the breath down to the lower belly, imagine a balloon filling and emptying beneath your hands as the breath comes in and out. As you exhale the belly falls. Take five breaths here.
- Move the hands upwards to the side of the ribcage. As you breathe in, first expand the belly, as before, then feel the ribs lift too as the lungs fill the chest. Exhale first emptying the chest then the belly. Take five long calm breaths here.
- Place the hands in the centre of the chest, just below the collarbones and draw the breath in, first from the belly, then up through the chest as the ribs lift, then right up to this space below your fingertips. Feel the very top of the lungs expand. As you exhale the breath leaves first from the upper chest, then the middle chest and finally the belly. Take five long grounding breaths here.

This might take a few goes to get the hang of but is worth persevering with as the benefits to mind and body are considerable. If you are doing some yoga stretches before bed, this calming breath practice is perfect straight afterwards and will ease the mind and body into sleep.

5. Taking Off the Rucksack

This is a visualisation exercise to help release stress in the mind and body—and to enjoy the feeling of relief. Some of the exercises above for children and teenagers have visualisation at their heart and it's a well-established mental tool. The brain uses it as a rehearsal because it stimulates the same regions as when we actually perform the action. Many sportspeople and performers use this technique to prepare themselves by triggering sensory cues. If you doubt the efficacy, try the exercise recommended for children on page 186.

I do this exercise when lying in bed and almost always fall asleep, so if you're ready for sleep, it can be a great way to drift off. When doing it with young people, I have to gently rouse them at the end, which always feels a shame to me, but I love hearing their experiences and knowing they can try this themselves any time they feel they are carrying the world on their shoulders.

- Get yourself comfortable lying down and take a few minutes to settle the body. Close the eyes. Take some slow deep breaths to calm the mind. Focus on being here right now, with nothing else to do, nowhere to be. Time for yourself.
- Imagine you are standing outdoors, in a place that is special to you. It might be a beach or a park, beside a lake or in a forest. If nowhere comes to mind, create a beautiful place instead where you feel safe and alone. Look around at what you can see. Notice any sounds, birdsong or waves rippling on the shore. Feel the warm sun on your skin. Notice any smells, perfume from flowers or the salty sea smell.
- Now, look down at your feet. You are wearing big, heavy, clompy boots. Maybe you can feel their weight as they anchor you firmly on the ground. You can feel them tightly on the foot and ankle. Your feet inside are heavy.
- Keep looking down. Now you become aware that you have an incredibly heavy rucksack on your back. You can feel the straps digging into your shoulders and the weight pressing down on your lower back. Your feet sink down further.
- Lean forwards to take the weight and slowly begin to lift your feet and take small steps forward, looking down the whole time. The rucksack is full of huge heavy rocks. Each of these represents something or someone

that you are worried about. You carry the rucksack, on your back, slow steps forward feeling each step and connecting the rocks to all your responsibilities and stress. Feel the trudge and the tedium.

- Stop now! You don't have to do this anymore. In this moment, there is nothing you need to do about the rocks. Let the rucksack slide slowly off your back. You hear it thud onto the ground behind you. Notice the relief and the new lightness in your shoulders, neck and back. Look up at the beautiful surroundings. Stretch.
- Turn around now, bend and open the top of the rucksack. Lift out the first heavy rock, feeling the weight in your hands. It has writing on it—the name of this particular worry. Look down at it before you throw it to one side. Letting go. Lift out the next rock, look at its name and roll it away from you. Keep doing this until the bag is empty, rocks strewn all around you. Lift the rucksack up and turn it upside down. It is light as a feather. Breathe in the fresh air around you.
- Time to take the boots off now. Let them sit beside the rocks and start walking away along the shore or lake or forest path. Notice the light and the breeze and the sweet scents, the birdsong. Feel the warm ground under your bare feet.
- Your feet are so light, your body moves easily and freely. Maybe you feel like running or skipping or dancing. Give yourself full permission to enjoy this freedom, allow the good feeling to grow, and stay in this lovely place for as long as you want.

This not only helps release stress in the short term, but the more you practise it the easier it will get. Tricking your brain into letting go of worry, even for a short period of time, means you can better enjoy those occasions which can sometimes be spoiled by a head full of worries. It won't make your worries disappear but is a great coping mechanism to avoid feeling swamped. And it's much better for the body to be flooded with dopamine than cortisol.

6. Calming Turmeric Latte

This delicious milky drink, sometimes called *haldi doodh*, makes a perfect evening substitute for that caffeine-loaded cuppa. Turmeric is anti-inflammatory and a powerful antioxidant. It is known for its relaxing and soothing qualities and can help if you have restless sleep. **Note** that turmeric is not suitable for anyone pregnant or breastfeeding, or who has surgery scheduled in the next two weeks. It's also not advisable for anyone taking aspirin, ibuprofen or acetaminophen as it may lessen the effects. Aside from that, a milky turmeric drink is not only tasty but has a host of healthy ingredients to send you off for a good night's sleep.

- *Ingredients*:

  1 x cup of milk (cow's milk is fine unless you have a blocked nose, otherwise oat, almond or soy)
  1 x small pinch of turmeric powder
  1 x very small pinch of black pepper (to aid absorption)
  Grated or finely sliced small piece of fresh ginger
  Honey to taste (optional)

- *Method:*

  Mix everything together, apart from the honey, and warm over a low heat. Once it reaches boiling point, immediately lower the heat and let it simmer for 5–10 minutes. Add honey to taste if needed then pour into a glass and enjoy.

7. **Gratitude Practice**

This has been covered in the chapter above as a life-enhancing practice with solidly scientific credentials. It's not just for kids though; it strengthens adult neural pathways too. We know that consciously choosing to experience feelings of gratitude supports greater health, happiness and self-knowledge. The brain releases feel-good chemicals such as dopamine, oxytocin and serotonin when we take the time to reflect on what we appreciate about our daily life, relationships and the wider world. I have kept a Gratitude Journal for over a decade and record daily whatever I have appreciated that day. When I look through the journals, a pattern clearly emerges: the small, simple things really matter. Combining a gratitude practice with mindfulness enhances the ability to notice what is actually in front of us, in the present moment. Here's how to start.

- You don't have to write anything down, just taking a few minutes at the end of the day to reflect and feel grateful is absolutely fine. A journal, however, offers the ability to flick back over previous days and weeks. This can be fascinating and affirming—especially on those days when nothing has gone right and you feel low.
- Once relaxed and prepared for sleep, cast your mind back over the day and recall a moment that felt good. However simple it may be (the sun on your face, a child laughing, nice-smelling soap) and hold the thought in your mind.
- Minds are so quick to jump from one thought to another. Hold onto this one, breathing slowly and allowing yourself to rest in the good feeling. Be thankful for whatever the moment offered. With each breath, let the feeling grow bigger and warmer.
- Repeat this twice more if you can. Or continue writing your list. Small things can feel magical but the big ones are good too—fresh air, music, great TV, chocolate, so go as big or small as you want.
- Once you've been doing this for even a couple of days, you may find yourself noticing something during the day and think that it will be good for your list later on. The more we do this, the better things we are able to see and appreciate in our lives.

8. Beditation

As the name suggests, this is a form of meditation you can do in bed that will calm the body and the mind and help you fall asleep. It was created by the brilliant Mindfulness in Schools Project and I've adapted it here for adults after seeing it work successfully for teenagers. The post-course feedback frequently puts this at the top of the practices they find most helpful. You might find that you drop off before you've got very far in this body scan, and the more you do it, the more that brain/body link will strengthen making it a go-to tool when you find sleep elusive.

- Settle yourself comfortably into bed and allow the eyes to close. Is there anything you can do to be 10% more relaxed? Make any adjustments and take a few long deep breaths.

- Become aware of the touch of the bedclothes. Feel the connection between the body and the mattress. Notice the contrast between the sensations on the face and the body below the covers. Allow each breath to relax the body a little bit further, feeling heavier, softer.
- Take the attention into the feet. Notice the touch of the covers on the heels, the toes, the ankles. Allow every tiny bone, muscle and tendon to release and let go. You might notice a fizzy or warming sensation when you focus on a body part, that's normal, just notice it's there.
- Move the attention slowly up the legs, allowing the shins, the calves and knees to soften and relax and settle.
- Those big thigh muscles that work so hard for us during the day, supporting us, can let go now. Feel them release, ready to rest.
- Moving up to the hips and groin, feel the bones, muscles, tendons, all softening. The lower back releases all tension, feels warm and heavy. Notice the whole of the lower body at rest.
- The belly is where we often carry our stress. Use the out-breath to let go of the tension there, you might get a gurgle of encouragement. Release it, there's nothing to do now, nowhere to be.
- Move the focus upwards now to the chest and heart. Feel the ribcage soften, all the tiny muscles there releasing tension. You may notice a warm sensation in the heart region. Allow it to expand by breathing into the space behind the breastbone. This feeling of warmth can spread through the whole of the body.
- The shoulders and neck are other tension hotspots, so send your focus now into the muscles across the shoulders, deep into the areas that may be knotted or painful. Allow everything to feel heavy, soft and breathe out any stress that has gathered there.
- Move the attention to the head which feels so heavy on the pillow, like a watermelon! Feel the scalp and ears relaxing. Let any tension from the jaw drain out and feel the tongue soft in the mouth. Feel the cheeks release. The eyes are gently resting, allow the area around the eyes to become heavy, all the little muscles relaxing. Finally, the forehead smooths outwards, and all tension disappears.
- Focus outwards, if you're still awake, to the whole of the body, resting, heavy and free of tension. Every cell in the body is relaxed. Allow each breath to take the body a little deeper into this lovely relaxation.

Final Thoughts

As this chapter and book come to an end, I am hopeful that, among the many suggested practices, you will find a way to support yourself and your child with their sleep. It's good to mix and match them and to give everyone a real "toolbox" of practical things to try in different circumstances. When you combine these mindfulness and relaxation tools with the sleep hygiene advice and get a good routine in place, sleep and bedtime problems may be a thing of the past and the whole family can benefit from the joys of a good night's sleep.

As we know, poor sleep affects many aspects of our lives and can make us feel pretty awful. For me, the most significant loss is when tiredness spoils our ability to enjoy life. This is profoundly important for our children and young people who all deserve to make the most of the opportunities around them and to thrive. Improving the quality and quantity of sleep can make the world a more enticing, stimulating and enjoyable place to be, and I wish this with all my heart for every child and every parent/carer. Sleep tight!

Resources

Professional Help/Crisis Support
For urgent help phone 111, option 2.

Contact your family doctor to discuss issues and request referrals to mental health professionals *www.nhs.uk* explains the options and how to access services.

The Samaritans can be contacted on 116 123 free from any phone, 24 hours a day 365 days a year.

SANEline for people with or supporting someone else with a mental health problem – 0300 304 7000.

The Mix is a service for people under 25. You can call them on 0808 808 4994 and request support by email.

Mindfulness Courses for Adults
If you are an adult interested in learning more about mindfulness with a trained teacher, look for people offering theses gold standard courses in your local area: 8-week MBCT (Mindfulness Based Cognitive Therapy) or MBSR (Mindfulness Based Stress Reduction) courses for adults. They are available online but there is no substitute for face-to-face learning here and especially for being in the presence of other like-minded folk.

Mindfulness Courses for Children and Young People
These are best delivered in the classroom by trained practitioners. Visit my website for details *www.mindfulkidscornwall.co.uk* and talk to the leaders in your child's school about offering the robustly evidenced .b and Paws b courses from the Mindfulness in Schools Project *https://mindfulnessinschools.org*

Books

Why We Sleep: The New Science of Sleep and Dreams by Matthew Walker (Penguin Random House, 2017)

Stand Tall Like a Mountain: Mindfulness and Self-Care for Anxious Children and Worried Parents by Suzy Reading (Aster, 2019)

Mindfulness: a Practical Guide to Finding Peace in a Frantic World by Mark Williams and Danny Penman (Piatkus, 2011)

Brainstorm: the power and purpose of the teenage brain by Daniel J Siegel (Scribe Publications, 2014)

The Sleep Revolution: transforming your life, one night at a time by Arianna Huffington (Harmony, 2016)

Healthy Sleep Habits, Happy Child by Dr Marc Weissbluth (Ballantine Books, 2021)

The Idiot Brain: a neuroscientist explains what your head is really up to by Dean Burnett (Guardian Faber Publishing, 2017)

The Happy Brain: the science of where happiness comes from by Dean Burnett (Guardian Faber Publishing, 2019)

The Phone Addiction Workbook: how to identify smartphone dependency, stop compulsive behaviour and develop a healthy relationship with your devices by Hilda Burke (Simon & Schuster, 2019)

Ten Keys to Happier Living: a Practical Handbook for Happiness by Vanessa King *(Headline, 2016)*

Be Happy Be You; the Teenage Guide by Penny Alexander and Becky Goddard-Hill (Collins, 2020)

The Self-Care Kit for Stressed-Out Teens: Healthy Habits and Calming Advice to Help You Stay Positive by Frankie Young (Vie, 2020*)*

Breathe Out: A Creative Guide to Happiness for Teen Minds – an illustrated journal filled with exercises to support wellbeing, written in association with the mental health charity MIND *(Michael O'Mara, 2020)*

The Little Book of Gratitude: create a life of happiness and wellbeing by giving thanks by Dr Robert A Emmons (Hachette UK, 2016)

The Thankful Book by Todd Parr (Little, Brown 2012)

Gratitude is My Superpower: a children's book about giving thanks and practising positivity by Alicia Ortego (My Superpower Books, 2021)

More Than a Woman by Caitlin Moran (Ebury Press, 2021)

A Mindfulness Guide for the Frazzled by Ruby Wax (Penguin Books, 2016)

I Think, I Am! Teaching kids the power of affirmations by Louise Hay & Kristina Tracy (Hay House Inc, 2020)

Experience Your Good Now!: learning to use affirmations by Louise L Hay (Hay House Inc, 2020)

You Matter by Delia Smith (Mensch Publishing, 2022)

Websites and Apps

There are a plethora of these to consider and choose from, I have listed a few below. As with all online mental health resources they are not a replacement for professional crisis support which can be sought in ways listed here.

1. *www.actionforhappiness.org* Action for Happiness is a fantastic charity dedicated to raising global levels of happiness by inviting us all to "keep calm, stay wise, be kind". Their website is packed full of insightful

information about simple ways to increase feelings of happiness. The app gives you friendly, daily happiness nudges.

2. *www.calmforkids.com* has some great yoga exercises and meditations for children aimed at calming, balance and concentration.
3. *www.mindfulnessinschools.org* is a great resource for information about ways to support young minds and will arm you with the science behind the curriculum. It can help you open a conversation with your child's school about introducing mindfulness.
4. *www.calm.com* this website and app has a wealth of calming sounds, relaxation guides and tracks including Harry Styles reading a calming story!
5. *www.theinnerhour.com* this app is designed to help with anxiety, depression, stress and anger as well as improving happiness and sleep. You can set a plan to focus on and follow the tips and advice.
6. *www.headspace.com* this brilliant and popular app sets out to help you "be kind to your mind" and has a huge choice of resources around meditation, stress and sleep.
7. *https://freedom.to* this app enables you to temporarily block websites and apps on your phone and devices which enables you to focus without interruption.
8. *www.offthegridapp.com* this free digital detox app helps you "get off your phone and get on with your life". Features include locking your phone while you socialise in person, letting your contacts know you are temporarily off grid and scheduling times when you want your phone to leave you in peace.
9. *www.randomactsofkindness.org* has great ideas of ways we can help other people in our community

Research

The Prince's Trust eBay Youth Index (February 2019) *www.princes-trust.org.uk*

The Prince's Trust and YouGov Young People in Lockdown report (May 2020) *www.princes-rust.org.uk*

The Prince's Trust Tesco Youth Index (January 2021) *www.princes-trust.org.uk*

Young Minds *www.youngminds.org.uk*
Department for Education report *State of the Nation 2019: children and young people's wellbeing* – find at *www.gov.uk*

Interview Tristan Harris: *Tech for Good*, Radio 4 *One to One* 04.05.21

The Social Dilemma (2020) American docudrama film directed by Jeff Orlowski and written by Orlowski, David Coombe and Vickie Curtis. It is a deep dive into how social media nurtures addiction, manipulates people's views, emotions and behaviour, and spreads disinformation to maximise profit. It examines the role of social media on mental health, particularly of adolescents. A must-see for parents.

The Mindfulness in Schools Project has collected many research papers on the impact of mindfulness on the wellbeing of young people. The following have informed me and I am very grateful for the rigorous work undertaken by all those involved:
The immediate and sustained effects of the .b mindfulness programme on adolescents' social and emotional wellbeing and academic functioning (September 2011) by Sarah Hennelly
Mindfulness Training in Primary Schools Decreases Negative Affect and Increases Meta-Cognition in Children (2016) by Charlotte E Vickery & Dusana Dorjee

Effects of Physical Exercise on Cognitive Functioning and Wellbeing: Biological and Psychological Benefits (April 2018) by Laura Mandolese et al, University of Naples Survey *Out of School Out of Pocket,* May 2019 *www.gkandpartners.com*

Dr Vyas Lee's practice in London *www.vyasleepractice.com*

Charities Offering Help
The Sleep Charity – founded by Vicki Dawson, dedicated to improving sleep for young people. Check out the Teen Hub and the free digital book *http://thesleepcharity.org.uk*

Young Minds *www.youngminds.org.uk*

MIND *www.mind.org.uk*

Mental Health UK *http://mentalhealth-uk.org*

Acknowledgements

During my early career in publishing I saw first-hand how much work goes into putting books onto shelves for readers, and how many people contribute to the process. This did not prepare me for what it takes from the author's perspective, however, and there are many people I must thank who have supported, advised and educated me during the writing and journey of this book.

My first heartfelt thanks must go to Sir Anthony Seldon whose visionary work bringing wellbeing classes to the pupils at the school he led well over a decade ago now, set me on the path to becoming a teacher of these vital skills. His support for my work and his generous endorsement of this book, mean the world.

Dr Faith Orchard's work at the University of Sussex has vital implications for understanding the relationship between sleep and mental health in adolescents. I thank her for her time and wish her continued success. Thanks also to Dr Jenna Vyas-Lee for sharing aspects of her vital work and supporting me in my writing.

The organisations I am a member of provide continual professional support and the opportunity to extend my practice and expand my learning and I am grateful to the British Sleep Society and The Association of Child and Adolescent Mental Health. Foremost in my thanks is the wonderful Mindfulness in Schools Project, whose brilliant courses enable the flourishing of young people and who have welcomed me to their team of global teachers. Christian Kerr at Calm For Kids provided me with the skills to teach the yoga practices that I have used with hundreds of children to support physical, mental and emotional health.

The schools in Cornwall who have invited me in to work with their young people have enabled me to learn a huge amount, as well as to offer my skills and experience. Thank you to all the teachers, children and parents who have allowed me the privilege of working with, and learning from, your kids. I am particularly grateful to Catherine Biddick, headteacher at Mount Hawke Academy who has welcomed me into her school for many years now. Being able to work with the children, many of whom I have taught from age 6 through to 11 has been deeply rewarding.

Thanks must go to my long-time yoga teacher and friend, Barry Elms, whose yoga nidra is a thing of beauty and which I have adapted for children in this book.

My one-time boss and friend, the extraordinary Debbie Owen, provided practical advice and support throughout, including directing me to the brilliant Rosemary Scoular and Natalia Lucas at United Agents. They enthusiastically took me on as a client, and submitted an early draft of this book. I am grateful to them for all their endeavours on my behalf and for holding my hand through the rejections and near-misses and rewrites. This book is better for all those improvements, and I am glad we remain on the best of terms.

Thanks to everyone at Austin Macauley for picking up the baton and taking this book on after I'd almost given up hope of it making its way into the world.

This book would never have made it here without the miracle of my friend of 30 years, successful novelist Josie Lloyd. She badgered, scolded, gave detailed feedback, commiserated, whooped and remained by my side throughout; thankyou my lovely.

Nicky Corbishley threw her formidable energy and enthusiasm behind my endeavours from day one and I am grateful for the decades of friendship, love and support.

My first readers have been invaluable for their insight, wisdom, time generously given, and wholehearted belief in what I wanted to achieve. Zoe Weatherhead and Mary Yucel—thank you both for everything you contributed and for your professional and personal support.

Dr Ceri Idris-Evans gave her useful feedback, thank you. Anna Fazackerley, journalist extraordinaire, has been a loyal cheerleader and provider of invaluable support and advice.

To my neighbours, especially Adam Roseveare for the author photograph, thanks for all the support and Friday night drinks. Sophie Tricard, Helen Cockram and all the Wenty girls have been on my side throughout and I am grateful for those 40-year friendships. For sustained friendship and enthusiastic support thanks are due to Vanessa, Sylvia, Harriet, Tam, Deb, Diane, Liz, Anouk; and to Fiona Cant for her bedtime bear, and Becky for cover art ideas.

Thanks also go to my dad, Mike, and my sister, Louise, for always believing I could get this done and for their loyalty and love. I think my mum would be proud of me. She always knew when I'd stayed up late reading and was pretending to be asleep. Thanks also to all my supportive Howarth in-laws.

Finally, I must thank my most invaluable resource: my lovely family. My incredible children Dylan, Lenny and Kitty have given me the opportunity to be that most rewarding of life's roles: a mum. They have taught me so much and brought me more joy than I can possibly express. My beloved husband Paddy, to whom this book is dedicated, made the world good and right from the moment we met. Long may the adventure continue.